PSYCHOLOGICAL FOUNDATIONS OF
MUSICAL BEHAVIOR

PSYCHOLOGICAL FOUNDATIONS
OF MUSICAL BEHAVIOR

By

RUDOLF E. RADOCY
Associate Professor of Music Education and Music Therapy
The University of Kansas
Lawrence, Kansas

and

J. DAVID BOYLE
Professor of Music Education
The Pennsylvania State University
University Park, Pennsylvania

CHARLES C THOMAS • PUBLISHER
Springfield • Illinois • U.S.A.

Published and Distributed Throughout the World by
CHARLES C THOMAS • PUBLISHER
BANNERSTONE HOUSE
301-327 East Lawrence Avenue, Springfield, Illinois, U.S.A.

© *1979, by* CHARLES C THOMAS • PUBLISHER
ISBN 0-398-03841-4
Library of Congress Catalog Card Number: 78-11823

With THOMAS BOOKS *careful attention is given to all details of
manufacturing and design. It is the Publisher's desire to present
books that are satisfactory as to their physical qualities and artistic
possibilities and appropriate for their particular use.* THOMAS
BOOKS *will be true to those laws of quality that assure a good
name and good will.*

Printed in the United States of America
N-11

Library of Congress Cataloging in Publication Data

Radocy, Rudolf E
    Psychological foundations of musical behavior.

    Bibliography: p.
    1. Music—Psychology. I. Boyle, J. David joint author. II. Title.
[DNLM: 1. Music. 2. Music therapy. 3. Psychology, Educational be-
havior. ML3830 R131p]
ML3830.R15   780'.15   78-11823
ISBN 0-398-03841-4

PREFACE

Psychological Foundations of Musical Behavior was born during a dreary day in Atlantic City during the 1976 national convention of the Music Educators National Conference. The authors, having heard a considerable amount of agreement regarding the need for a new psychology of music textbook, made the decision to write. After two years of outlines, drafts, telephone calls, revisions and discussion, the results now are in the reader's hands.

The authors have exercised their professional judgments, based on teaching psychology of music and conducting related research and scholarly inquiry, regarding content. Naturally, some arbitrary decisions were necessary, and the authors' scholarly biases are reflected. Given their chosen content, however, the authors have tried to make this book comprehensive, comprehensible, and contemporary. Traditional areas of study are represented, and the authors have tried to explain what their experiences suggest are difficult topics. Many references are contemporary, although, with time, this book inevitably will be obsolete as new research is reported.

Special acknowledgement must be extended to those who assisted significantly in this book's preparation. Gratitude is expressed to The University of Kansas for granting one author (Rudolf E. Radocy) a sabbatical leave at a critical time. George Duerksen and Harlan Hoffa provided professional encouragement and support. Holly Ping, June Kautz, and Barbara Gordy provided able secretarial assistance. The editorial staff of Charles C Thomas, Publisher was helpful in the final stages of manuscript preparation. Finally, appreciation is extended to the numerous students at The University of Kansas and The Pennsylvania State University whose educational triumphs and traumas helped shape this book.

J. DAVID BOYLE
RUDOLF E. RADOCY

CONTENTS

PSYCHOLOGICAL FOUNDATIONS OF MUSICAL BEHAVIOR

Chapter One

INTRODUCTION

PURPOSE

THIS BOOK PROVIDES THE READER with a comprehensive overview of human musical behavior, as viewed from a psychological perspective. Music has been a cultural component since a time prior to recorded history. Organizing sound for functional and aesthetic purposes provides many fascinating (if not always answerable) questions. Description, prediction, and explanation of composition, as well as performance, and listening behavior are challenging and unfinished tasks. This book focuses questions and general interest in such description, prediction, and explanation for the benefit of psychologists, musicians, educators, and anyone else with a serious interest in music.

An understanding of human musical behavior has utility for the musician in the studio, on the stage, in the classroom, or in a commercial setting. Why are there preferences for certain sounds? How relevant is acute pitch discrimination? What psychophysical processes underly musical perception? Is there a physical basis for musical taste? Are some individuals "naturally" musical? Why is a deviation from stereotyped performance practice a "stroke of creative genius" when done by a well-known conductor but "failure to understand the literature" when done by an amateur? Knowledge of human musical behavior in its many manifestations is essential for addressing these and numerous other questions.

Contemporary musicians and educators, struggling to balance conflicting philosophies and societal demands, may find utility in developing understanding and familiarity with human musical behavior. Does music really motivate and/or sedate students?

3

What physiological changes may occur in listening to music? Why are children more receptive to "different" music in the primary grades than in later years? How related is musical capacity or ability to intellectual and manual abilities? Again, although this book does not promise definitive answers, the information provided can focus relevant inquiry.

SCOPE

Traditional domains of the psychology of music include psychoacoustics, measurement and prediction of musical ability, functional music, cultural organization of musical patterns, music learning, and the affective response to music. A glance at the Contents indicates that the traditional domains have suggested relevant chapters; in addition, attention has been given to the psychological foundations of rhythm, melody, harmony, and musical preferences.

The authors freely admit to a behavioristic perspective. Musical behavior is one aspect of human behavior; consequently, it must be subject to the same genetic and environmental controls which govern all human behavior. A concern for what people *do* with musical stimuli, in natural as well as laboratory situations, is expressed throughout the book.

Behavior, as used herein, means the activity of living dynamic human beings. Such activity is directly observable and is of interest either in itself or as external evidence of some internal state. Cognition, the internal processes of memory and "thinking," may be behavior in a covert sense, but the only way to study objectively such covert behavior is to study overt manifestations thereof. Perception is a process of sensing the environment; it obviously is essential for behavior. Perception may be studied only through evidence of its results. Musical behavior includes performance, listening, and creative activity involved in composition. The study of musical behavior thus necessarily includes related cognitive and perceptual processes. That which people *do* with music is musical behavior. So, too, is that which music *does* to people.

As Gaston (1968, p. 7) indicates, musical behavior is studied through psychology, anthropology, and sociology. This book primarily reflects a psychological study, as psychology is the study of human behavior. Nevertheless, the authors have not hesitated to look beyond the general body of psychological literature. Sociology, anthropology, philosophy, and acoustics are germane areas from which the authors have drawn valuable material.

PREVIEW

In planning this book, the authors have considered the dynamic (in the sense of moving and ever-changing) aspects of musical performance and listening as well as important influences of prior experiences on present behaviors. No human musical activity is solely the result of willful individual interaction with music. Cultural influences, learning, and biological constraints are as crucial as motivation, reward, and any "inherent" properties of the musical stimulus.

As Gaston (1957, p .26) has stated:

> To each musical experience is brought the sum of an individual's attitudes, beliefs, prejudices, conditionings in terms of time and place in which he has lived. To each response, also, he brings his own physiological needs, unique neurological and endocrinological systems with their distinctive attributes. He brings, in all of this, his total entity as a unique individual.

Without certain psychoacoustical phenomena related to the perception and processing of pitch, loudness, and timbre, music would not exist, at least as it is presently known. The second chapter will discuss basic descriptions and relationships involving those phenomena. Considerable attention will be given to perception, judgment, and measurement, as well as physical and psychophysical events.

Music, a dynamic art form, exists in time; some organization of tonal durations is present in all music. The third chapter discusses rhythmic behaviors and what is involved in producing and responding to rhythms. The authors believe that the rhythmic response is a learned one; no person "has rhythm" on any absolute inherent basis.

Definitions and opinions regarding melody and harmony differ; it is debatable whether they exist in all music. Nevertheless, they are vital considerations in much Western music, and the terms are used freely by musicians and nonmusicians. The fourth chapter considers horizontal and vertical pitch organization, tonality, scales, and value judgments, as well as related pedagogical issues.

The fifth chapter studies the question of why people have music. There are varying opinions; the chapter considers philosophical, functional, and cultural issues, particularly the selected theories on (1) the origins of music, (2) functional uses of music, and (3) music as a cultural phenomenon.

Chapter Six is concerned with the "chills up the spine" effect and other indications of an affective response to music. There is no question that physiological changes can occur with music. But what is their nature? What is the influence of training? What is meant by "beautiful" in music?

Television viewers may have encountered the tuna who continually is frustrated when he attempts to be selected by a canning company. In spite of displaying his self-designated characteristics of "good taste," such as reading Shakespeare, playing tennis or polo, and buying an expensive television set but not watching it, the underseas egomaniac always is told that the tuna processors want not tuna with "good taste," but rather want tuna that "tastes good." The pun notwithstanding, maintaining an appearance because of presumed indication of a certain preference or taste relates to the seventh chapter, which examines musical preferences and influences thereon.

Music's utility as a stimulator, tranquilizer, and reward, of particular concern to music therapists as well as music educators, is discussed in the eighth chapter. Attention is given to ceremonial, industrial, and commercial as well as therapeutic aspects.

Measurement and prediction of musical ability have been stressed in psychology of music. Construction and publication of aptitude and "talent" measures indicate a desire for student selection, but such measures also represent assumptions regarding the nature and manifestation of musical ability. Although this is not a measurement book, the ninth chapter considers several approaches to measuring musical ability and underlying rationales.

Music teachers obviously must be concerned with music learning—not just in the traditional sense of memorization, but also in the sense of learning to perform, analyze, and organize musical ideas. The tenth chapter presents basic learning considerations and offers practical applications to music learning.

The final chapter examines some future research directions. As more knowledge regarding neural circuitry, dual sensory responses, and social pressures is accumulated and assimilated, there may be profound effects upon the study of musical behavior.

Throughout the chapters is the authors' bias that music is a human phenomenon. Individuals bring their prior experiences to the performance and listening situations, where such experiences interact with all the dynamic aspects of human intercourse. There is much to be learned regarding musical behavior. Its complexities can overwhelm the student, teacher, and researcher. Seemingly far-fetched and distantly related ideas may begin to appear with surprising frequency. One must believe that musical behavior is, in the last analysis, another form of human behavior— it is no more, and no less. As Gaston (1968, p. 21) said, "Music is not mystical nor supernatural—it is only mysterious."

REFERENCES

Gaston, E. T. Factors contributing to responses to music. In E. T. Gaston (Ed.), *Music Therapy 1957*. Lawrence, Kansas: The Allen Press, 1957.

Gaston, E. T. Man and music. In E. T. Gaston (Ed.), *Music in Therapy*. New York: MacMillan Publishing Company, 1968.

Chapter Two

PSYCHOACOUSTICAL FOUNDATIONS

P SYCHOACOUSTICS IS A BRANCH of psychophysics, the study of sensory responses to physical stimuli. When one studies auditory sensations, one studies psychoacoustics. Questions regarding comparative pitches and loudness, assigning pitch and timbre sensations to tonal clusters and, indeed, perceptions of all tonal properties essentially are psychoacoustical questions. Without psychoacoustical phenomena, music (as we know it) could not exist. After presenting brief overviews of the production and transmission of musical sounds (which may be omitted by anyone familiar with elementary acoustics of music), this chapter considers reception of musical sounds and psychoacoustical phenomena organized around the basic psychological tonal properties of pitch, loudness, and timbre.

PRODUCTION OF MUSICAL SOUNDS

Basic to any sound is vibration—something moves back and forth. If the vibration is periodic, i.e. vibrates with a regularly recurring motion, it may lead to sensation of musical tone. Sources of musical sounds include vibrating strings, air columns, metal plates, metal bars, and membranes.

Consider a vibrating pendulum, one of the simplest illustrations of vibration and related properties. The pendulum, once displaced and thereby set into motion, will swing back and forth. Although the distance it swings will decrease gradually, the pendulum will swing long enough for an observer to note that it regularly returns to the point at which it began to swing. Every so often, with regularity, it completes a *cycle*. A cycle is the complete journey of a vibrating object from an original point through

8

both extremes of displacement and back to the original point. The time required for the cycle's completion is the *period*. The number of cycles completed in a given amount of time is the *frequency*. The distance between a vibrating object's original location and its point of maximal displacement is the *amplitude*. One readily can observe and describe a cycle, period, frequency, and amplitude in relation to a vibrating pendulum.

Although their individual cycles cannot be seen, in the ordinary sense, vibrating objects producing musical sounds also vibrate in cycles and with a certain period, frequency, and amplitude. Musical sounds generally are a complex of individual vibrations; they contain numerous frequencies. Musical sounds can be analyzed into their individual component frequencies, but one usually hears a given musical sound as having just one frequency.

Not all vibrations are perceivable as sound, of course. A minimal amount of power (intensity) is necessary, and human ears normally respond to an approximate frequency range of 20 to 18,000 cycles per second [called Hertz, abbreviated Hz, in honor of Heinrich Hertz (1857-1894), who conducted early research with electromagnetism]. Individuals vary in their frequency sensitivity, particularly regarding the upper limit. Sounds considerably lower than 20 Hz may be heard under artificial conditions.

The production of musical sounds, then, requires that something be set into periodic vibration. If it vibrates with acceptable frequency and intensity, and those vibrations somehow can be transmitted to a listener, music is possible.

TRANSMISSION OF MUSICAL SOUNDS

Transmission, as used here, refers to the propagation or spread of a disturbance through the air from a sound source to a listener. We are not considering electrical or electronic transmission or sound's travel through media other than air.

Consider a row of upright dominoes. If they are placed at a critical distance from each other, a person can produce an amusing ripple effect by pushing the first domino into its neighbor. This is somewhat analogous to what happens when a disturbance spreads through the air from a sounding musical instrument to a listener.   The vibrating body disturbs air particles around it. Those particles bump other particles, which in turn bump others.   Unlike the dominoes, each particle can move back and forth as long as the source of the disturbance continues to vibrate. However, just as the first domino does not travel to the end of the row, no one air particle travels from the musical source to the listener.   It is the disturbance which travels.

A disturbance spreading through air is a *longitudinal* disturbance, i.e. the overall disturbance travels in the same direction as the slight movement of each particle.   (In *transverse* disturbances, the overall disturbance travels in a direction perpendicular to the slight movement of each particle.   Transverse disturbances do not occur in a gas.)   A travelling disturbance or a chain of travelling disturbances often is called a *wave*.   A sound wave is a series of disturbances travelling through a medium.

Waves may travel directly from a sound source to a listener. They may encounter a surface which represents a sudden change in properties of the medium; then, the wave will be *reflected,* although some of its energy will be absorbed by the reflecting surface.   Reflection represents a sudden direction change for the wave; a gradual change in direction often results from *refraction,* a gradual "bending" of the waves owing to a gradual change in medium properties such as temperature or density.   We can sense sounds from sources not aligned directly with our ears or obscured from view because of *diffraction,* the ability of a wave to "go around corners" or pass through a small opening.

A travelling wave represents changing locations of particles as they undergo bumping and the resulting displacements.   Accompanying the continual changes in particle location are changes in pressure.   When particles are compressed more closely together than they are in an undisturbed state, the pressure increases.   When particles are spread further apart (rarefacted) than they are in an undisturbed state, the pressure decreases.   This means that a periodic pressure fluctuation occurs at any point in a travelling wave in air.   Such periodic pressure fluctuations, minute though they are, are the form in which Beethoven symphonies, Handel oratorios, rock tunes, and third grade recorder ensemble sounds reach our ears.

RECEPTION OF MUSICAL SOUNDS

From Air to Inner Ear

The periodic pressure fluctuations accompany the travelling wave as it enters the ear. The obvious external or cosmetic portion of the ear is the pinna; the meatus, or "hole in the head," is the entrance to the auditory canal. The travelling wave passes through the auditory canal and encounters the eardrum or tympanic membrane, which separates the outer and middle ear.

The eardrum responds to the pressure fluctuations by moving in and out. (Incredibly tiny amounts of pressure change are sufficient to move the eardrum.) Connected to the eardrum is the middle ear's chain of three small bones (hammer, anvil, and stirrup or incus, malleus, and stapes), which are connected in turn to another membrane, the oval window. The eardrum's motion is transmitted through the bones to the oval window, which separates the middle and inner ear.

The oval window's motions are conveyed to the fluid contained in the snail-shell-shaped inner ear or cochlea. The fluid in turn is excited into wavelike motions which are detected by the basilar membrane, an appendage, fastened below the oval window, which runs through almost the entire length of the cochlea. Details regarding basilar membrane activity still are subject to further investigation, but, essentially, the membrane moves up and down in a manner depending upon the frequencies of the fluid's vibrations. Higher frequencies elicit maximal membrane movement closer to the oval window end or base; lower frequencies elicit maximal movement closer to the "far" end or apex of the basilar membrane. Combinations of frequencies, such as most musical tones, excite the membrane at several locations. Where, when, and how much the basilar membrane is excited provides basic information for perception and organization of the psychological sensations basic to music.

From the time the original vibrating body disturbs the surrounding medium until the resulting disturbance reaches the basilar membrane, the form of energy expended is mechanical. It is a matter of movement. Lying alongside the basilar membrane are hair cells, collectively known as the organ of Corti, which sense the membrane's movements and function as transducers. A transducer is a device which converts one form of energy to another (microphones and loudspeakers are common examples); the hair cells convert mechanical energy to electrochemical energy and start auditory signals on their way to the brain.

From Inner Ear to Brain

The characteristic vibration of the basilar membrane innervates (excites) the hair cells. There are about 25,000 cells in the human basilar membrane (Whitfield, 1967); they are arranged in inner and outer cells in relation to the membrane's edge. The cells innervate the neural fibers of the acoustic nerve. The hair cells differ functionally, as evidenced by the guinea pig's *inner* cells producing a cochlear microphonic (an electrical discharge obtained by inserting an electrode into the cochlea) proportional to the *velocity* of basilar membrane movement while the *outer* cells produce a cochlear microphonic proportional to the amount of basilar membrane *displacement* (Dallos et al., 1972). Furthermore, few outer cells appear to be affected by the efferent neural pathway while all inner cells appear to be affected (Davis, 1962).

Even a single-tone stimulus activates a large portion of the cochlear neural fibres; two tones which are very slightly different activate respective areas along the basilar membrane which overlap considerably. The boundaries between activated and unactivated areas apparently help signal the stimulus frequency(ies). Intensity apparently is signalled in terms of the number of activated fibres and the frequency of neural discharge (Whitfield). The basic information regarding frequency, intensity, and waveform properties is passed to and through the neural pathways to the auditory cortex, in rough accordance with the schematic diagram in Figure 2-1 (Whitfield; Roederer, 1975). Although the auditory cortex is the "ultimate destination," neural processing occurs prior to the cortex; some perception necessary for basic musical decision making is completed at subcortical levels. Frequency discrimination, for example, probably is complete at the collicular level (Whitfield, p. 163).

The complicated combination of neural pathways leading from the cochlea to the brain may be grouped into the ascending and descending auditory pathways. The ascending pathway (known as *afferent* because the signals go toward the brain) includes the spiral ganglion, the dorsal and ventral cochlear nucleus complex, the superior-olivary complex, the nuclei of the inferior colliculus and lateral lemniscus, the medial geniculate body, and the auditory cortex. The descending pathway (known as *efferent* because the signals go away from the brain) includes higher descending neurons and the olivo-cochlear bundle (Gacek, 1972). Existence of the efferent pathway is important musically because, although its information handling capacity is less than that of the afferent

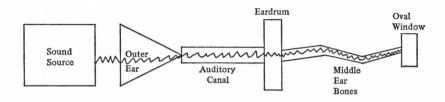

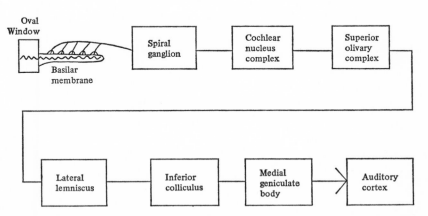

Figure 2-1. Diagram of auditory transmission from sound source to auditory cortex.

pathway, it can increase or decrease excitability of the hair cells, particularly the inner cells (Davis, 1962).

The purpose of the above abbreviated description of the travel of a sound encoded in a pressure fluctuation at a musical source to its encoding as an electrochemical discharge directed toward the auditory cortex is to enable the reader to have some idea of the structures involved. Readers interested in more detailed knowledge may consult Stevens and Warshofsky (1965) for a highly readable and profusely illustrated description; more technical and physiologically oriented descriptions are available in hearing texts such as Whitfield.

PITCH PHENOMENA

Pitch pervades most music, yet it often is ill-defined and confused with other phenomena. Pitch is defined herein as the sensation resulting from relative placement of a sound on a high-low continuum. Such placement is learned; it is the assignment of apparent location. As such, pitch is a metathetic (place) variable, rather than a prothetic (magnitude) variable (Stevens, 1975), although there may be some prothetic aspects of pitch.

The following discussion of pitch phenomena is organized around clarification of its relationship to frequency, various kinds of pitch processing, phenomena resulting from pitch combinations, absolute pitch, and attempts to measure pitch.

Frequency-Pitch Relationship

In general, people may experience a pitch sensation from any sufficiently periodic sound in the range of approximately 20 to 18,000 Hz. The upper limit fluctuates widely with individuals; under special conditions even the lower limit can be exceeded: Whittle, Collins, and Robinson (1972) successfully presented highly intense frequencies as low as 3.15 Hz to subjects seated in a cabinet in such a manner that their entire bodies were immersed in uniform sound pressure.

Pitch varies largely as a function of frequency variation, but each minute frequency change does not elicit a pitch change. Classical psychophysics developed the concept of the just noticeable difference (jnd) or difference limen, an amount by which a stimulus must be changed in order for an observer to detect a difference a certain criterion percentage of the time. The jnd for frequency discrimination (and hence detection of discrete pitches) varies greatly with methodology as well as people (Woodworth and Schlosberg, 1965) ; the size of the jnd varies with the stimulus frequencies such that it is smaller (in terms of Hz) for lower frequencies (Nordmark, 1968; Moore, 1974). Despite its fluctuation, the jnd usually lies well within the limits necessary for functional musical discrimination.

The pitch associated with a particular frequency may vary despite the lack of any change in the physical vibration rate. The classic study of Stevens (1935) often is cited as evidence that the pitch of a tone can change with an increase in the intensity of a tone sounding with a constant frequency. Three observers adjusted the intensities of comparison tones to make them equivalent in pitch to standard tones in high (> 3000 Hz), medium (1000-3000 Hz), and low (< 1000 Hz) frequency ranges. Observers disagreed regarding the amount of intensity changes necessary to match pitches, but it was noted that high frequencies tended to increase in pitch with increased intensity, medium frequencies did not change in pitch with an intensity increase, and low frequencies decreased in pitch. The 1935 classic, over generalized and not always replicable, has been updated by Terhardt (1974b), who obtained the classic results at 2000 Hz and partially obtained them at 4000 Hz. There was individual variability; people vary in the extent to which they are pitch-shifters. With a 40 decibel (db) increase in intensity level (40 db represents an increase in power of 10,000:1) of a standard, the frequency of a variable tone matched to the standard shifted down, on the average, by 2 percent at 200 Hz, down by 0.75 at 1000 Hz, up by 1.5 percent at 4000 Hz, and up by 2.5 percent at 6000 Hz. The effect of a pitch change of a constant frequency sounded with changing intensity apparently is genuine for *pure* tones, but it cannot be assumed as characteristic of all listeners.

Another example of the changing pitch of a constant frequency is binaural diplacusis, in which one tone is heard with a different pitch in each ear. This bizarre condition is difficult to research because it fluctuates in the listener; its relation to music processing appears to be noncritical (Sherbon, 1975), although in some clinical instances it must play a role in music perception.

Frequency is a physical property of musical tones; pitch is a psychological property. They are not perfectly related, and they are not the same thing.

Pitch Processing of Single Pure Tones

A "pure" tone is a tone of just one frequency. Except for some of the sounds produced by electronic means, there are no pure tones in music, although certain flute and organ tones come close to being pure. Musical tones are complex; they contain a mixture of frequencies. Nevertheless, much has been learned about the behavior of the auditory system with the aid of pure tones. Furthermore, all complex tones may be analyzed into pure tone components, so knowledge of pure tone processing is useful.

Pure tones, being of one frequency, actually are less clear in pitch than complex tones. For a given duration of sound, a high frequency tone can be determined with greater accuracy than can a low one. A certain minimal amount of time is necessary for pitch perception of a given frequency; the greater the frequency, the shorter the time period may be (Kock, 1935).

Stevens, Davis, and Lurie (1935) used the remarkable similarity of guinea pig cochleas to those of humans to study the relationship of particular membrane stimulations to pitch perception. Using the output of an electrode placed in contact with a guinea pig's cochlea, they saw, via an osilloscope, that higher tones were localized among the membrane near the oval window end, tones around 2000 Hz near the middle, and lower tones closely near the far (helicotrema) end. They noted throughout that two tones could be differentiated provided that areas of the membrane differing by .025 mm were stimulated. This study illustrates what is basically responsible for particular pure tone perceptions: the place of greatest stimulation along the basilar membrane.

The stimulation areas (or resonance maxima) on the membrane have been mapped (Von Bekesy, 1960). For example, 5000 Hz stimulates the membrane maximally about 10 mm from the base (oval window end). Two thousand Hz has its resonance maximum at approximately 16 mm; the relatively low frequency of 200 Hz has its resonance maximum about 300 mm from the base (apex end).

Detection of a difference between two pure tones requires that the location of resonance maxima for the two tones be different. In terms of frequency difference (Δf), this translates in one study to from 3 to 0.5 percent of the initial frequency for pure tones of a constant intensity (Zwicker, Flottorp, and Stevens, 1957); at 100 Hz, a change to 103 or 97 Hz is necessary, while at 2000 Hz, the frequency must change to 1990 or 2010 Hz. These figures are for a continuous sounding, slowly changed tone; the subject's task sometimes is called frequency resolution. The jnd for any sort of frequency distinction is not a precise unchanging value; it varies with frequency, intensity, duration, and rate of change (Roederer, 1975).

Pitch Processing of Combined Pure Tones

Tones which contain only one frequency when they leave their respective sound sources may combine in the air and reach the ear in the form of a tonal superposition; a sound wave is determined by the interaction or interference of both waves. Any sound wave, in the sense of a pattern of displacements, is determined at any given time by the frequency and intensity of each component. When there is only one component, as in the case of a pure tone, the wave is simply dependent upon that tone's frequency and intensity, but a combination of pure tones makes a superposed waveform which depends not only on the two vibrations' frequencies and combined intensity but also on their relative phase.

Phase refers to the part of a regularly recurring cycle which is complete at a particular time. The moon may appear as new, a quarter crescent, full, or elsewhere at various predictable times of the month—one can speak of phases of the moon. So too may a vibration cycle be at varying degrees of completion or phase—the vibrating particle is at its original position or displaced in varying amounts in one direction or another. *Two* vibrations' cycles may or may not be at the same phase. Both may be starting and completing cycles at identical times, in which case they are in zero phase or the same phase relative to each other. One may be behind the other; for example, one vibration cycle may be at a point of maximal displacement while the other is at the original position of rest. In this case, they are out of phase. The superposed waveform will be influenced by relative phase. It is even possible to have, for two tones of identical frequency, a combined waveform which shows less amplitude than either individual waveform because of the destructive interference resulting from the individual waves, in effect, working against each other. Of course, the combined waveform may be stronger than either component, which will happen when the tones are in phase and constructive interference results.

The combination of pure tones, which in a way is similar to a complex tone, will stimulate the basilar membrane strongly at more than one location. If the frequency difference (Δf) between the two tones is of sufficient size, which could be as low as 6 percent but is more likely to be from 12 to 20 percent or more (Cardozo, 1974), there is a clear discrimination of two separate tones. If Δf is insufficient, a sensation of roughness, beating, or unison will result. The distance along the membrane that must be exceeded to promote a clear two-tone sensation is known as the *critical band width;* according to Roederer (1975), it has a value of approximately 1.2 mm. In terms of Hz, it varies with frequency from about 25 to over 2000 Hz; different studies give somewhat different results (Plomp, 1976; Moore, 1977).

The concept of a critical band width as a minimal distance between points of stimulation and the corresponding sensation may be illustrated easily through the sense of touch, as suggested by Roederer (1975), borrowing the analogy from Von Bekesy (1960). One person touches another's underarm skin with two pencil points simultaneously. The person being touched must indicate whether he or she is being touched in one place or two. It will be found that a certain minimal distance must be exceeded for it to become obvious that a person is being touched in two places rather than one.

Thus, frequency discrimination of two simultaneous pure tones also is primarily dependent on the location of basilar membrane stimulation. The jnd for frequency discrimination of two simultaneous tones is considerably larger than the jnd for detecting changes in a single pure tone (Roederer, 1975). However, musicians rarely deal with pure tones.

Pitch Processing of Complex Tones

A complex tone contains more than one frequency. It differs from a combination of pure tones in that the waveform from one sound source is complex. A bowed violin string, a plucked guitar string, a blown trumpet, and a human voice all output a complex waveform which is a mixture of individual frequency components.

The individual frequency components include a *fundamental* frequency (generally the lowest frequency) and higher frequencies which may be in a harmonic or inharmonic relationship. In a harmonic relationship, the higher frequencies are in an integral multiple relationship with the fundamental, i.e. nondecimal whole numbers multiplied by the fundamental frequency will give the frequencies of the higher components or *harmonics*. In an inharmonic relationship, the higher components are related in a nonintegral multiple manner. Musical complex tones show *varying degrees of harmonicity.** The more nearly harmonic the relationship, the more obvious is the pitch sensation.

The relative strengths of the particular frequency components vary. Diagrams of complex tones, made via spectrum analyzers or other analytic electronic equipment, show, within limits, the

---

*The terms partial, harmonic, and overtone sometimes are used interchangeably. This is unfortunate because they have different meanings. A *partial* is any component of a complex tone, regardless of any mathematical relationship or lack thereof. A *harmonic* is any frequency (not necessarily a component of a particular tone) which is in an integral multiple relationship with the fundamental frequency. (The fundamental itself is the first harmonic, $f \times 1 = f$.) An *overtone* is any harmonic *other than* the fundamental which is in a particular complex tone. Any component of a complex tone is a partial; it may or may not be a harmonic. Any integral multiple of the fundamental frequency is a harmonic; it may or may not be a partial or an overtone (Backus, 1969).

particular component frequencies and their intensity levels. Curiously, the fundamental frequency is not always the strongest component, despite the fact that the pitch associated with the complex tone almost always is the pitch elicited by the fundamental.

A complex mixture of frequencies may stimulate the basilar membrane at eight or more locations; such stimulations often exceed the critical band width. Yet a complex tone is heard with one distinct pitch. Why? The answer lies in the fact that the basilar membrane serves as an analyzer and information passer for complex tones—the pitch assignment primarily occurs higher in the auditory pathway.

Understanding pitch perception of complex tones requires understanding that the auditory system uses information regarding *periodicity*. Periodic motion is regularly recurring motion; sound waves are periodic. The simplest kind of wave arises from a pure tone; one is diagrammed in Figure 2-2. (Wave diagrams such as this, similar to oscilloscope tracings, should be conceived as a pattern of particular displacements frozen in time.) A complex wave appears in Figure 2-3. In both instances, there is a pattern: sooner or later, the waveform *repeats* itself; it has periodicity. This rate of repetition or repetition frequency is extremely important musically.

A complex tone with component frequencies of 100, 200, 300, 400, and 500 Hz will make a wave with a repetition frequency of 100 Hz. So will a complex tone containing only the 400 and 500 Hz components. In either case, the pitch sensation for 100 Hz

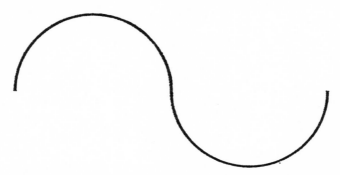

Figure 2-2. Displacement pattern arising from a pure tone.

Figure 2-3. Displacement pattern arising from a complex tone.

will be assigned. A complex tone with component frequencies of 50, 150, and 200 Hz will make a wave with a repetition frequency of 50 Hz, as will a complex tone with components of 400, 450, and 500 Hz. In each case, the pitch sensation for 50 Hz will be assigned. The repetition frequency is detected by the process of *fundamental tracking,* which yields a sensation of *periodicity pitch,* also known as subjective pitch, virtual pitch, and residual pitch.* Such pitch sensations even can be assigned to the incredibly complex waveforms associated with noise (Rainbolt and Schubert, 1968).

The strength of periodicity pitch and its assignment beyond the cochlea are illustrated in a study by Houtsma and Goldstein (1972). Using earphones, they presented randomly chosen paired upper harmonics, without the fundamental, monotically (two harmonics to one ear) and dichotically (one harmonic to each ear) to three experienced musicians. The musicians were able to recognize melodies which the fundamental would have formed equally well in both conditions, even though the harmonics could not combine in either ear in the dichotic condition. The presence of the fundamental in the cochlea is not necessary for fundamental tracking, which is a centralized neural process.

Periodicity pitch apparently results from superposition of the neural excitation patterns elicited by individual tonal components.

---

*Strictly speaking, residual pitch probably should refer only to periodicity pitch determined by the eighth and higher harmonics.

Each individual component, if presented as a pure tone, would elicit its own unique pattern. When the components occur in a complex tone, there is a combined neural excitation. This occurs even when part of the information comes from one ear and part comes from the other, as happens in dichotic presentation. If the frequencies are not strictly harmonic, an unambiguous pitch nevertheless is experienced with dichotic presentation (Van den Brink, 1974), although it is likely that the pitch is higher than the pitch normally associated with the repetition frequency.

Although central (in the neural network) rather than peripheral (in the cochlea) pitch processing obviously is necessary for fundamental tracking, the means by which it occurs is not yet known in detail. Goldstein (1973) views the "central pitch processor" as a recognizer of patterns associated with stimulation along the basilar membrane. The central processor estimates the frequency in accordance with a best matching stored (learned) pattern of periodic signals. Wightman (1973) theorizes a model in which spatial distribution (along the basilar membrane) information is twice transformed. Frequency is coded by place, and intensity is coded by amount of neural activity at each place, then a mathematical operation called autocorrelation is performed in which the spatial information becomes time information. Both views imply a learned recognition of designated periodicity patterns.

The particular frequency components which appear to be the major determinants of a complex tone's pitch may vary with the fundamental frequency; this is the concept of spectral dominance (Ritsma, 1970). Plomp (1967b) had fifteen subjects judge complex tones in which the fundamental was reduced in Hz by 10 percent while the higher harmonics simultaneously were increased by 10 percent as compared with unaltered complex tones. The altered tones were judged as higher, despite their lower fundamentals. Plomp concluded that beyond fundamental frequencies of about 1400 Hz, the fundamental itself is the prime determinant of complex tone pitch, while for complex tones with fundamentals of roughly 700 to 1400 Hz the second and third harmonics are crucial. The third and higher harmonics are the pitch determinants for tones with a fundamental in the range of about 350 to 700 Hz; below 350 Hz the fourth and higher harmonics are crucial. All Plomp's dividing regions are well within the common musically useful frequency range.

Curious effects involving a shift in periodicity pitch for two-component complex tones may be demonstrated under laboratory conditions. With adjacent harmonic frequencies, such as 480 and 600 Hz (fourth and fifth harmonics of 120 Hz), the pitch corresponds to that elicited by the missing fundamental, which is the waveform repetition frequency. But shifting frequencies away from a harmonic situation, while maintaining a constant frequency difference, such as to 520 and 640 Hz, results in a pitch shift upward. Exactly why this happens is unclear (Smoorenburg, 1970).

The pitch perception of a complex tone need not be a unitary sensation. Individuals can learn to "hear out" some of the partials in a complex tone when the frequency separation exceeds the critical band width (Plomp, 1964).

Relative phase of the components may influence complex tone pitch perception when the signals consist of three harmonics above the eighth. Below the eighth harmonic, pitch perceptibility of complex tones apparently is uninfluenced by phase (Bilsen, 1973).

Of profound musical importance, complex tone pitch perception is related to waveform periodicity, although not simply so. Music as it is currently known could not exist without periodicity pitch. It is a complicated and, as yet, unexplained affair to which psychologists and musicians should direct increasing attention.

Combination Tones

When two different frequencies are sounded together, such as in a violin double stop or in a harmonic interval on an organ, a third, generally lower, pitch may be heard in addition to the pitches associated with the two primary frequencies. This is a so-called combination tone. Combination tones equivalent in frequency to the difference between the two primary tones $(f_2 - f_1)$ probably are the most common. Combinations represented by

$2f_1 - f_2$ and $3f_1 - 2f_2$ also are audible; in theory, many other combinations resulting from multiples of the lower tone (f_1) and upper tone (f_2) are possible.

The phenomenon of the combination tone (also called a subjective tone) is real, but there is disagreement regarding its nature. Defining a combination tone as a tone not present in the sound stimulus but heard by the ear can be misleading. There are at least three ways in which a combination tone-like sensation may be experienced.

Periodicity pitch, detected by the neural process of fundamental tracking, was discussed above. It may be possible to experience a periodicity pitch sensation from a combination of frequencies not arising from the same source. Backus (1969) implies that a combination tone really is nothing more than the ear's ability to detect a waveform repetition frequency.

It is easy to produce a very strong third sound by putting two inputs into one speaker, as with a synthesizer, electronic organ, or two audio oscillators. The third frequency is represented physically in the soundwave; it results from heterodyneing, in which two signals of nearly the same frequency mix and fluctuate in amplitude (Strange, 1972, p. 10). It is misleading to call these sounds true combination tones.

The third way of experiencing a combination tone-like sensation is to experience a true combination tone, which results from cochlear distortion. Such a tone requires a minimal intensity level of the primary frequencies which is well beyond threshold. Plomp (1965) found that subjects heard more combination tones at higher sound pressure levels; 51-57 db marked the detectability threshold, i.e. the sensation level at which combination tones just become audible. At customary listening levels for many people combination tones are avoided because the ear does not distort sufficiently, although there are large interindividual differences. Audiblity also may vary with the particular combination tone (Plomp, 1976).

The major problem in recognizing a true combination tone as something distinct from periodicity pitch or electronic hocus-pocus is agreeing that there is distortion in the ear. In simple language, what is being referred to here as distortion is a tendency of the basilar membrane to move more than it should in simple response to a given amount of stimulation. Excess movement could cause hair cell stimulation at extra places, thereby creating extra sound sensations. Contemporary evidence suggests that such distortion is genuine. Sweetman and Dallos (1969) showed that guinea pig cochleas evidence distortion; the question is not whether there is distortion, but whether it is electromechanical or just mechanical. Dallos and Sweetman (1969) demonstrated that harmonics of a low-frequency fundamental, which could give rise to combination tones, are more prominent at the low-frequency end of the guinea pig cochlea than they are at the regions which their particular frequencies would suggest. Goldstein (1970) showed that a "cancellation tone" of identical frequency as a combination tone, adjusted for proper amplitude and relative phase, could cancel the combination tone. By taking advantage of the Mossbauer effect, which entails using an implanted radioactive substance to trace basilar membrane displacements, Rhode and Robles (1974) observed nonlinearity, i.e. distortion, in the cochlea of a squirrel monkey. Given such evidence, it seems reasonable that tonal sensations can arise through cochlear distortion.

Combination tones can interact with other components to increase tonal complexity; they can alter the way a tonal stimulus is heard. They probably will be continually studied; musical utility may be found.

Intervals

An interval is a simultaneous or successive sounding of two tones, pure or complex. Some musicians call a simultaneous interval harmonic and a successive interval melodic. Psychology of music has been concerned with apparent consonance, pitch, and size of intervals.

CONSONANCE-DISSONANCE. Study of consonance has been confused by varying uses of the label as well as different views of what causes a consonance classification. Almost half a century ago, Peterson and Smith (1930) asked subjects to evaluate mistuned intervals and report "unnatural" ones, thereby equating certain tunings with consonance. Bugg (1933) reported that subjects were confused when asked to classify intervals as consonant on the basis of fusion, blending, smoothness, and purity (all of which have nonauditory connotation), as if they were synonymous terms. He felt that a problem with consonance was that it is not necessarily a pleasantness-unpleasantness dimension; affective reactions somehow must be removed from consonance. More recently, Terhardt (1974a) has divorced psychoacoustic consonance (the absence of roughness) from any musical interval sensations: Psychoacoustic consonance is a matter of frequency distance, whereas musical intervals are ratio phenomena. Difficulties with consonance theories and judgments obviously are related to psychologists' and musicians' inabilities to agree regarding a definition.

Musicians generally regard consonance as a relatively restful and passive state of auditory sensation while dissonance is a relatively agitated and active state. Seconds, the augmented fourth, and sevenths currently are considered dissonant in an abstract sense while unisons, thirds, fourths, fifths, sixths, and octaves are considered consonant. Since such judgments can change with time and context, Lundin (1947) proposed what probably is the most espoused explanation of consonance: It is a matter of cultural conditioning. Prior physical theories, resorting to numerical relationships, beats, fusion, and genetics, all are lacking because of incorrect interpretations of physiology or failure to consider mistuned consonances.

Since Lundin's declaration, however, investigators have continued to consider alternatives, often with recognition that musicians may merely label intervals by using consonance or dissonance as a synonym or qualifying adjective for interval names. Van de Geer, Levelt, and Plomp (1962) asked ten subjects who were not professional musicians to judge twenty-three pure tone intervals on a seven-point scale for each of ten bipolar adjectives. In addition to consonant vs. dissonant, subjects considered dimensions such as high vs. low, active vs. passive, and rough vs. smooth. The subjects' ratings were factor analyzed and three common core variables emerged to explain the overall variation in ratings. The only factor to which consonant-dissonant related was an evaluation factor: The nonmusical subjects evaluated the intervals in terms of consonance-dissonance, euphonious-diseuphonious, and beautiful-ugly. The authors concluded that nonmusicians tend to evaluate intervals rather than name them on a ratio basis.

Plomp and Levelt (1965) used nonmusicians in updating the old theory that dissonance results from beats among partials. They related consonance to the critical band width; the most dissonant intervals were those with a frequency difference corresponding to about one-fourth of the band width. For increasing frequency levels, the width of the most dissonant interval increases. The amount of consonance for particular interval distances varied differently for different frequency ranges. The essence of Plomp and Levelt's findings is that partials from the two tones comprising an interval align along the basilar membrane. If the resulting stimulations are identical or separated by a critical band width, consonance is promoted. If they lie within a critical band width and are not identical, dissonance is promoted. This may be called a theory of "colliding harmonics" (Roederer, 1975); it is important because it suggests that, at least for people lacking musical training, there may be some physical basis for a consonance phenomenon.

Although not studying consonance, Siegel and Siegel (1977) demonstrated that musicians do tend to categorize intervals rather than evaluate them. Six subjects, all with excellent relative pitch and interval naming ability, judged thirteen intervals, ranging from 20 cents* flatter than a perfect fourth through 20 cents sharper than a perfect fifth, arranged in 20-cent steps. The randomly presented intervals were judged against a standard perfect fourth, augmented fourth, and perfect fifth. In addition to classifying intervals, the subjects evaluated their size and indicated whether they were in tune. Subjects were quite accurate at categorization, but *within* the interval categories there was little change in perceived interval size. Subjects judged only 37 percent of the intervals as out-of-tune when in fact 77 percent were.

It is unlikely that the terms consonance and dissonance will disappear, so musicians probably should give greater consideration to what is meant by consonance and dissonance. It is especially important to remember that the phenomenon exists in the musically

---

*A cent is 1/100 of a tempered scale half step. It is a convenient measure of the physical distance between two tones comprising an interval because that distance in cents will not vary with frequency range.

naive, independently of interval names, while musicians label intervals on the basis of experience and training.

APPARENT PITCH. An interval is two tones which, when sounded together, *may* have a unitary pitch sensation. For many listeners there is no such tonal fusion, and the concept of intervalic pitch is vague.

Farnsworth (1938) had 276 subjects, half "musical" and half "nonmusical," listen to single tones followed by two-tone intervals containing the single tone as the upper or lower member. They apparently were asked to indicate which interval matched the tone's pitch; subjects had difficulty with the task. Slightly more musical than nonmusical subjects favored the interval with the standard in the soprano. In another part of the study, subjects compared a 512-1024 Hz and 645-767 Hz interval. Musical subjects tended to hear the larger interval as higher; nonmusicians tended to hear the larger interval as lower. Farnsworth did this to show that Stumpf's principle, which he later cited in his text (1969), required revision.

In its original form, Stumpf's principle stated that any simultaneous interval has a pitch equivalent to that of the lower tone. In Farnsworth's modification, the interval's pitch tends to be equivalent to that of the upper tone, except for those who are musically untrained, and for some basses.

Except to the extent that periodicity pitch is formed, intervalic pitch probably is too elusive: Harmony is *not* a unitary pitch sensation. One mystery in psychology of music is why two simultaneous sound sources, like two violin strings, usually produce an interval while a tone from a single sound source, or even a noise which is more complicated acoustically than the interval, produces a unitary pitch sensation. The answer probably lies in the brain's ability to use various cues related to localization and transient waveform characteristics (Roederer, 1975).

APPARENT SIZE. Musical intervals usually are specified by the scale degree (third, fifth, sixth, etc.) of their upper tones in relation to the lower tones, subject to modification by accidentals (minor, major, augmented, etc.). Another way is to specify the interval ratio; each interval has in its simplest (just) form a characteristic ratio. An octave's upper frequency is related to its lower frequency as 2 is to 1. A perfect fifth's upper frequency is in a 3:2 ratio with its lower frequency. Other characteristic ratios are 16:15 for a minor second, 9:8 for a major second, 6:5 for a minor third, 5:4 for a major third, 4:3 for a perfect fourth, 7:5 for an augmented fourth, 5:3 for a minor sixth, 8:5 for a major sixth, 9:5 for a minor seventh, and 15:8 for a major seventh. In performance practice there is considerable deviation from the simple ratios; the tempered scale, even when perfectly tuned, lacks the characteristic ratios except for the octave. The most specific way to indicate physical interval size is in cents (one cent = 1/1200 of an octave). For example, an octave is 1200 cents; a perfect fifth (3.2 ratio) is 702 cents; the less-than-perfect fifth of the tempered scale is 700 cents. The number of cents in an interval may be computed via the formula

$$n = 3986.31 \ [\log(f_2/f_1)],$$

where n is the number of cents of the desired interval, f_2 is the frequency of the upper tone, and f_1 is the frequency of the lower tone (Backus, 1969).

However an interval is measured physically, there is also a psychological sensation of interval size. For musicians, "a fourth is a fourth" and "a fifth is a fifth" may be true regardless of frequency range, as suggested by the Siegel and Siegel study discussed above. All identically named intervals have a degree of perceptual similarity, regardless of particular frequency components, which aids in identification and musical utility. But if an interval, particularly a successive interval, is evaluated rather than simply categorized, its apparent size may vary with frequency range. There is conflicting evidence regarding the direction of change. Some maintain that physically equal intervals appear to increase in size with increasing frequency (Stevens, Volkmann, and Newman, 1937; Stevens, 1975); others say that intervals in lower frequency ranges have greater "melodic distance," which implies that they appear to become smaller with increasing frequency (Winckel, 1967). Apparent interval size poses a continuing and interesting problem.

Beating

A perceptible rise and fall in apparent loudness is associated with the simultaneous sounding of two slightly different frequencies. The beat frequency for a mistuned unison is equivalent to the difference between the two frequencies; the further away the frequencies are from each other, the faster is the beating. With sufficient frequency separation, the beating becomes a roughness. Once the separation corresponding to the critical band width is reached, a sensation of two tones results.

Beating is caused by periodic changes in the superposed waveform. Beating of a mistuned unison is *first order* beating; it is a result of peripheral, i.e. cochlear, auditory processing. Beating of a mistuned interval other than a unison, particularly an octave, fourth, or fifth, is *second order* beating (Roederer, 1975), which may result from the peripheral interference of combination tones or, especially at lower frequencies, from central neural processing (Plomp, 1976). *Binaural* beating, a special kind, may occur when a separate input is provided to each ear.

First order beating may be useful in tuning. Piano tuners often count beats to obtain the proper tempered tuning of designated intervals. Instrumentalists are confident that they are in tune when the first order beats disappear. However, tuning by eliminating the beats between a reference tone and a tone to be tuned may be ambiguous to the tuner because of uncertainties regarding the direction of deviation. Corso (1954) had a violinist, a bassoonist, an alto saxophonist, and two clarinetists tune to a piano and a variety of electronic tone sources. In one experimental condition the performer played alone, then with the reference tone to enable a comparison using beating. In the other condition the performer first listened to the reference tone, then played alone. Neither procedure produced more accurate tuning than the other. Corso suggested that unison tuning is more dependent on pitch-matching than on beat elimination. One should not regard tuning by beat elimination as a necessarily superior method.

Second order beating, also known (unfortunately) as the beating of mistuned consonances, is more ambiguous than first order beating. It is not obvious just what is fluctuating. Second order beats are strong when the beating interval, such as a mistuned fourth or fifth, is below 500 Hz. The beats become progressively weaker above 1000 Hz. The beats, when audible, do not disappear when noise is introduced to cover (mask) possible peripheral effects such as combination tones; evidence strongly suggests central processing of second order beats. (Plomp, 1967a).

If a different sound is presented to each ear in such a manner that the sounds cannot possibly mix until they reach the neural pathways, binaural beats may result. In an intensive study regarding detection limits for binaural beats, Perrott and Nelson (1969) found that beat detection was most likely around 500 Hz. Likelihood of detection decreased with higher frequencies; beyond 1500 Hz, there were no binaural beats. The stimulus conditions varied regarding the difference in Hz between the tones; with higher standard frequencies greater interear frequency differences produced more obvious binaural beats. For smaller frequency differences subjects reported a "fused" auditory image, waxing and waning. For larger frequency differences, a rapid flutter was reported while each individual pitch retained its identity in its particular ear.

Similar sounds presented binaurally indeed may fuse into one wavering sensation, rather than maintaining individual pitch identities (Tobias, 1972). The stimulus duration and the small amount of time required for the stimulus to grow to its maximal level influence fusion (Perrott, Briggs, and Perrott, 1970).

Perception of binaural beats may have some nonauditory implications. According to Tobias (1972), women normally hear binaural beats at lower frequencies than men, but the frequency levels increase at the onset of menstruation, then decline, then increase slightly fifteen days later.

Beating is of obvious musical importance. One reason that one French horn amplified to ten times its output cannot sound like ten horns is that the complex beating among the ten horns' outputs adds a quality of "richness" to which listeners have become accustomed. (This is the so-called chorus effect (Backus, 1969).) Beating in exposed orchestral passages which is not dismissed as vibrato may make listeners cringe. Binaural beats require high quality headphones and are not usually exploited musically, but they may offer interesting possibilities for those who wish to experiment with new musical effects.

Absolute Pitch

The phenomenon of absolute pitch is often astounding to those who do not possess it and may be viewed as quite ordinary and a bit of a nuisance by those who do. Also known as perfect pitch, absolute pitch exists when one can correctly identify a tone by letter name without reference to any external standard. To correctly label a sound as "C" when only a C is heard is quite different from being presented with a tone labelled as F, and then being asked to label C in relation. Many a musician acquires relative pitch, the ability to name tones in relation to a known external standard by utilizing interval relationships, but the acquisition of absolute pitch is no simple matter.

The presence of absolute pitch in persons who have not had extensive musical training suggests some extra perceptual ability, possibly even genetically transmitted. It has been suggested that "tonal chroma," cyclical tonal characteristics with octave-octave consistency, are responsible for absolute pitch (Bachem, 1954).

For some authorities, absolute pitch is a matter of deliberate learning. Meyer (1956) believed in the memorization of tone height with practice. Corso (1957) found that some tonalities were easier to judge than others; ascending scales were more conducive to tonality recognition than random scale patterns or chord sequences. Such differences were believed related to learned habit as well as technical considerations. Cuddy (1968) suggested that internalizing A440 as a reference tone was more effective than trying to learn each tone individually. He noted that judgments of pure tones were related to musical training and that judgments of piano tones were specifically related to piano training. Internalizing a particular reference would enable one to display absolute pitch, but differential degrees of accuracy with different performance media suggest learning a pseudoabsolute pitch by using auditory cues other than frequency, e.g. timbre characteristics.

A somewhat more contemporary view of absolute pitch development relates learning tonal identification to a critical age period, roughly four to seven years, when pitch has a greater salience, in speech and in music, than it does in later life. Jeffress (1962) noted that some supposedly tone-deaf individuals were from India and spoke a language in which pitch is insignificant. Sergeant (1969) showed that a majority of surveyed adults possessing absolute pitch experienced intensive musical training during the critical period. De Gainza (1970) indicated that isolated sounds attracted her small children, but with maturity form, structure, and tonal relations replaced individual pitch saliency. The ear can observe and perceive details, but it also can perceive structure, which, in music, may become more important than the details which foster absolute pitch development. The critical period view is called *imprinting,* in analogy with the maternal connection a hatched duckling makes with the first moving object it encounters. During the critical period a label is highly associable with a tonal sensation.

In investigating absolute pitch, it is important to use varied stimuli and avoid relative pitch cues. It is not enough to "come within a third" or label only certain tones produced by instruments with which the individual is familiar. Many individuals probably can learn to identify *certain* tones *some* of the time, but to insist that they can identify *any* tone *all* of the time is misleading. If absolute pitch is desirable, more consideration of imprinting is necessary, and experiments should be planned accordingly.

Pitch Measurement

Pitch may be measured in various ways, but any technique must use a human observer (or an apparatus built to simulate one). The stroboscope and digital frequency counter measure frequency, not pitch.

Pitch matching often is used as a measure. Intonation problems are pitch matching problems; to say that someone is "out-of-tune" is to say that, in some observer's subjective judgment, a produced sound does not match a standard.

A judgment that one tone is higher or lower than another may suffice, but quantitative comparisons of pitch require more detail. There is an interesting quantitative pitch scale known as the *mel* scale (scale in the measurement, not the musical sense). On the mel scale 1000 Hz of frequency, 40 db above the hearing threshold, are equivalent to 1000 mels of pitch sensation. The changes in mels for given frequency changes are not equivalent, e.g. a pitch sensation of 2000 mels, "twice as high" as 1000 mels, is elicited by 3120 Hz, not 2000 Hz. A frequency of 500 Hz is 602 mels; 500 mels requires a frequency of approximately 390 Hz. A lucid table of frequency-mel equivalents appears in Stevens (1975).

The mel scale was established by the psychophysical method of fractionation (Stevens, Volkmann, and Newman, 1937). Five observers set variable frequencies to sound half as high as standards of 125, 200, 300, 400, 700, 1000, 2000, 5000, 8000, and 12,000 Hz, and the resulting average values were developed into the mel scale. It was noted that there was considerable variability; for 1000 Hz the frequency equivalent to half pitch was set at 391, 485, 590, 622, and 640 Hz, and that the observer who was a trained musician had trouble disregarding octave sensations and could not conceive of a "zero" pitch.

In 1940, Stevens and Volkmann had twelve observers use a tunable electric piano to divide each of the frequency intervals 40-1000, 200-6500, and 3000-12000 Hz into four equal pitch intervals. The observers also adjusted a variable tone to sound half as high as various standards. Results of the respective methods of bisection and fractionation agreed closely, and the mel scale had further credence.

The mel scale appeared useful. Stevens (1954) maintained that jnds for pitch are subjectively equal when measured in mels, although they of course vary when measured in Hz. But in a practical sense, particularly to musicians, the mel scale suggests pitch relationships which just do not hold. For a musician, an *octave* is "twice as high." This may be an artifact of musical training; Allen (1967) had ten musical and ten nonmusical subjects rate the similarity of twenty-three test tones to a 1000 Hz standard. The musical subjects rated the test tones forming an octave with the standard as significantly more similar than did the nonmusical subjects. Perhaps the mel scale relationships cannot hold for musical subjects because of indoctrination to the octave.

Beck and Shaw (1962) presented piano tones ranging from 131 to 4,186 Hz in relation to a 131 Hz and 523 Hz standard. The subjects made magnitude estimations* of the comparison pitches in relation to the standards and assigned numbers to represent their judgments of the octave relationship between each comparison tone and the standards. For the 131 Hz standard the magnitude estimations of pitch distances gave results "close" to the mel scale, although octave judgments were rather consistently below those predicted by the mel scale. For the 523 Hz standard, with considerable variability, lower comparison tones yielded results smaller than mel scale predictions while higher comparisons yielded larger results. In general, and more importantly, musical subjects tended to give magnitude estimations which were smaller than those of nonmusical subjects. When pure tones rather than piano tones then were used, more conformity to the mel scale was found for all subjects. In this and in a later study (Beck and Shaw, 1963) the authors conclude that pitch estimates are influenced by the choice of standards and multiple judgments. The mel scale's complexity is obvious.

Radocy (1977) had musicians and nonmusicians listen to successive intervals at five different frequency levels. Some intervals were in a 2:1 mel relationship; some were physical octaves, and the others were neither. Subjects simply classified each interval as to whether its upper tone was less than twice as high, twice as high, or more than twice as high as the lower tone. In general, nonmusicians heard all intervals as larger, but in no instance did a majority of listeners, musicians or nonmusicians, classify a 2:1 mel relationship as twice as high. Octaves generally were considered twice as high, but not always.

The search for a quantitative pitch measure continues. The

---

*Magnitude estimation is a technique for estimating apparent strengths or distances simply by assigning numbers to represent apparent proportionate amounts. It is discussed in detail below.

mel scale obviously has problems. An octave, a 2:1 frequency relationship, is not always a 2:1 pitch relationship, but then what is?
In addition to its placement or location aspect (metathetic), pitch
may have a degree of pitch definity (prothetic), e.g. an oboe pitch
usually is more definite than a cymbal pitch. Perhaps some sort
of measure can be developed to take this into account as well as
the relation to frequency.

LOUDNESS PHENOMENA

Loudness is an obvious but complex property of sound. Musical performances may be evaluated readily as "too loud" or "too
soft" by very unsophisticated listeners. Considerable pedagogical
effort is directed by music educators toward improving a student's
sensitivity or musicality by using more effective dynamic contrasts in performance.

Curiously, although human ears are sensitive to a range of
sound power of about one trillion to one, minute loudness distinctions have not attained the importance of minute pitch distinctions in Western music. Loudness notation generally is en-
trusted to symbols for dynamic levels and words indicating a
gradual change. Furthermore, although six basic dynamic levels—
pp, p, mp, mf, f, ff—have been used for approximately 200 years,
few instrumentalists have a dynamic range capable of attaining
those six discrete levels. This generally is not due to limitations
of musical instruments. Restricted musical dynamic ranges and
solo passages equal in loudness to full orchestral passages, characteristic of films and television, may be partly responsible, but the
general artistic demand for a range and variation seems restricted
(Patterson, 1974).

Our loudness discussion is organized around distinguishing
loudness from intensity, volume, and density, measurement of
loudness and systematic relations emerging therefrom, masking,
loudness summation, and dangers of prolonged exposure to high
loudness levels.

Intensity-Loudness Relationship

Intensity and loudness are not interchangeable terms. Intensity is an objectively measured physical property, an amount

of power. It often is expressed in power units per unit area, as in watts per square meter. Loudness is a subjective sensation of the magnitude or strength of sound. It requires an animate perceiver (or a machine built to simulate one).

Loudness's major determinant is the amount of sound intensity, but the intensity-loudness relationship is not on a simple one-to-one basis. A minimum time, often about .015 sec, is necessary for a sound to build to its maximal loudness; prolonged steady sounds may appear to diminish in loudness owing to auditory fatigue or habituation (Roederer, 1975). The influence of how long a sound takes to reach its maximal intensity ("rise" time) on loudness varies with the sound's frequency and complexity. Rise time generally is more influential for lower frequencies and pure tones (Gjaevenes and Rimstad, 1972). More importantly for music, the intensity-loudness relationship is confounded by frequency. Details of the confounding are discussed as part of the measurement of loudness level below; the confounding essentially means that equal intensities do not elicit equal loudness across all audible frequencies. This is because the ear's sensitivity varies with frequency.

Volume

It is most unfortunate that volume, which implies an amount of space or capacity, commonly is used as a synonym for loudness, which is an amount of strength or a magnitude. Volume is the apparent size or extensity of a sound; most would say that a tuba tone is more voluminous than a flute tone of equal intensity.

People generally are not trained to judge volume. Their criteria are unstable, and more conspicuous differences between tones may obscure volume differences. Nevertheless, in an early study (Stevens, 1934b), five observers matched paired tones in volume by changing intensities. Tones judged equivalent in volume were compared for frequency and intensity differences. It was noted that volume differences were greater at lower intensity levels for all frequencies. However, an increase in intensity level brought a more rapid volume increase at higher than at lower frequencies.

That volume depends in a complex way on frequency and intensity was demonstrated with forty-six observers by Terrace and

Stevens (1962). They plotted frequency-intensity combinations necessary for equal volume judgments and formed a "vol" scale of measurement in which 1 vol equals the apparent volume of 1000 Hz at 40 decibels of sound pressure level. They found that regardless of frequency, at around 140 db all tones sounded equal in volume. In general, higher frequencies required greater intensities for equivalent volume, and the rate of growth in volume (as intensity increased) varied with frequency.

Volume's existence as an independent tonal attribute is questionable. Volume has no quasi-parallel relationship with any single physical attribute in the way that loudness is related to intensity or pitch is related to frequency. Nevertheless, the ability of observers to make reliable volume judgments which relate lawfully to frequency-intensity combinations, independently of loudness, suggests that the volume concept is more than fanciful thinking.

Density

Density, the apparent compactness of a sound, is another tonal attribute which lacks one distinct quasi-parallel physical relationship. It also is questioned regarding its independent existence, and it may be merely the opposite pole of volume.

Stevens (1934a) had four observers equate different paired frequencies in density by varying one tone in intensity. Differences in settings between equal density and equal loudness judgments were noted. Opposite to volume judgments, judgments of equal density required that lower frequency tones be louder than higher frequency tones. For a given frequency, the louder the tone, the more dense it appeared.

Guirao and Stevens (1964) later found that density grows in a lawful way with increases in intensity, but the rate of growth is slower at higher frequencies.

Observation that volume decreases while density increases with increasing frequencies and that lawful relationships apparently exist between increasing intensity and corresponding increases in volume and density suggested a relationship between *loudness* and some *combination* of volume and density. It indeed was found that loudness judgments are proportional to the products of vol-

ume and density judgments, and, furthermore, that softness judgments are proportional to the products of smallness and diffuse-
ness judgments. Such proportionality was more clearcut for
noise than tone, but the concept of loudness as a synthesis of volume and density is intriguing (Stevens, Guirao, and Slawson,
1965).

Measurement of Loudness

Quantification of loudness, a challenging and controversial
task because of the many complications, may be approached in
terms of quantifying the tonal stimulus, in which case one is not
really quantifying the loudness sensation, or in terms of quantifying the response to the stimulus magnitude.

STIMULUS MEASURES. Since intensity is defined as an amount
of power per unit area, it must be quantified in terms of a power
unit per area unit. Watts per square meter are common units for
sound intensity. Most sound intensities are rather small values;
one watt per square meter is a rather intense sound which approaches the upper limit of hearing. The threshold of hearing at
1000 Hz is around .000000000001 w/m². Negative powers of ten
often are utilized in expressing such tiny numbers; the above
threshold is 10^{-12} w/m².

Sound intensity usually is expressed in terms of intensity *level*
rather than pure intensity. Intensity level implies a comparison
of a particular intensity to some baseline value, just as the fourth
floor of a building is the fourth floor in comparison to the ground.
The comparisons implied by intensity levels of sound are ratio
comparisons which use the unit known as the decibel.

Decibels are measures of power ratios. They are not limited
to measure of sound; light and electric current also may be measured in decibels. Decibels are best defined in terms of the formula by which they are computed. For sound intensity,

$$D = 10 \; [\log \; (I/I_0)],$$

where D is the number of decibels, I is the particular intensity
which the decibel value places on a level, and I_0 is the baseline
value. A logical baseline is the intensity at the threshold of hearing; hence 10^{-12} w/m² often is used.

It is important to recognize two consequences of a decibel

value being a shorthand way to express a ratio comparison. One, a relatively small range of decibels encompasses a relatively large range of acoustic powers. Two, one cannot simply combine decibels to obtain an intensity level for tonal combinations.

An intensity of 10^{-6} w/m^2 (.000001 w/m^2) has an intensity level of 60 db. An intensity of 10^{-5} w/m^2 (.00001 w/m^2) has an intensity level of 70 db. That 10 db difference represents a tenfold (10:1) increase in power—.00001 is ten times .000001. An intensity level of 80 db is attained by an intensity of .0001 w/m^2 (10^{-4}); the difference between 80 and 60 db represents a one hundredfold (100:1) increase in power—.0001 is 100 times .000001. *Any* 10 db difference means that one sound has ten times the intensity of the other. A 20 db difference always represents one hundred times the intensity; 30 db, one thousand times; 40 db, ten thousand times, etc. The decibel scale is logarithmic; equal decibel amounts stand for equal ratios.

Two decibel values may not be summed directly in any acoustically meaningful way. Two intensity levels of 60 db do not total 120 db—they total approximately 63 db. Each intensity corresponding to a 60 db level is .000001 w/m^2; .000001 w/m^2 +.000001 w/m^2 = .000002 w/m^2, not .00001 w/m^2, which has a level of 70 db, and *obviously not* 1.0 w/m^2, which has a level of 120 db. By working backwards in the decibel formula, adding the intensities themselves, and finding the level for the sum of intensities (a formidable task unless a calculator with logarithmic functions is available), one can show that any intensity level increases by approximately 3 db when combined with an equivalent level. If the combined intensity levels are not equal, the result will be something less than 3 db added to the higher level: 60 db + 59 db ≈ 62.6 db, e.g.

Sound pressure level is a more common stimulus measure than intensity level because it is easier to measure, and it relates logically to the concept of pressure variations being responsible for sound. Sound pressure level (SPL) is expressed in decibels which are computed differently in relation to a different baseline. The formula is:

$$D = 20 \ [\log \ (P/P_0)],$$

where D is the number of decibels, P is a particular pressure value, and P_0 is a baseline pressure. A common baseline is .00002 newtons per square meter. With SPL decibels, a difference of 20 decibels represents a tenfold increase in sound pressure level; 40 decibels represents a one hundredfold increase, etc. Most decibel measures in psychoacoustic literature are indicators of SPL; investigators should specify clearly the baseline and the property, intensity level or SPL.

RESPONSE MEASURES. One way to measure the loudness sensation is to refer individual loudness sensations for particular frequency and intensity combinations to a reference frequency. Fletcher and Munson (1933) made so-called equal loudness contours (sometimes called Fletcher-Munson curves today) by having eleven observers make 297 observations of comparative loudness. Schneider et al. (1972) derived equal loudness contours by noting different rates of loudness growth with intensity at different frequencies. Molino (1973) showed that the spacing between equal loudness contours varied with the standard frequency to which judgments must be related, although overall curvatures were consistent across differing standards. Whittle, Collins, and Robinson (1972) extended equal loudness contours to 3.15 Hz under laboratory conditions. Although there are individual differences, studies yielding equal loudness contours, a sample of which appears in Figure 2-4, show several things about the ear's behavior.

Understanding equal loudness curves (or contours) is facilitated by realizing that any point on an equal loudness curve is equally as loud as any other point on the same curve. Furthermore, each point on any curve represents a particular frequency-intensity combination. In Figure 2-4, the horizontal axis represents frequencies and the vertical axis represents intensity levels.

Frequency's confounding influence on the intensity-loudness relationship is evidenced by the fact that the curves indeed are *curved*. If a given intensity elicited a given loudness sensation regardless of frequency, the curves would appear as straight lines. One can note that the curves "go down" as frequency increases to around 2000 Hz, thereby indicating increasing auditory sensitivity. Beyond about 3000 Hz, sensitivity decreases and the curves "go

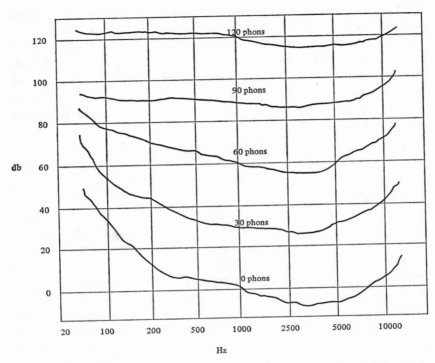

Figure 2-4. Sample equal loudness curves. The curves connect frequency-intensity level combinations which are judged to be equally loud as a 1000 Hz standard of a given intensity level. These particular curves are hypothetical, but they approximate those of several studies.

up." The amount of change is less at higher loudness levels.

Each curve has a *phon* value. Phons are arbitrarily equivalent to decibels at 1000 Hz; e.g. a 1000 Hz tone of 60 db also is 60 phons. Any other frequency judged as equal in loudness to the 1000 Hz—60 db standard also is 60 phons. Phons, the measurement unit for loudness *level* (not loudness), thus are measures of equivalency to the intensity level of some standard.

Equal loudness curves are based on averages of observation. Individual judgments will vary, and they will be influenced by the types and presentation conditions of stimuli. The curves provide a good representation of characteristic auditory behavior, but the loudness comparisons they permit are only at the less than, equal to, and greater than level.

Laboratory attempts to measure loudness in terms of how much louder one sound is than another have used observers' productions and/or estimations of various loudness distances or ratios. A *sone* scale of loudness, based on estimates of apparent ratios, and a *lambda* scale, based on equal-appearing intervals and ratios are alternative ways of describing apparent loudness relationships (Beck and Shaw, 1967). Methodology influences the results of loudness estimates and production. The Method of Constant Stimuli, in which predetermined tones are presented in random order, biases responses toward the middle of the stimulus ranges; the extreme loudnesses are under- or overestimated. The Method of Adjustment, in which the subject adjusts a tonal stimulus to match a conceptualization of another stimulus, biases responses in relation to the stimulus range and the starting position of the adjustment apparatus. The Method of Limits, using ascending and descending series of stimulus tones, biases in relation to range and direction (Warren, 1970). Despite procedural difficulties, a large body of evidence suggests that equal *stimulus ratios* produce equal *response ratios*. This is known as the *power law,* and it merits separate and detailed treatment.

The Power Law

Development of the power law, also known as the psychophysical law, has occurred largely through the work of S. S. Stevens. Symbolization of the power law varies; in Stevens's text, published posthumously with his widow's assistance, it is stated as

$$\Psi = \kappa\phi^\beta,$$

where Ψ is the sensation magnitude, ϕ is the stimulus magnitude, and β is an exponent which indicates the growth rate of the sensation in relation to stimulus growth (Stevens, 1975). (The κ is an experimental constant depending on units of measurement; Attneave (1962) says that it depends on the reference stimulus.) The β value varies with the stimulus; when β is greater than 1.00, the sensation grows faster than the stimulus. When it is less than 1.00, the sensation grows more slowly than the stimulus. Values for β, called power functions, which Stevens reported include:

0.67, for the loudness sensation elicited by a 3000 Hz tone.

0.50, for the brightness sensation elicited by a brief light flash.

1.00, for the apparent visual length of a projected line.

1.40, for the apparent taste of salt.

0.80, for the hardness experienced in squeezing rubber.

3.50, for the sensation of electric shock experienced from a current applied to the fingers.

The power law is believed to result from a general tendency of human sensory systems to perceive equal sensation ratios for equal stimulus ratios. The size of the sensation ratio is expressed as a power function of the stimulus ratio by the power law. For example, it works out, in accordance with the loudness power function of .67, that any increase of 9 db (remember, decibels are ratio comparisons) of SPL increases loudness in *sones* by a factor of two for the standard condition. (One sone is the loudness of a band (frequency spread) of noise centered on 3150 Hz sounding at an SPL of 32 db.) (Stevens, 1972; 1975).

Many measurements used to investigate the power law for loudness and other prothetic continua were obtained through magnitude estimation. In magnitude estimation, as it is usually practiced, the observer assigns numbers to stimuli in such a manner as to relate the stimuli on a proportionate basis. For example, if the first tone is judged "100" and the second tone is judged to sound half as loud the observer will call it "50." Over twenty years ago Stevens (1956b) described recommended magnitude estimation procedure regarding stimulus ranges, session lengths, presentation orders, and numbers of subjects. It is *not* necessary to give an observer a predetermined standard; he or she may use any numbers which seem to represent his or her sensations.

In his text, Stevens reports (p. 28) data from an early magnitude estimation experiment. Eight 1000 Hz tones, with SPLs ranging from 40 to 110 db in increments of 10 db were presented. Subjects assigned numbers in accordance with their individual standards; the numbers were converted to a common scale and averaged.* The stimulus SPLs and their corresponding average magnitude estimations were:

(SPL)	(Average Magnitude Estimate)
40	1.1
50	2.1
60	5.0
70	10.0
80	18.0
90	40.0
100	90.0
110	200.0

The ratio between each pair of adjacent SPL's is 3.2 to 1. The ratios between corresponding pairs of average sensation estimations range from 1.9 to 2.4. The power function estimate, computed at each level of correspondence by dividing the logarithm of the sensation ratio by the logarithm of 3.2 (the stimulus ratio), varies from .51 to .70. The overall power function for this experiment is obtained by averaging the seven estimates and is equal to .64.

Subjects' tendencies to "center" ratio judgments were noted in a task requiring subjects to halve and double apparent loudness of 1000 Hz at 30, 60, 90, or 120 db SPL. At low SPLs, decibel changes were greater for doubling than halving; the opposite was true at high SPLs (Stevens, 1957a). Such magnitude *production* biases were related to earlier noted magnitude *estimation* biases in which faint tones were underestimated while strong tones were overestimated (Stevens, 1956a). It became an established practice to confirm magnitude estimations with magnitude productions to balance the systemic errors, e.g. Hellman and Zwislocki, 1968.

Stevens (1957b; 1970; 1971) frequently argued that his power law should replace the Weber-Fechner law as the basic statement of psychophysical relationships because of (1) his findings that jnds for prothetic continua, such as loudness, are not of constant

*Averaging of magnitude estimations is via the median or the geometric mean of each set of estimations. The median is the middle value; the geometric mean is the nth root of a geometric series of n terms, i.e. $\sqrt[n]{(X_1)\ (X_1)\ (\ldots)\ (X_n)}$.

size, (2) the (to him) futility of scaling psychological magnitudes via confusion, and (3) apparent power functions in neural effects. The Weber-Fechner law, incorporating an assumption that equally often noticed differences are psychologically equal, states that the sensation is equal to a constant multiplied by the logarithm of a ratio relating the stimulus to a threshold or baseline. The Weber-Fechner law predicts a logarithmic rather than the power relationship (Ekman, 1959). On the grounds that perceptual invariance under differing environmental conditions has been observed, e.g. that which appears twice as large as something else maintains that appearance on a cloudy day; Yilmaz (1967) has favored the power law in the belief that it enables encoding of the environment in a maximally useful way.

The different values observed for the power functions in different sensory continua, possibly resulting from different "couplings" of neural mechanisms (MacKay, 1963), have been utilized to substantiate power law relationships through cross-modality matching. In cross-modality matching, one prothetic continuum, such as loudness, is matched by adjusting another, such as vibration, brightness, or strength of handgrip.* Stevens (1966) obtained matches of loudness with ten other continua and found that the resulting equal sensation functions were in accordance with the individual power functions.

Power law relationships have been criticized because of the averaging of individual magnitude estimations and productions and a belief that such sensory judgments are a part of learning and indoctrination. In defense, two studies are particularly interesting. Stevens and Guirao (1964) obtained magnitude estimates and productions for a 1000 Hz tone from eleven observers individually. Each observer yielded an approximately similar function. Bond and Stevens (1969) had five five-year-old children adjust a lamp's brightness to match the apparent loudness to a 500 Hz tone set at eight different levels. If stimulus-sensation relations for loudness depend on learning, the children's results

---

*In a way, the assignment of numbers to represent sensations, as in magnitude estimation, is a type of cross-modality matching. The numbers are part of the sensory continuum of numerosity.

should have differed from those of adults. But they did *not* differ. Predicted relations were obtained.

Experimental arrangements have troublesome influences on results obtained with magnitude estimation. Stimulus range, location of the first stimulus presented within the range, and the standard and its associated number cause variation. Poulton (1968) cites these difficulties and insists that Stevens's impressive results are artifacts of using trained observers and restricted experimental conditions.

Investigation of any phenomenon may alter that phenomenon, and measuring loudness via magnitude estimation is no exception. Furthermore, individuals will vary in their sensations and in their abilities to express them with numbers. The power function for loudness will vary with the stimulus condition; loudness generally grows more rapidly with lower frequencies. In spite of complexities, criticisms, and contradictions, implications of the power law, as demonstrated through magnitude estimation, for the musician are:

1. Loudness grows systematically with intensity as a function of natural perceptual processes.
2. Individuals are capable of making far more subtle loudness judgments than traditional dynamic markings suggest.

Masking

As is obvious from ordinary experience, one sound, normally perfectly audible by itself, can become inaudible in the presence of a louder sound. This phenomenon is called *masking*. That which is made inaudible is the mask*ed* tone (or noise); that louder sound which makes the softer sound inaudible is called the mask*er*. Orchestral woodwind players sometimes will disregard certain passages because they are not "exposed." Such players feel that other instruments will mask the sound of the disregarded passage, so it need not receive special attention in practice sessions.

A quantitative relationship between loudness and masking was noted by Fletcher and Munson (1937), who related it to early attempts to measure loudness. Egan and Hake (1950) conducted a classic study of the masking effects of a pure tone of 400 Hz and a 365-465 Hz band of noise centered on 410 Hz. The threshold of hearing in quiet was determined at various frequencies for the five subjects, then the masker was introduced. Subjects adjusted the masked tones to make them audible again; the amounts of adjustments required were plotted to show the *masking curve* for each masker. Egan and Hake noted that noise was a more efficient masker because it lacked the problems with beating and combination tones experienced with certain masking tone-masked tone frequency relationships.

Masking curves diagram attempts to mask a variety of tones with a given tone or noise. Masking curves, a sample of which appears in Figure 2-5, characteristically show maximal masking

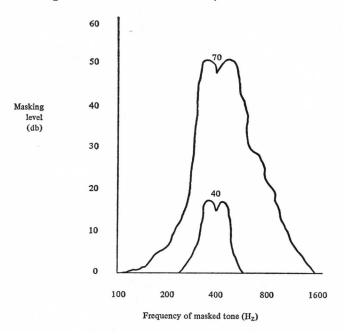

Figure 2-5. Typical masking curves, drawn for 400 Hz masking tones at 40 and 70 db. The height of each curve shows the increase in db necessary in order to "unmask" a masked tone. These curves are hypothetical, but they are similar to published curves.

effect near the frequency of the masker. At lower intensity levels of the masker, the curve declines symmetrically; masking effects below the masking frequency are about as extensive as masking effects above the masking frequency. However, the masking curve is asymmetrical at higher masker intensity levels; masking is more extensive for frequencies above the masker. Dips and ambiguous regions often appear in masking curves for tones at places near a harmonic relationship between the masking and masked tones. It is important in interpreting masking curves to recognize that the curve's height represents a *difference* in the strength of a sound between (1) when the masked sound was just audible in the masker's absence and (2) the point to which the masked sound must be raised to make it audible in the masker's presence.

A newer technique for studying masking holds the masked tone (sometimes called a probe frequency) constant and varies the masking tone. This apparently permits closer investigation of areas where the masking and masker frequencies coincide (Vogten, 1974). The levels to which the masking tone must be altered to mask the constant masked tone may be plotted to form a *tuning* curve, which is opposite (inverted and extended to the left) in shape to conventional masking curves (Zwicker, 1974).

In addition to simultaneous masking, forward and backward masking are possible in the laboratory. In forward and backward masking, the masking sound respectively precedes or follows the masked by a very brief time period. Forward masking probably is a matter of reduced auditory sensitivity or prolonged neural stimulation from the masker. Backward masking is mysterious; it must result in some way from incomplete processing of the masked sound (Moore, 1977).

Masking is useful in investigations of various psychoacoustical conditions. The relationship of combination tones to masking is investigated continually; even combination bands of noise have been observed (Greenwood, 1971). Presenting the masked tone binaurally and in opposite (180°) phase sometimes makes it less and sometimes more detectable in the presence of a masking tone of the same frequency (Wightman, 1969). In addition to auditory masking, a type of *perceptual* masking may result when a "meaningful" stimulus, such as a speech pattern, is used as a masker: The masking effect of speech is greater than that of random noise (Carhart, Tillman, and Greetis, 1969).

Loudness Summation

Individual loudnesses sum to form combined loudness. This obvious mathematical fact is perceptually complex and of musical importance because sounds summate differently under different conditions.

Fletcher (1946), using an early tone synthesizer, demonstrated that complex tones sound louder than pure tones. Stevens (1956a) noted that separate noise bands (and, by analogy, groups of frequencies) are not simply additive. Even frequencies widely separated from each other can have a mutually inhibitive effect.

Zwicker, Flottorp, and Stevens (1957) showed that loudness summation for pure tones depends on frequency separations in relation to the critical band width. When the frequency spacing (Δf) between simultaneous pure tones is increased to a critical point (Δ f $\approx$ 100 Hz for a 500 Hz standard, $\approx$ 180 Hz for a 1000 Hz standard, $\approx$ 350 Hz for a 2000 Hz standard), the loudness sensation increases. A similar loudness increase was noted when the width of a noise band was increased beyond a certain point. At low SPLs, with wide frequency spacing, there is no summation; the total loudness is equivalent to the loudest individual tone. Loudness summation appears greatest for tones at a loudness level of 50 to 60 phons; uniform spacing of frequency components produces greater loudness than nonuniform spacing.

When a stimulus with designated SPL is presented binaurally it sounds louder than when it is heard with only one ear. In one study (Reynolds and Stevens, 1960), monaural loudness grew with a power function of .54, while binaural loudness grew with .60. The ratio between monaural and binaural loudness for corresponding stimuli grew as a function of SPL with an exponent of about 0.066. The superiority of two-eared hearing thus becomes greater as the stimulus magnitude increases.

The critical frequency difference for loudness summation vanishes under conditions of dichotic presentation—separate frequencies to each ear. For between ear differences of 0 to "several thousand" Hz, Scharf (1969) noted that dichotic pairs remained equally loud. Dichotic summation occurred even when the tonal sensation was of two separate localized tones, one in each ear. This is logical in relation to previous studies showing ordinary loudness summation related to the basilar membrane's critical band widths because dichotic presentation prevents phenomena which are dependent on the critical band width.

In one of his last published works, Stevens (1972) outlined a computational procedure, based on careful laboratory observations, for the perceived loudness of a noise divided into one-third octave bands. By analogy, it may apply to mixtures of complex tones. The procedure uses a standard reference of a one-third octave band centered on 3150 Hz, the sone as defined above, the power law for loudness, equal loudness contours for noise, and the summation rule

$$S_t = S_m + F(\Sigma S - S_m),$$

where S_t is the total loudness, S_m is the loudness of the loudest sound, ΣS is the sum (in sones) of the loudness of all bands, and F is a tabled value which varies as a function of the loudest band.

Individuals demonstrating loudness summation must be cognizant of relative phase, particularly with two individual loudnesses. Destructive interference can produce a tonal superposition which has a waveform of smaller amplitude than either component waveform. Chapin and Firestone (1934) found that the relative phase of a 108 Hz fundamental and a harmonic influenced loudness, as well as tone quality. The amount of phase influence may be small; Schubert and Nixon (1970) found little influence of relative phase on the ability to hear octaves at a sufficiently loud level to detect them amidst a noise background. But phase influences are possible, and controlled investigations of loudness summation should specify the phase relationships.

Dangers to Hearing

Exposure to sound at high intensity levels can cause a temporary threshold shift; i.e. a greater amount of intensity is necessary in order for the listener to just perceive a sound. Temporary threshold shifts may depend on the amount of SPL in the critical bands around the affected frequencies as well as the exposure time (Yamamoto et al., 1970). Under conditions of prolonged exposure such threshold shifts may become permanent.

Musicians and others have questioned effects of high intensity levels on rock-and-roll musicians, whose characteristic styles often demand high loudness levels. Jerger and Jerger (1970) measured the hearing sensitivity of nine rock-and-roll performers just prior to a performance and within an hour of the performance's conclusion. Eight performers showed a threshold shift of at least 15 db for at least one frequency in the 200-8000 Hz range; some losses were as high as 50 db. The shift influenced frequencies which may appear high for many musical purposes, but intelligibility of speech suffers with a loss of high frequency sensitivity because consonants become blurred.

Rintelmann, Lindberg, and Smitley (1972) exposed twenty females with normal hearing to taped rock-and-roll at an SPL of 100 db on two occasions. One tape contained 60 minutes of continuous music; the other had one minute of ambient (chance, random, background) discotheque noise at an SPL of 80 db inserted after each three minutes of music. The temporary threshold shift was significantly less for the intermittent listening condition, although recovery (return to normal hearing threshold) time was about the same for both conditions. The authors noted that 50 percent of the subjects in the intermittent condition and 80 percent in the continuous condition were "endangered" in accordance with published standards restricting daily exposure to high sound levels.

Rock-and-roll is not the only culprit, of course, and hearing loss is not the only implication. Stephens and Anderson (1971) determined the "threshold of discomfort" or uncomfortable loudness level for a 1000 Hz tone and also administered personality measures to a group of British subjects. The higher the hearing threshold, the lower was the uncomfortable loudness level. There were significant negative correlations, i.e., a tendency for a group to be high on one trait and low on another between uncomfortable loudness level and introversion, test anxiety, and motivation to avoid failure.

The danger to hearing is more than propaganda from those who do not like particular musical styles or who are unduly bothered by noisy environments. As musicians work with and listen to high intensity sounds, they must at least consider the implications for their hearing and the hearing and psychological comfort of others.

TIMBRE PHENOMENA

Timbre or tone quality is the tonal attribute that distinguishes sounds of identical pitch, loudness, and duration. An oboe and a viola can play an A of identical frequency and sound pressure level for an identical time period, but they sound different. Timbre, because of its multidimensionality and the difficulty of separately controlling separate dimensions, lacks the amount of research literature characteristic of pitch and loudness. Considered here are timbre's relationship to waveform, timbre recognition, and measurement.

Waveform-Timbre Relationship

Waveform, the pattern of displacements associated with a soundwave, is the closest quasi-parallel physical property to the psychological property of timbre. A complex waveform depends on the particular component frequencies, the number of frequencies, the relative strengths of the frequencies, and the relative phases among the frequencies (Backus, 1969). Different musical instruments sound differently to a large extent because of their different frequency combinations and interactions. As will be discussed below, however, waveform is not a sufficient control of timbre sensations.

The influence of phase differences on timbre perception merits special attention because it has been believed that waveform differences attributable to phase make no difference in timbre. Recent evidence is that there *are* indeed differences attributable to phase relationships. Although static phase differences between contrasting two-tone stimuli separated by silence may be rather difficult to detect, observers readily can detect a changed phase inserted within a constantly sounding signal, particularly when the change is 60° or more out of phase (180° is totally out of phase)

(Raiford and Schubert, 1971). In Patterson's (1973) study, listeners made no differences in pitch matches of complex tones under two different phase conditions, but there were timbre differences. Plomp and Steeneken (1969) showed convincingly that, while phase effects are not as great as effects of relatively harmonic strengths, there are independent phase effects on the timbre of tones having equal loudness and pitch.

Influences Other than Waveform

A particular waveform is insufficient to represent physically a particular timbre. The onset (initial transience, attack, rise time) of a tone is vital in timbre, as are transient fluctuations within a sound's steady state.

Onset refers to the "opening section" or "buildup" in a sound. Silence cannot instantly become a steady-state sound; a certain time must elapse while more and more energy is supplied to the vibrating system. Once the energy supplied is equal to the energy lost through friction, the steady state is reached.

Winckel (1967) has discussed extensively onset effects from theoretical and experimental standpoints. Onset times vary with different instruments; the trumpet has a rapid onset of about 20 milliseconds while the flute requires 200 to 300 milliseconds. Individual complex tone partials have their own rates of growth. Every tonal attack includes an initial very rapidly decaying smear of inharmonic as well as harmonic frequencies; the sharper the attack, the greater the range of the smear and the shorter the onset time. Onset behavior inherent in the vibrating system is modified by idiosyncrasies of the player, the instrument (or voice), and the acoustical environment. It is clear that attempts to compare "good" and "bad" sounds via the oscilloscope or to imitate orchestral instruments with organs and economy-model synthesizers are unlikely to be fruitful because of inability to duplicate onset behavior.

A millisecond (.001 sec.) is a rather short period of time to most people; 300 milliseconds is less than a split second. Anyone who questions the importance of the brief onset for timbre, however, needs only to experiment with removing the initial portions of taped musical tones. In studies such as that of Elliott (1975), experienced musicians had considerable difficulty in identifying common orchestral instruments when the onset portions of the tones were absent.

The steady-state portion of most musical sounds is not truly "steady"—there are numerous fluctuations in waveform and vibrato rates. Such transient tonal aspects also influence timbre.

Grey's (1977) subjects compared computer-synthesized tones of equal pitch, loudness, and duration for "similarity." The tones were synthesized to match natural oboe, clarinet, saxophone, English horn, French horn, flute, bassoon, trumpet, and string tones. The similarity ratings were found to be organized along three dimensions. One was the spectral energy distribution which resulted from the particular waveforms. Another was related to the low and high frequencies in the onset, and the other was related to spectral fluctuations.

In the free-field listening situation characteristic of a concert hall, reverberant sound dominates for the greater part of the audience. The waveform's makeup differs from point to point, so even steady-state tones have different timbres at different locations (Plomp and Steeneken, 1973).

Tone Source Recognition

The basilar membrane stimulation pattern resulting from a particular complex waveform's characteristics probably is the physiological basis for timbre perception, at least in the case of a steady-state waveform (static case) (Plomp, 1970).

Roederer (1975) discusses dynamic ("in context") tone source recognition as a matter of timbre perception, resulting from neural processing of waveform information, storage in memory with a learned label, and comparison with prior information. The sensation of a clarinet sound as opposed to a trumpet sound may be experienced by anyone with normal hearing, but the distinction between the two in terms of labels requires learning, which likely results in actual neural modifications of cortical structures.

Instruments vary greatly in price, for many reasons, and one occasionally wonders regarding their timbre differences. Illustrative is a study by Vattano, Cross, and Morgan (1976), who had nine musicians and nine nonmusicians listen to passages played on three unseen violins. One violin was valued at $300.00, one at $2,000, and one at $5,000. Subjects, particularly the musicians, were able to detect the differences in desirable timbre, but they were mostly between the $300.00 and $2,000 models. Analysis of the physical makeup of the tones showed that the more expensive instruments did have more relative strength in the higher harmonics as compared to the "cheap" one.

Subjects' tendencies to downgrade timbre in making performance quality distinctions were demonstrated by Madsen and Geringer (1976), who had fifty subjects rank order eight sets of accompanied trumpet performances of the first phase of "Twinkle, Twinkle, Little Star." Each set was a combination of good or bad tone quality and sharpness, flatness, or accurate intonation. The "best" and "worst" of twenty versions were selected by a panel of judges to represent good and bad tone quality for each set. Intonation was varied by setting a tunable electronic keyboard to be 25 cents flat, 50 cents sharp, or in tune in relation to the trumpet. The overall rank order for the eight sets was:

(1) good quality, sharp;
(2) bad quality, sharp;
(3) good quality, in tune;
(4) bad quality, in tune;
(5) good quality, flat;
(6) bad quality, flat.

The preference for sharpness, often noted (Roederer, 1975), dominated preference for tone quality. When analyzed separately, there were statistically significant differences in preference due to intonation but not to quality.

Measurement of Timbre

One consequence of timbre's multidimensionality is the lack of any measurement unit for timbre analogous to the mel for pitch and the sone for loudness. Attempts to measure timbre usually rely on subjective qualitative descriptors such as "rich," "mellow," "thin," "buzzy," "comical," "noble," etc., which may be verified by examining orchestration texts.

In one verbal descriptor study (Truax, 1972), fourth grade students assessed flute, oboe, clarinet, trumpet, and French horn excerpts with twelve five-point scales based on pairs of bipolar adjectives. For eight adjective pairs (bright-dark, light-heavy, clear-hazy, delicate-rugged, shallow-deep, thin-full, small-large, smooth-rough), the children ranked the instruments in an identical order: flute, oboe, clarinet, trumpet, horn. The other adjective pairs yielded inconsistent rankings. Timbre perceptions apparently were influenced by the differing musical content of the examples.

In a more elaborate study, Von Bismarck (1974a;b) presented twenty-five 200 Hz complex tones with varying waveforms, five steady-state vowel segments, and five bands of noise to eight musicians and eight nonmusicians, who classified each sound along thirty seven-point scales formed by bipolar adjectives. Statistical analysis yielded four factors which explained 91 percent of the variability in classification. The most important attribute of timbre was *sharpness* (as in one pole of "dull-sharp," not high in pitch) attribute, which seemed to depend on the upper frequency in a complex sound and the comparative progressive reduction in the strengths of upper partials, i.e. slope of the spectral envelope. Von Bismarck demonstrated that sharpness can be doubled or halved, just as loudness, and thereby suggested another basic tonal property. Perhaps other measurement attempts will suggest that timbre not be measured as a unitary property.

The aforementioned Grey study used a multidimensional scaling technique, feasible with a computer, to order subjective tonal similarity comparisons in geometric space. This is a sophisticated technique for explaining timbre distinctions, and may suggest a trend for the future as more intricate mathematical operations become practical.

SUMMARY

Chapter Two has presented considerable information related to music's psychoacoustical foundations. It is difficult to simplify that which is inherently complex, but the main points in the chapter include the following:

1. Musical sounds depend on rapid atmospheric pressure fluctuations resulting from physical vibration, generally of a periodic nature.
2. Pressure fluctuations are transmitted as mechanical vibrations to the inner ear, where they are processed and converted to electrochemical signals directed to the brain.
3. Pitch, a tone's apparent relative location on a high-low continuum, is dependent on the physical property of frequency, but the pitch-frequency relationship is not perfect.
4. Pitch assignment for a pure tone depends upon the area of basilar membrane stimulation.
5. A combination of pure tones forms a sensation of unison, beating, roughness, or two tones in accordance with the frequency separation of the tones.
6. The amount by which a frequency must be changed in order to elicit a pitch difference varies with the individual, the occasion, and the frequency range.
7. The pitch of a complex tone depends upon the periodicity pitch resulting from the waveform repetition frequency detected through the central neural process of fundamental tracking.
8. Periodicity pitch may shift away from waveform repetition frequency under certain conditions.
9. Combination tones result from cochlear distortion; they are distinguished from periodicity pitch in that they require more than minimal intensity level for perception and are peripheral rather than central effects.
10. Consonance or dissonance usually is considered as another label for various intervals by musicians and as an evaluated tonal phenomenon by nonmusicians.
11. Consonance and dissonance judgments depend heavily on training and experience, but there may be some physical basis for consonance as a tonal phenomenon because of the basilar membrane alignment of tonal components.
12. Why complex tones from separate sound sources generally result in harmony while individual complex tones yield a unitary pitch sensation is unclear.

13. The apparent size of a musical interval of constant ratio may vary with frequency range.
14. First order beating, an apparent rise and fall in loudness of a mistuned unison, is a peripheral effect.
15. Second order beating, an apparent waxing and waning or fluttering of a mistuned nonunison interval, is a central pitch processing effect.
16. Binaural beats and fusion may be created by feeding separate sounds to each ear.
17. Absolute pitch, the ability to name a tone without reference to any external pitch standard, may be related to learning label-sensation associations at a critical age.
18. Attempts to measure pitch as distinct from frequency via the mel scale have been somewhat disappointing.
19. Loudness, the apparent strength or magnitude of a tone, depends largely on intensity, but the intensity-loudness relationship is not perfect.
20. Loudness is distinct from volume, the apparent size or extensity of a tone, and density, the apparent tonal compactness; but loudness may be a product of volume and density interactions.
21. Decibels are measures of the physical dimensions of intensity level and sound pressure level, not of loudness.
22. Equal loudness curves connect frequency-intensity combinations which produce loudness levels equivalent in phons.
23. Equal loudness curves show how frequency confounds the intensity-loudness relationship; a given intensity does not lead to an equal loudness sensation across all frequencies.
24. Loudness may be measured via various estimation and production techniques; the sone scale has been derived therefrom.
25. The power law shows that loudness grows in a lawful manner in relation to growth in sound intensity; the growth rate varies with stimulus conditions.
26. One sound may mask another and particular masking behaviors may be quantified through masking curves.

27. Loudness summation depends on the particular component frequencies, their degrees of separation, and relative phase as well as individual loudness; there is no simple additive process.

28. Exposure to music at high intensity levels can degrade hearing sensitivity.

29. Timbre, apparent tone quality or color, depends on the factors influencing waveform as well as onset and transient waveform characteristics.

30. Tone source recognition depends on learning as well as timbre perception.

REFERENCES

Allen, D. Octave discriminability of musical and non-musical subjects. *Psychonomic Science*, 1967, 7, 421-422.

Attneave, F. Perception and related areas. In S. Koch (Ed.), *Psychology: A Study of a Science* (Vol. 4). New York: McGraw-Hill, 1962.

Bachem, A. Time factors in relative and absolute pitch determination. *Journal of the Acoustical Society of America*, 1954, 26, 751-753.

Backus, J. W. *The Acoustical Foundations of Music*. New York: W. W. Norton, 1969.

Beck, J., & Shaw, W. A. Magnitude estimations of pitch. *Journal of the Acoustical Society of America*, 1962, 34, 92-98.

Beck, J., & Shaw, W. A. Single estimates of pitch magnitude. *Journal of the Acoustical Society of America*, 1963, 35, 1722-1724.

Beck, J., & Shaw, W. A. Ratio-estimations of loudness intervals. *American Journal of Psychology*, 1967, 80, 59-65.

Bilsen, F. A. On the influence of the number and phase of harmonics on the perceptibility of the pitch of complex signals. *Acustica*, 1973, 28, 60-65.

Bond, B., & Stevens, S. S. Cross-modality matching of brightness to loudness by 5-year olds. *Perception and Psychophysics*, 1969, 6, 337-339.

Bugg, E. G. An experimental study of factors influencing consonance judgments. *Psychological Monographs*, 1933, 45 (2). (Whole No. 201).

Cardozo, B. L. Frequency discrimination at the threshold. In E. Zwicker and E. Terhardt (Eds.), *Facts and Models in Hearing*. New York: Springer-Verlag, 1974.

Carhart, R., Tillman, T. W., and Greetis, E. S. Perceptual masking in multiple sound backgrounds. *Journal of the Acoustical Society of America*, 1969, 45, 694-703.

Chapin, E. K., & Firestone, F. A. The influence of phase on tone quality and loudness; the interference of subjective harmonics. *Journal of the Acoustical Society of America*, 1934, 5, 173-180.

Corso, J. F. Unison tuning of musical instruments. *Journal of the Acoustical Society of America*, 1954, *26*, 746-750.

Corso, J. F. Absolute judgments of musical tonality. *Journal of the Acoustical Society of America*, 1957, *29*, 138-144.

Cuddy, L. L. Practice effects on the absolute judgment of pitch. *Journal of the Acoustical Society of America*, 1968, *43*, 1069-1076.

Dallos, P. S., & Sweetman, R. H. Distribution pattern of cochlear harmonics. *Journal of the Acoustical Society of America*, 1969, *5*, 37-45.

Dallos, P., Billone, M. C., Durrant, J. D., Wang, C. Y., & Raynor, S. Cochlear inner and outer hair cells: functional differences. *Science*, 1972, *177*, 356-360.

Davis, H. Advances in the neurophysiology and neuroanatomy of the cochlea. *Journal of the Acoustical Society of America*, 1962, *34*, 1377-1385.

DeGainza, V. H. Absolute and relative hearing as innate complementary functions of man's musical ear. *Council for Research in Music Education*, 1970, *22*, 13-16.

Egan, J. P., & Hake, H. W. On the masking pattern of a simple auditory stimulus. *Journal of the Acoustical Society of America*, 1950, *22*, 622-630.

Ekman, G. Weber's law and related functions. *Journal of Psychology*, 1959, *23*, 343-352.

Elliott, C. A. Attacks and releases as factors in instrument identification. *Journal of Research in Music Education*, 1975, *23*, 35-40.

Farnsworth, P. R. The pitch of a combination of tones. *American Journal of Psychology*, 1938, *51*, 536-539.

Farnsworth, P. R. *The Social Psychology of Music* (2nd ed.). Ames: Iowa State University Press, 1969.

Fletcher, H. The pitch, loudness, and quality of musical tones. *American Journal of Physics*, 1946, *14*, 215-225.

Fletcher, H., & Munson, W. A. Loudness. *Journal of the Acoustical Society of America*, 1933, *5*, 82-108.

Fletcher, H., & Munson, W. A. Relation between loudness and masking. *Journal of the Acoustical Society of America*, 1937, *9*, 1-10.

Gacek, R. R. Neuroanatomy of the auditory system. In J. V. Tobias (Ed.), *Foundations of Modern Auditory Theory* (Vol. 2). New York: Acadamic Press, 1972.

Gjaevenes, K., & Rimstad, E. R. The influence of rise time on loudness. *Journal of the Acoustical Society of America*, 1972, *51*, 1233-1239.

Goldstein, J. L. Aural combination tones. In R. Plomp and G. F. Smoorenburg (Eds.), *Frequency Analysis and Periodicity Detection in Hearing*. Leiden: Sijthoff, 1970.

Goldstein, J. L. An optimum processor theory for the central formation of the pitch of complex tones. *Journal of the Acoustical Society of America*, 1973, *54*, 1496-1516.

Greenwood, D. D. Aural combination tones and auditory masking. *Journal of the Acoustical Society of America*, 1971, *50*, 502-543.

Grey, J. M. Multidimensional perceptual scaling of musical timbres. *Journal of the Acoustical Society of America*, 1977, *61*, 1270-1277.

Guirao, M., & Stevens, S. S. The measurement of auditory density. *Journal of the Acoustical Society of America*, 1964, *36*, 1176-1182.

Hellman, R. P., & Zwislocki, J. J. Loudness determinations at low sound frequencies. *Journal of the Acoustical Society of America*, 1968, *43*, 60-64.

Houtsma, A. J. M., & Goldstein, J. L. The central origin of the pitch of complex tones: Evidence from musical interval recognition. *Journal of the Acoustical Society of America*, 1972, *51*, 520-529.

Jeffress, L. A. Absolute pitch. *Journal of the Acoustical Society of America*, 1962, *34*, 987.

Jerger, J., & Jerger, S. Temporary threshold shift in rock-and-roll musicians. *Journal of Speech and Hearing Research*, 1970, *13*, 221-224.

Kock, W. E. On the principle of uncertainty in sound. *Journal of the Acoustical Society of America*, 1935, *7*, 56-58.

Lundin, R. W. Toward a cultural theory of consonance. *Journal of Psychology*, 1947, *23*, 45-49.

MacKay, D. M. Psychophysics of perceived intensity: a theoretical basis for Fechner's and Stevens's laws. *Science*, 1963, *139*, 1213-1216.

Madsen, C. K., & Geringer, J. M. Preferences for trumpet tone quality versus intonation. *Council for Research in Music Education*, 1976, *46*, 13-22.

Meyer, M. On memorizing absolute pitch. *Journal of the Acoustical Society of America*, 1956, *28*, 718-719.

Molino, J. A. Pure-tone equal-loudness contours for standard tones of different frequencies. *Perception and Psychophysics*, 1973, *14*, 1-4.

Moore, B. C. J. Relation between the critical bandwidth and the frequency difference limen. *Journal of the Acoustical Society of America*, 1974, *55*, 359.

Moore, B. C. J. *Introduction to the Psychology of Hearing*. Baltimore: University Park Press, 1977.

Nordmark, J. O. Mechanisms of frequency discrimination. *Journal of the Acoustical Society of America*, 1968, *44*, 1533-1540.

Patterson, B. Musical dynamics. *Scientific American*, 1974, *231* (5), 78-95.

Patterson, R. The effects of relative phase and the number of components on residue pitch. *Journal of the Acoustical Society of America*, 1973, *53*, 1565-1572.

Perrott, D. R., & Nelson, M. A. Limits for the detection of binaural beats. *Journal of the Acoustical Society of America*, 1969, *46*, 1477-1481.

Perrott, D. R., Briggs, R., & Perrott, S. Binaural fusion: Its limits as defined by signal duration and signal onset. *Journal of the Acoustical Society of America*, 1970, *47*, 565-568.

Peterson, J., & Smith, F. W. The range and modifiability of consonance in certain musical intervals. *American Journal of Psychology*, 1930, *42*, 561-572.

Plomp, R. The ear as a frequency analyzer. *Journal of the Acoustical Soci-*

ety of America, 1964, *36,* 1628-1636.

Plomp, R. Detectability threshold for combination tones. *Journal of the Acoustical Society of America,* 1965, *37,* 1110-1123.

Plomp, R. Beats of mistuned consonances. *Journal of the Acoustical Society of America,* 1967, *42,* 462-474. (a)

Plomp, R. Pitch of complex tones. *Journal of the Acoustical Society of America,* 1967, *41,* 1526-1533. (b)

Plomp, R. Timbre as a multidimensional attribute of complex tones. In R. Plomp and T. G. Smoorenburg (Eds.), *Frequency Analysis and Periodicity Detection in Hearing.* Leiden: Sijthoff, 1970.

Plomp, R. *Aspects of Tone Sensation.* London: Academic Press, 1976.

Plomp, R., & Levelt, W. J. M. Tonal consonance and critical bandwidth. *Journal of the Acoustical Society of America,* 1965, *38,* 548-560.

Plomp, R., & Steeneken, H. J. M. Effect of phase on the timbre of complex tones. *Journal of the Acoustical Society of America,* 1969, *46,* 409-421.

Plomp, R., & Steeneken, H. J. M. Place dependence on timbre in reverberant sound fields. *Acustica,* 1973, *28,* 50-59.

Poulton, E. C. The new psychophysics: Six models for magnitude estimation. *Psychological Bulletin,* 1968, *69,* 1-19.

Radocy, R. E. Pitch judgments of selected successive intervals: Is twice as frequent twice as high? *Psychology of Music,* 1977, *5* (2), 23-29.

Raiford, C. A., & Schubert, E. D. Recognition of phase changes in octave complexes. *Journal of the Acoustical Society of America,* 1971, *50,* 559-567.

Rainbolt, H. R., & Schubert, E. D. Use of noise bands to establish noise pitch. *Journal of the Acoustical Society of America,* 1968, *43,* 316-323.

Reynolds, G. S., & Stevens, S. S. Binaural summation of loudness. *Journal of the Acoustical Society of America,* 1960, *35,* 1337-1344.

Rhode, W. S., & Robles, L. Evidence from Mossbauer experiments for nonlinear vibration in the cochlea. *Journal of the Acoustical Society of America,* 1974, *55,* 588-596.

Rintelmann, W. R., Lindberg, R. F., & Smitley, E. K. Temporary threshold shift and recovery patterns from two types of rock and roll music presentation. *Journal of the Acoustical Society of America,* 1972, *51,* 1249-1254.

Ritsma, R. J. Periodicity detection. In R. Plomp and G. Smoorenburg (Eds.), *Frequency analysis and periodicity detection in hearing.* Leiden: Sijthoff, 1970.

Roederer, J. G. *Introduction to the physics and psychophysics of music* (2nd ed.). New York: Springer-Verlag, 1975.

Scharf, B. Dichotic summation of loudness. *Journal of the Acoustical Society of America,* 1969, *45,* 1193-1205.

Schneider, B., Wright, A. A., Edelheit, W., Hock, P., & Humphrey, C. Equal loudness contours derived from sensory magnitude judgments. *Journal of the Acoustical Society of America,* 1972, *51,* 1951-1959.

Schubert, E. D., & Nixon, J. C. On the role of phase in the audibility of octave complexes. *Journal of the Acoustical Society of America,* 1970, *47,* 1100-1106.

Sergeant, D. Experimental investigation of absolute pitch. *Journal of Research in Music Education,* 1969, *17,* 135-143.

Sherbon, J. W. The association of hearing acuity, diplacusis, and discrimination with musical performance. *Journal of Research in Music Education,* 1975, *23,* 249-257.

Siegel, J. A., & Siegel, W. Categorical perception of tonal intervals: Musicians can't tell *sharp* from *flat. Perception and Psychophysics,* 1977, *21,* 399-407.

Smoorenburg, G. F. Pitch perception of two-frequency stimuli. *Journal of the Acoustical Society of America,* 1970, *48,* 924-942.

Stephens, S. D. G., & Anderson, C. M. G. Experimental studies on the uncomfortable loudness level. *Journal of Speech and Hearing Research,* 1971, *14,* 262-270.

Stevens, J. C., & Guirao, M. Individual loudness functions. *Journal of the Acoustical Society of America,* 1964, *36,* 2210-2213.

Stevens, S. S. Total density. *Journal of Experimental Psychology,* 1934, *17,* 585-592. (a)

Stevens, S. S. The volume and intensity of tones. *American Journal of Psychology,* 1934, *46,* 397-408. (b)

Stevens, S. S. The relation of pitch to intensity. *Journal of the Acoustical Society of America,* 1935, *6,* 150-154.

Stevens, S. S. Pitch discrimination, mels, and Kock's contention. *Journal of the Acoustical Society of America,* 1954, *26,* 1075-1077.

Stevens, S. S. Calculation of the loudness of complex noise. *Journal of the Acoustical Society of America,* 1956, *28,* 807-832. (a)

Stevens, S. S. The direct estimation of sensory magnitudes-loudness. *American Journal of Psychology,* 1956, *69,* 1-25. (b)

Stevens, S. S. Concerning the form of the loudness function. *Journal of the Acoustical Society of America,* 1957, *29,* 603-606. (a)

Stevens, S. S. On the psychophysical law. *Psychological Review,* 1957, *64,* 153-181. (b)

Stevens, S. S. Matching functions between loudness and ten other continua. *Perception and Psychophysics,* 1966, *1,* 5-8.

Stevens, S. S. Neural events and the psychophysical law. *Science,* 1970, *170,* 1043-1050.

Stevens, S. S. Issues in psychophysical measurement. *Psychological Review,* 1971, *78,* 426-450.

Stevens, S. S. Perceived level of noise by Mark VII and decibels (E). *Journal of the Acoustical Society of America,* 1972, *51,* 575-601.

Stevens, S. S. *Psychophysics.* New York: Wiley, 1975.

Stevens, S. S., & Volkmann, J. The relation of pitch to frequency: a revised scale. *American Journal of Psychology,* 1940, *53,* 329-353.

Stevens, S. S., & Warshofsky, F. *Sound and hearing.* New York: Time, Inc., 1965.

Stevens, S. S., Davis, H., & Lurie, M. H. The localization of pitch perception on the basilar membrane. *Journal of General Psychology,* 1935, *13,* 297-315.

Stevens, S. S., Guirao, M., & Slawson, A. W. Loudness, a product of volume times density. *Journal of the Acoustical Society of America,* 1965, *69,* 503-510.

Stevens, S. S., Volkman, J., & Newman, E. B. A scale for the measurement of the psychological magnitude pitch. *Journal of the Acoustical Society of America,* 1937, *8,* 185-190.

Strange, A. *Electronic Music.* Dubuque, Iowa: W. C. Brown, 1972.

Sweetman, R. H., & Dallos, P. Distribution pattern of cochlear combination tones. *Journal of the Acoustical Society of America,* 1969, *45,* 58-71.

Terhardt, E. Pitch, consonance, & harmony. *Journal of the Acoustical Society of America,* 1974, *55,* 1061-1069.(a)

Terhardt, E. Pitch of pure tones: Its relation to intensity. In E. Zwicker and E. Terhardt (Eds.), *Facts and Models in Hearing.* New York: Springer-Verlag, 1974.(b)

Terrace, H. S., & Stevens, S. S. The quantification of tonal volume. *American Journal of Psychology,* 1962, *75,* 596-604.

Tobias, J. V. Curious binaural phenomena. In J. V. Tobias (Ed.), *Foundations of Modern Auditory Theory* (vol. 2). New York: Academic Press, 1972.

Truax, B. S. Development of a verbal technique for identifying children's musical concepts of instrumental timbre (Doctoral dissertation, The Pennsylvania State University, 1971). *Dissertation Abstracts International,* 1972, *32,* 6482A. (University Microfilms No. 72-13, 945)

Van der Geer, J. P., Levelt, W. J. M. & Plomp, R. The connotation of musical consonance. *Acta Psychologica,* 1962, *20,* 308-319.

Van den Brink, G. Monotic and dichotic pitch matchings with complex sounds. In E. Zwicker and E. Terhardt (Eds.), *Facts and Models in Hearing.* New York: Springer-Verlag, 1974.

Vattano, F. J., Cross, H. A., & Morgan, R. J. Perception of qualitative differences in violins. *Psychology of Music,* 1976, *4* (2), 3-8.

Vogten, L. L. M. Pure-tone masking: a new result from a new method. In E. Zwicker and E. Terhardt (Eds.). *Facts and Models in Hearing.* New York: Springer-Verlag, 1974.

Von Bekesy, G. *Experiments in Hearing.* New York: McGraw-Hill, 1960.

Von Bismarck, G. Timbre of steady sounds: a factorial investigation of its verbal attributes. *Acusctia,* 1974, *30,* 146-149.(a)

Von Bismarck, G. Sharpness as an attribute of the timbre of steady sounds. *Acustica,* 1974, *30,* 159-172.(b)

Warren, R. M. Elimination of biases in loudness judgments for tones.

Journal of the Acoustical Society of America, 1970, *48,* 1397-1403.

Whitfield, I. C. *The Auditory Pathway.* London: Arnold, 1967.

Whittle, L. S., Collins, S. J., & Robinson, D. W. The audibility of low-frequency sounds. *Journal of Sound and Vibration,* 1972, *21,* 431-448.

Wightman, F. L. Binaural masking with sine wave maskers. *Journal of the Acoustical Society of America,* 1969, *45,* 72-78.

Wightman, F. L. The pattern-transformation model of pitch. *Journal of Acoustical Society of America,* 1973, *54,* 407-416.

Winckel, F. *Music, Sound and Sensation.* (T. Binkley, trans.) New York: Dover, 1967.

Woodworth, R. S., & Schlosberg, H. *Experimental Psychology* (rev. ed.). New York: Holt, Rinehart, and Winston, 1965.

Yamamoto, T., Takagi, K., Shoji, H., & Yoneada, H. Critical band with respect to temporary threshold shift. *Journal of the Acoustical Society of America,* 1970, *48,* 978-987.

Yilmaz, H. Perceptual invariance and the psychophysical law. *Perception and Psychophysics,* 1967, *2,* 533-538.

Zwicker, E. On a psychoacoustical equivalent of tuning curves. In E. Zwicker and E. Terhardt (Eds.). *Facts and Models in Hearings.* New York: Springer-Verlag, 1974.

Zwicker, E., Flottorp, G., & Stevens, S. S. Critical band width in loudness summation. *Journal of the Acoustical Society of America,* 1957, *29,* 548-557.

Chapter Three

RHYTHMIC FOUNDATIONS

R HYTHM is an essential component of all musics, whether it be music of primitive societies, music of traditional Western styles, or music of a contemporary popular style. Despite its musical importance, the study of rhythm in performance "has been almost totally neglected in the formal training of musicians since the Renaissance" (Cooper and Meyer, 1960, p. v).

This is not to suggest, however, that rhythm as a phenomenon has not been studied considerably. To the contrary, it has been studied both intensively and extensively from many perspectives. Winick's (1974) annotated bibliography of rhythm in music includes nearly 500 sources. Innumerable definitions and explanations of rhythm and its various attributes have been offered. Theorists have developed elaborate "systems" and analyses of musical rhythm. Philosophers have offered theories of rhythm. Psychologists also have developed rhythmic theories, although their theories purportedly have an empirical base and are concerned primarily with responsiveness to rhythm. In addition, they have studied rhythm as both a stimulus and response (Lundin, 1967) and, in recent years, have become increasingly concerned with rhythmic perception. Other writers have been concerned with exploring developments in rhythm from the time of the ancient Greeks to the present, while still others have sought to examine musical rhythms in relation to rhythms in nature. A smaller group of writers has been concerned with notation systems. Persons concerned with influencing human behavior through music have recognized and studied rhythm's role in music used to modify nonmusical behaviors. Performing musicians, in addition to depending on rhythm to lend structure and hold performances together, use rhythm as one means of enhancing expression or creativity. Music teachers have examined rhythm from a pedagogical perspective.

Persons concerned with understanding the psychological foundations of rhythmic behavior are faced with the perplexing problem of synthesizing an overwhelming body of literature into a conceptual framework which will provide a basis for dealing with rhythmic behavior. Such a framework necessarily requires an examination of (1) rhythm's function in music, (2) rhythmic structures in music, (3) theories of response to rhythm in music, (4) psychological processes underlying rhythmic behaviors, and (5) the development and evaluation of rhythmic behaviors. This chapter provides such an examination.

Function of Rhythm in Music

"When the musics from all cultures of the world are considered, it is rhythm that stands out as most fundamental. *Rhythm is the organizer and the energizer.* Without rhythm, there would be no music whereas there is much music that has neither melody nor harmony." (Gaston, 1968, p. 17) .

Cooper and Meyer (1960, p. 1) also view rhythm as fundamental to music: "To study rhythm is to study all of music. Rhythm both organizes and is itself organized by all the elements which create and shape music processes." Mursell (1956, pp. 254-257) , whose study and writings concerning rhythm spanned forty years, cites additional functions of rhythm in music as it relates to man:

1. Rhythm gives life, sparkle, reality, and expressiveness to the performance of music.
2. A grasp of and feeling for rhythm adds immensely to the pleasure of listening.
3. A sense of rhythm can carry one over technical hurdles in performing music.
4. A live feeling for rhythm facilitates music reading.
5. Rhythm is the best and most natural starting point for musical creation.

Clearly, rhythm's primary function in music is to give order.

Music is a temporal art which must be organized in such a way that it is comprehensible. Rhythm, in its broadest sense, *"is everything pertaining to the temporal quality (duration) of the musical sound"* (Apel, 1944, p. 640). It is the organization of sound's durational attributes which indeed allows sound to become music. When comprehensible organization is lacking, the listener does not perceive the sound as music.

Rhythm provides the forward movement of music, thus making music a dynamic energizing force. Music with little rhythmic movement elicits less dynamic responses than music in which rhythmic movement is active. As noted above, rhythm provides the life to music, and a "feel" or "sense" of rhythm as the dynamic force within music facilitates a person's interactions with music both as a performer and a respondent.

Whether as a performer or respondent, an individual's interaction with rhythm in music can result in aesthetic experience (Sachs, 1953, p. 18). The increasing importance of rhythm as an aesthetic device is readily apparent when one compares its prominence and complexity in twentieth century music with its role in renaissance, baroque, classical, and romantic music.

Most traditional definitions of rhythm allude in some way to rhythm as the organizational and dynamic force in music.* Even with a general agreement regarding rhythm's basic function in music, there is, as Creston (1964, p. v) notes, a need "to separate the chaff from the wheat." Discussions of rhythm and its attributes yield little consensus, and a clear understanding of the basic attributes of rhythm in music is essential to understanding the psychological foundations of rhythmic behavior. The next section attempts to clarify some of the confusion regarding the various attributes of rhythmic structures in music.

RHYTHMIC STRUCTURES IN MUSIC

Descriptions of the attributes of musical rhythm are many and varied. There is some commonality of terms employed in these descriptions, but common meanings are not always applied to these terms. Mursell (1937, p. 190), for example, recognizes two

---

For a discussion of various definitions of rhythm, see Creston, 1964, pp. v-vi.

attributes of musical rhythm: (1) the underlying beat and (2) the phrase rhythm. Cooper and Meyer (1960, p. 3) recognize three basic modes of temporal organization in music: (1) pulse, (2) meter, and (3) rhythm. Gordon (1971, pp. 67-69), in a departure from traditional use of terminology in explaining rhythmic organization in music, maintains that rhythm is comprised of three basic elements: (1) tempo beats, (2) meter beats, and (3) melodic rhythm. Relationships resulting from combinations of these three basic elements comprise "rhythmic patterns" which "elicit musical meaning . . . in the mind of the listener" (Gordon, 1971, p. 69). Creston (1964, pp. 1-44), writing from a composer's vantage point and considering rhythm in terms of "the organization of duration in ordered movement," a view consistent with the authors' perceptions of the function of rhythm in music, identifies four basic aspects of rhythm: (1) meter, (2) pace, (3) accent, and (4) pattern.

Creston views the traditional terms "time" and "tempo" as somewhat indefinite and inaccurate and replaces them with the terms "meter" and "pace" respectively. Most current writings also use meter in place of time, although substitution of pace for tempo is not so common. "Accent is used in the traditional sense (emphasizing a beat), but "pattern" refers to any subdivision of a pulse or beat into smaller units, e.g. a ♩ into 𝅘𝅥𝅮𝅘𝅥𝅮, 𝅘𝅥𝅭𝅘𝅥𝅮, 𝅘𝅥𝅮𝅘𝅥𝅮𝅘𝅥𝅮, 𝅘𝅥𝅯𝅘𝅥𝅯𝅘𝅥𝅯𝅘𝅥𝅯 etc.

While all the above schemes for explaining the organization of rhythm structure have merit, this discussion will not adhere strictly to any one scheme; rather, it draws from the common aspects of several of the schemes and, for the most part, uses conventional terminology.

Underlying the structural components is pulse, which is commonly referred to as beat. The beat is the basic unit of duration and divides duration into equal segments. A problem arises in discussion of beat with respect to meter. Meter signatures specify which unit of notation receives a beat; in practice, however, the unit designated by a meter signature as receiving the beat is not always the same as the beat which is felt in response to the music. Mursell (1937, pp. 189-198) uses the German term *Takt* to indicate the beat which is felt; Farnsworth (1969, p. 233) refers to it as the "true beat." Creston avoids the problem of two kinds of beats by referring to that which is indicated by the meter signature as "pulse" or "metrical pulse" and that which is felt as the "beat." Because other distinctions have been made between pulse and beat, e.g. pulse implies a series of points dividing duration into equal segments, while beat reflects equal segments of time having duration, however, some confusion arises in using the two terms. For this discussion, therefore, the term pulse will not be used. Rather, the beat indicated by a meter signature will be referred to as the *metrical* beat; the beat felt in response to music will be referred to as the *true* beat. Instances in which the beat felt coincides with the metrical beat will be referred to as beat. Metrical beat will be used only when referring to the beat indicated by a meter signature and when it does not coincide with the beat which is felt in response to music.

Meter involves the grouping of beats, usually metrical beats. Meter is primarily a function of notation and is indicated in music notation by bar lines. The idea is that the first note of each measure should receive an accent, thus delineating the meter. That music does not always conform mechanically to this pattern is obvious. This departure from the norm allows music to be an expressive medium rather than confining it to being mechanical or arithmetical.

When the tempo of music is quick, the effect on the listener often is to make the notated measure, rather than the metrical beat, the unit of the beat. These true beats are often grouped into several measures, thus creating the effect of a superimposed meter. Creston (1964, p. 3) has classified these groupings of beats as follows:

MONOMETER	meter of one measure
DIMETER	meter of two measures
TRIMETER	meter of three measures
TETRAMETER	meter of four measures
PENTAMETER	meter of five measures
HEXAMETER	meter of six measures, etc.

In other instances neither the metrical beat nor the measure are the same as the true beat; e.g. $\frac{6}{8}$ meter in moderate or faster tempo usually is felt in two's, with the 𝅘𝅥. functioning as the unit of the true beat.

Jacques-Dalcroze (1921, Musical Supplement, p. 1) suggested a plan whereby meter signatures would be more meaningful and which would avoid the confusion between the metrical beat and the true beat. The note which is to be the unit of the beat would be substituted for the lower number of the meter signature (see Figure 3-1).

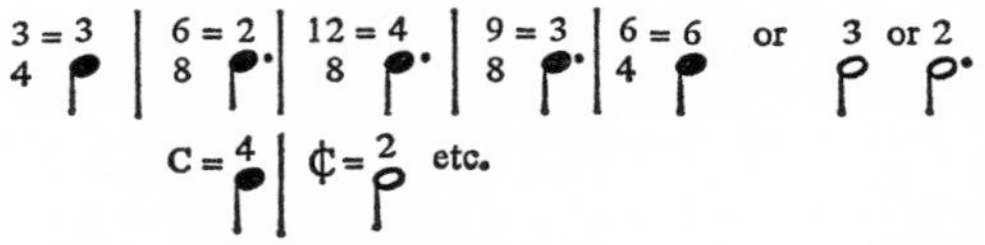

Figure 3-1. Jaques-Dalcroze's rationalized meter signatures. While Jaques-Dalcroze's suggestion has received some following in recent years, it is far from common practice, and musicians must continue to cope with distinguishing between the metrical beat and the true beat.

Tempo, or *pace* as Creston terms it, refers to the speed at which the beat recurs. Tempo in music notation is indicated in general terms by use of the traditional Italian terms, including (from slowest to quickest) *grave, largo, adagio, lento, andante, moderato, allegro,* and *presto.* More precise tempo indications are given in terms of metronome markings which indicate the number of times a given note value or unit of time recurs in one minute. The note value indicated may coincide with either the metrical beat or the true beat. A typical metronome indication is

𝅘𝅥 = M.M.80.   This means that the quarter note is the beat unit, and the beat would recur at the rate of 80 per minute. (Mälzel constructed the metronome in 1816, and M.M. is a standard abbreviation for Mälzel Metronome.)

Accent is the aspect of rhythm which makes prominent or emphasizes a beat. Creston (1964, pp. 28-32) recognizes eight types of accents: dynamic, agogic, metric, harmonic, weight, pitch, pattern, and embellished. A *dynamic accent* emphasizes a beat by means of tone intensity, i.e. the tone is louder than others. An *agogic accent* emphasizes by means of duration, i.e. the tone is longer than those preceding or following it. A *metric accent* basically reflects the particular grouping of true beats or metrical beats and often is a dynamic accent. A *harmonic accent* emphasizes a beat by use of dissonance or harmonic change on the beat. A *weight accent* expresses emphasis through change in texture. A *pitch accent* denotes emphasis on the highest or lowest tone of a group. *Pattern accents* occur on the initial tone of a melodic figure which is repeated. *Embellished accents* emphasize a beat through the use of melodic embellishments, e.g. mordents, trills, and grupetti.

Creston views accent as the "very life of rhythm," without which meter becomes monotonous, pace (his term for tempo) has no sense of motion, and pattern becomes a nebulous elaboration.

It is in discussions of how phrase or melodic rhythms are organized around the structure of beat, meter, and accent that there seems to be the greatest amount of disagreement. Mursell (1937, pp. 176-185) and Cooper and Meyer (1960, p. 6) recognize rhythmic grouping or units as the basic structural level for melodic rhythms. These units are derived from ancient Greek poetic meter, and involve the grouping of unaccented beats around an accented beat. The five basic units are

iamb	‿ —
anapest	‿ ‿ —
trochee	— ‿
dactyl	— ‿ ‿
amphibrach	‿ — ‿

in which the dash indicates an accent. The theory is that these units underlie the melodic rhythms of music. Yeston (1976, pp. 27-34), however, notes several problems in attempting to reduce rhythm to such basic units, particularly when laws of perception are considered. He maintains that attempts to analyze rhythm in these terms are overly reductive and not reflective of the realities of rhythmic variety.

Gordon (1971, pp. 67-71; 1976, pp. 31-58) and Creston (1964, pp. 34-43) view subdivisions of beats as the underlying structural units for melodic rhythms. Both Gordon and Creston agree that beats are subdivided into basically two's or three's. When the beat is divided into two equally spaced subdivisions (which he calls *meter beats*), Gordon labels this duple meter; when the beat is subdivided into three meter beats he labels it triple meter.* Creston refers to subdivisions of the beat as *patterns;* patterns are classified as *regular* or *irregular* and *simple* or *compound.* Regular patterns reflect subdivisions suggested by meter signatures; irregular patterns are subdivisions not suggested by the meter signature. Repeated patterns are called simple patterns; changing patterns are compound.

The temporal order in which sounds occur may be overridden in perceptual organization of rhythm. *Auditory stream segregation,* in which auditory input is organized into two simultaneous patterns on the basis of common elements rather than strict temporal order, and rhythmic or melodic *fission,* in which alternating tones form two separate melodic rhythms, are interesting cases of rhythm perception which are not uncommon in music.

When Bregman and Campbell (1971) presented a short cycle of six tones (three high and three low) at a rapid rate, their subjects invariably divided the sequences into two streams on the basis of frequency. The patterns actually perceived were only those which related elements in the same subjective stream. The perceptual split depended on the frequency difference and presentation rate; faster presentation rates required less difference between high and low tones in order to induce the streaming effect.

Auditory stream segregation on the basis of frequency differences is more likely when the tones are short and discrete. Frequency glides between the tones and longer tones result in a continuity which makes the temporal order easier to follow and discourages stream splitting (Bregman and Dannenbring, 1973).

Rhythmic fission was illustrated by Dowling (1968), who presented tone sequences, at about ten tones per second, which were

---

*The reader should keep in mind that Gordon's terminology for duple and triple meter is based on whether the beat is *subdivided* into two's or three's; conventional references to duple and triple meter, however, are based on whether accented *beats* are grouped in two's or threes.

constructed so that frequency difference between *successive* tones was *large* while the difference between *alternate* tones was *small*. Melody was detected among alternating tones of the same intensity and frequency range, especially when observers were directed in their listening. The rhythmic fission was intensified by intensity differences or stereophonic separation between the patterns.

In a later study, Dowling (1973) showed that two familiar melodies formed by alternating successive tones ("interleaved" melodies) are easily identified as the result of melodic fission when the two melodies' frequency ranges do not overlap. When frequency ranges do overlap, the task is more difficult, although listeners can track a familiar melody if it is prespecified, i.e. they know the melody in advance. All melodies were altered to a rhythm of alternating quarter notes and quarter rests, and the combined tonal sequences ("interleaved" melodies) were presented at a rate of eight tones per second.

The organization of auditory streams is context dependent; e.g. widely separated frequencies may be in one stream if other stimulus elements are noises. Two organizational principles, one of element similarity and one of temporal proximity, may conflict. Basically, auditory streams appear to form in such a manner that elements within a stream are maximally similar (McNally and Handel, 1977).

Regardless of how one analyzes melodic rhythms, there is common agreement that melodic rhythms overlay and entwine themselves around the beat. Melodic rhythms may vary infinitely; they may be even, uneven, use subdivision of beats, or involve durational values extending over many beats. It is the very freedom of melodic rhythm that provides a primary means for making music a dynamic energizing force.

While melodic rhythm with its free organization in relation to the substructure of beat, accent, and meter provides both variety and unity for musical structure, it must be recognized that many additional extensions of rhythmic structure are used to provide even greater interest. The potential of polyrhythms, multimeters, changing meters, changing tempi, and ametrical rhythms, in combination with the potential for rhythmic variety within conventional rhythmic structure, make rhythmic structure a truly dynamic and integral part of all music.

RESPONSE THEORIES

The basis for human response to music's rhythmic structure has been subject to much debate. Several theories have evolved concerning response to rhythmic structure which Lundin (1967, pp. 116-122) summarizes as (1) *instinctive,* (2) *physiological,* and (3) *motor.* Lundin also proposes a fourth theory, in which rhythm is viewed as a learned response.

Instinctive Theories

Seashore, the major proponent of the instinctive theory, states (1938, p. 138) that "there are two fundamental factors in the perception of rhythm: an instinctive tendency to group impressions in hearing and a capacity for doing this with precision in time and stress." He considers the capacity for rhythm as one of a hierarchy of musical talents, all of which are instinctive. He agrees that individuals differ in their rhythmic capacities, but he maintains that the capacity is an inherited trait, not a learned one.

Both Mursell (1937, p. 153) and Lundin (1967, p. 117) criticize this viewpoint. They argue that considering an individual's tendency to group auditory impressions as instinctive is contrary to accepted research findings. In their view, the response to rhythm involves some learning. Because of Seashore's views, there have been several investigations concerning the improvability of the performance of rhythm.

In a study in which the experimental task was to keep time with a rhythm pattern presented aurally, it was found that the capacity for motor-rhythm could be improved (Nielsen, 1930, p. 78). The improvement occurred during the early stages of training. In a similar study reported by Lundin (1967, p. 114), Henderson also found that rhythm performance could be improved. As a group, his subjects made distinct progress over a five-day practice period.

Whitson (1951, p. 56) investigated the improvability of rhythmic perception as measured by the Seashore rhythm test. He submitted a group of junior high school students to a short, ill-defined "formal course of rhythm training." On the basis of their significantly improved scores on the Seashore rhythm test, he concluded that rhythm perception can be improved through instruction.

Perhaps the most ambitious study of this type is the one by Coffman (1949). He selected eighteen seventh and eighth graders and twelve college students who had scored below average on the Seashore rhythm test and the Coffman rhythm discrimination test and gave them private or small group rhythm instruction for approximately three months. The training program was basically a kinesthetic approach, including eurhythmics,* an intensive course in drumming, and the more common tapping and clapping activities. This training, which was described as intensive remedial training, enabled both the seventh and eighth graders and the college students to significantly improve their scores on the Coffman and Seashore tests (Coffman, 1949, p. 74). (One may, however, suspect the statistical artifact of regression toward the mean because Coffman's subjects were selected for their low scores.)

When research such as the above is considered, it is clear that instinctive theories are inadequate for explaining response to rhythm.

Physiological Theories

Theories that rhythmic response depends upon recurring physiological processes are not new. The idea that man's heart beat serves as a basis for rhythm and tempo in music has been the most prevalent view, of which Jaques-Dalcroze (1921, pp. 79-82) was an avid supporter.

Evidence to support the heart beat theory is entirely lacking. Mursell (1937, p. 155) criticizes the heart beat notion on the basis that there is no mechanism known to psychology by which the heart beat gives us our sense of timing.

---

*Eurhythmics refers to a system of rhythmic movements devised by Jaques-Dalcroze (1921) and involves responding to, or *realizing*, rhythms through movement. The method is based on the principle that children should *experience* rhythm through movement prior to study of rules. Jaques-Dalcroze's eurhythmics, which includes twenty-two types of rhythmic exercises, are designed to facilitate a feeling for bodily rhythm and aural perception of rhythm.

Lund's (1939) study of the true beat in music also refutes the theory. Seventy-three college sophomores indicated the proper tempi for two popular tunes by adjusting a lever on a Duo-Art reproducing piano. Lund reports no significant relationships between students' preferred tempi and the rate of any of their objectively measured physiological processes and states (p. 70) that "the theory that the preferred 'true beat' in music is conditioned by some regularly recurrent physiological process has no support from the data of this study."

Another theory concerning physiological processes was advocated by McDougall, (1902, pp. 460-480) who maintained that a primitive rate of nervous discharge serves as the basis for human response to rhythm. Both Mursell and Lundin dismiss this theory because of its hazy view of a mind-body interaction.

Mursell (1937, p. 157) notes that attempts to explain rhythm in terms of regularly recurring bodily processes overemphasize the regularity of rhythmic occurrence. By and large, attempts to support physiological theories have relied on correlations, real or otherwise, between the tempi of music of selected composers and the various rates of physiological processes.

The "natural" rhythms of human physiology, including the menstrual cycle and cyclic changes in body temperature, wakefulness, and biochemistry, are too lengthy and variable to explain rhythmic responses to relatively short-term musical stimuli. A person's receptivity to musical stimuli may vary with cyclic phenomena, of course.

Motor Theory

The motor theory of rhythm holds that rhythm is dependent upon the action of the voluntary muscles. Lundin (1967, p. 120) states:

> We are able to grasp and respond to complex rhythms not on the basis of instincts or nebulous physiological mechanisms, but because we have a neuromuscular system which is complex and capable of being trained to make these responses.

Thus, according to this theory, rhythmic response is through an individual's own voluntary muscle action.

That nearly all investigations concerning the nature of

rhythmic experience find a motor or muscular factor lends support to motor theory advocates (Schoen, 1940, p. 21). Mursell and Lundin recognize the motor theory as the most plausible of the theories, but neither accepts it without reservation.

Mursell (1937, p. 162) maintains that *"the ultimate foundation of rhythm is to be found in mental activity."* He insists that mind and body cannot be separate, but must function as a totality in which the brain and the central nervous system are the controlling factors over voluntary movements.

Lundin (1967, p. 106) agrees that rhythmic response involves more than voluntary muscle movement. To him it is both a perceptual and a motor response. He maintains that responsiveness to rhythm is learned and cannot be accounted for solely by any of the above theories. Response to rhythm involves the total organism and cannot be explained in either/or terms of muscles or mental activity.

Rhythmic Response as Learned

Although he labels it a "modified motor theory," Lundin's (1967, pp. 106-113) account of rhythmic response reflects the view that rhythm is a learned response which involves both perception and motor response. Perception of rhythm requires observation of rhythmic stimuli and may or may not involve overt behaviors. It involves both perceptual *organization* of rhythmic stimuli and *discrimination* among stimuli. Lundin contends that the ability to organize and discriminate among rhythmic stimuli is dependent on learning. Hebb's (1949, pp. 22-37) discussion of the role of experience in perception lends strong support to Lundin's position.

Lundin also maintains that overt motor rhythmic responses have a perceptual base. Overt motor rhythmic responses reflect the clarity of an individual's perceptual responses.

Anyone who has taught music recognizes that students' rhythmic responses can be modified. To say that rhythmic responses can be explained independently of learning, therefore, is to ignore the facts. Rhythmic responses clearly involve a great deal of learning. While the extent of the interaction between learning and instinctive factors or the rates of physiological processes perhaps

never will be fully understood, motor response *is* inextricably related to rhythmic response, although it alone is inadequate for
explaining rhythmic response.   One must conclude, therefore,
that rhythmic response, as most psychological responses, is a
learned response which is facilitated by voluntary motor activity.
A discussion of the extent to which motor activity facilitates
rhythm response follows.

PSYCHOLOGICAL PROCESSES AND RHYTHMIC BEHAVIOR

The above views of Mursell and Lundin imply a close, complex interaction between motor activity and mental activity.
Other educators also have recognized that motor activity and
thinking go hand in hand. This section discusses some theoretical
and psychological bases underlying the theory of motor activity as
a facilitator of learning as well as some research which supports
the theory.

Theoretical and Psychophysiological Bases

Piaget, who has devoted a lifetime to epistemology, places
much importance upon early sensorimotor learning as the basis
of intellectual development.*

> In his scheme of things, a sensorimotor intelligence, not perception,
> provides the foundation for later intellectual development (and, . . .
> it is the matrix from which and in which perception itself originates
> and evolves). (Flavell, 1963, p. 472)

The studies of early sensorimotor experiences of chimpanzees
reported by Hebb (1958, p. 116) corroborate Piaget's view.
Chimpanzees whose sensorimotor experiences were limited greatly during infancy were much slower at learning simple tasks than
were other chimpanzees who had been allowed normal sensorimotor experiences during infancy.

Views that motor activity aids in thinking are not new. Indeed, the motor theory served as an impetus from which modern
views concerning the effect of movement on thinking have
evolved. The motor theory of thought was originally devised in
order to avoid postulating ideation to explain thinking. Hebb

---

*A discussion of Piaget's views regarding learning appears in Chapter Ten.

(1958, p. 58) states:

> It proposed that, when a man is thinking, what is really going on is that he is talking to himself, or making movements with his hands and fingers that are too small to be seen. Each word or movement of the hand produces a feedback stimulation that produces the next one, in a chain reaction: instead of ideation, therefore, what we have is a series of S-R reactions. The theory is no longer entertained as a complete explanation . . . but the conceptions which it developed concerning sensory feedback remain valid and important for the understanding of serial behavior.

Sensory feedback is usually of two kinds: exteroceptive and proprioceptive. Exteroceptive sensory cells are excited by events external to the body. Proprioceptive sensory cells are excited by *movements* of the body, and it is the proprioceptive feedback that is of particular relevance in understanding rhythmic behavior.

Proprioceptive feedback usually is equated with kinesthetic feedback. This feedback from movement has been called proprioception rather than kinesthesis. The change in terminology has occurred because the concept of kinesthesis generally is associated with introspection, whereas proprioception emphasizes receptor and sensory nerve action which can be determined neurophysiologically (Osgood, 1953, p. 29).

That proprioceptive pathways to the thalamus, cerebellum, and cortex exist is an established fact (Morgan, 1965, p. 258). There are three types of neural receptor cells for proprioceptive sensations: (1) "spray type" cells at different positions in the joints, (2) Golgi end organs, and (3) Pancenian corpuscles. These cells are actually in the joints rather than in the muscles.

Proprioceptive stimuli may travel to the cortex via either of two routes. The direct route is through the thalamus. The other, more diffuse and indirect, is through the reticular activating system. Morgan (1965, p. 41) reports that the various sensory inputs and outputs are not clearly separated in the reticular system.

Thus, neurophysiological findings support the contentions that sensory feedback from movement is related to higher mental processes. However, the precise role that proprioceptive impulses play in higher mediating processes is not known. It is, though, subject to much speculation.

Osgood (1953, p. 651) says "it may be that motor tone merely serves as a facilitative agent for mental activity in general." Hebb (1958, p. 60) maintains that thinking cannot be accounted for by central processes alone or by muscular feedback alone: Both mechanisms are involved.

At least two theories of perception have movement as one of their bases.   The theories proposed primarily are concerned with visual perception, but the principles involved also apply to perceptions through other sensory media.

Hebb maintains that eye movements are essential to visual perception.   He does not, however, insist perceptual integration is wholly the result of such motor activity.   Eye movements "contribute, constantly and essentially, to perceptual integration, even though they are not the whole origin of it" (Hebb, 1949, p. 37).

The sensory-tonic field theory of perception postulates that both proprioceptive and exteroceptive feedback are essential to perceptual integration (Allport, 1955, pp. 183-207).   This theory holds that it can be shown experimentally that sensory, i.e. exteroceptive, and tonic, i.e. proprioceptive, factors are equivalent with respect to their contributions to the dynamic outcome.

Perhaps the following statement best summarizes the status of the motor versus mental controversy:

> Actually the interrelation of motor and mental activity is one of cyclic and reciprocal interdependence. However, the nature of the problem and current trends in thinking make it necessary at this time to emphasize particularly the dependence of the mental upon motor activity. (Sperry, 1964, p. 429)

Movement and the Perception of Rhythm

The perception of rhythm, in the psychological sense, means "the perception of a series of stimuli as a series of groups of stimuli" (Woodrow, 1951, p. 1232).   It may or may not involve the reproduction of rhythm patterns.

In the last decades of the nineteenth century and the early decades of this century, the perception of rhythm was investigated frequently.   Introspective analysis was the accepted experimental technique of the times; thus, when evaluating the findings concerning the value of movement (or kinesthesis as it was called) as an aid in the perception of rhythm, this factor must be taken into consideration.

Boring (1942, p. 586) reports that all investigators during this time discovered that auditory rhythms tend to be accompanied by kinesthetic accentuation. Bolton, McDougall, Stetson, Miner, and Kofka were prominent among investigators reporting such findings.

Ruckmick (1913, pp. 305-359) attempted to answer once and for all the question concerning the role of kinesthesis in the perception of rhythm. In his much quoted study, he presented subjects with both auditory and visual rhythm patterns. The subjects were to verbally give their impressions of the groupings. His conclusions were that (1) the perception of rhythm may take place without accompanying kinesthesis, (2) there are individual differences in the amount of kinesthesis involved in the perception of rhythm, and (3) generally kinesthesis is connected most prominently with the initial clear perception of the type and form of rhythm.

In 1945 (p. 84), Ruckmick explained that the last conclusion meant that "kinaesthesis [sic] was essential for the establishment of a rhythm pattern" (Ruckmick, 1945, p. 84). It was only after a rhythm pattern had been established that kinesthesis ceased to be necessary for the perception of a rhythm.

From his review of Ruckmick's and other early studies concerning rhythmic perception, Boring (1942, p. 587) concluded that many perceptions are grouped by concomitant kinesthesis and many are not. "Kinesthesis is not a *sine qua non* of rhythm."

Rhythmic Perception vs. Rhythmic Behavior

As stated in Chapter One, perception is a process of sensing the environment. Because perception, as cognition, is essentially a covert process, investigators of perception generally study perception in terms of some overt manifestation of perception.* As

---

*For a more extensive study of the relationship between covert conceptual or perceptual activity and overt instrumental (movement) or symbolic (verbal) musical behaviors, the reader should consult Woodruff (1970, pp. 51-54) and Regelski (1975, pp. 11-15).

Rainbow (1977, p. 56) notes, perception in music historically has been measured by asking subjects to *demonstrate* the ability to do a task. Studies of rhythmic perception have asked subjects to demonstrate perception by reproducing a pattern through clapping or in the case of perception of beat or meter by stepping or marching in time to music. Rainbow's pilot study for his longitudinal investigation of the rhythmic abilities of preschool children, however, revealed that vocally chanting rhythms might be a more appropriate measure of rhythmic perception, particularly for young children.

Thackray's (1968) investigation of rhythmic abilities sought to clarify the distinction between rhythmic perception and rhythmic performance and to investigate the extent to which the two are related. A factor analysis of the correlation coefficients among his seven rhythmic perception subtests revealed a fundamental factor in rhythmic perception: *the ability to perceive and memorize a rhythmic structure as a whole, and to analyze it consciously* (Thackray, 1968, p. 15). Thackray's rhythmic perception test battery essentially involved *discrimination tasks,* and the responses required were symbolic, i.e. verbal, rather than instrumental, i.e. movement. Thackray concluded that there are three essentials for rhythmic perception: (1) ability to count, (2) time discrimination, and (3) loudness discrimination.

Thackray also devised a five-part rhythmic performance test which required subjects to reproduce rhythmic patterns through movements. He found a "positive but not especially high" (.65) correlation between subjects' score on the rhythmic perception and rhythmic performance tests. A factor analysis of the combined batteries revealed a substantial factor of general rhythmic ability running through the tests. His results suggest that this general rhythmic factor is measured appreciably better by the performance tests than by the perception tests. The best individual measure is the reproduction of the rhythm of a melody.

Thackray's (1968, p. 45) general conclusion regarding the relationship between rhythmic perception and rhythmic performance is stated thusly:

Although rhythmic ability is complex, there is a common factor running through all the forms of rhythmic activity which we have considered, which might be defined as the ability to perceive rhythmic structures in respect to the three elements of timing, duration and intensity, and to perform rhythmic movements in which these qualities are clearly defined.

As will be apparent in the following discussion, researchers' use of terminology has not been consistent with Thackray's distinction between perceptual behaviors and performance behaviors. Although the authors recognize that perception underlies rhythmic behaviors, they believe that it is clearer to examine the overt behavior, whether it be symbolic (verbal) or instrumental (movement), and avoid attempts to classify it as perceptual or performance.

DEVELOPMENT OF RHYTHMIC BEHAVIORS

Rhythmic behaviors include a broad spectrum of behaviors, ranging from simple tapping of the toe in time with the beat to the sightreading of intricate rhythms. The development of rhythmic behaviors has been the subject of much speculation, research, and trial and error. This section examines research findings and music teachers' views regarding the development of rhythmic behaviors. In addition, it reviews approaches to measuring rhythmic behaviors.

Research on the development of rhythmic behaviors basically is developmental or experimental. Developmental research can be either longitudinal or cross-sectional. Longitudinal studies investigate a groups' rhythmic abilities (or whatever trait one wishes to study) over an extended period of time, whereas cross-sectional studies investigate a trait in different groups at various age or developmental levels. Although longitudinal studies are the preferred methodology, nearly all studies of the development of rhythmic behaviors are cross-sectional. None involves the study of a given group for a period greater than one year.

Developmental Research

Although there are some exceptions, nearly all developmental research regarding rhythmic behaviors examines one of two rhythmic behaviors: (1) the ability to keep time with the beat of music and (2) the ability to repeat a given rhythm pattern. The variables in the different studies are numerous, thus making it difficult to understand clearly the status of rhythmic behaviors at different age or developmental levels. Some studies examine rhythmic behaviors in isolation from any melodic behaviors, while others examine rhythmic behaviors in conjunction with behaviors related to pitch organization.

Studies of infants' rhythmic development, however, necessarily involve a research strategy different from the types just mentioned. The investigator must observe the infants' rhythmic behaviors, either freely emitted or in response to rhythmic stimuli. Most studies of infants' musical behaviors support Fridman's (1973, p. 264) basic hypothesis which was derived from her study of infants and young children: "The first cry of the newborn is the generator not only of the spoken language and of musicality, but also of movement and of musical rhythm." She maintains that each phonic manifestation of a baby from birth to age one has an equivalent rhythm which in turn creates "new motor auditive stereotypes of different rhythms." Following is Fridman's (p. 268) list of babies' phonic manifestations and their equivalent rhythms:

Crying	— Quick
Breathing	— Regular or fast
Moaning	— Slow
Sucking	— Fast
Swallowing	— Fast
Hiccoughing	— Spasmodic
Eructation	— Spasmodic
Sneezing	— Spasmodic
Trilling	— Slow & intonated, with intervals
Babbling	— Intonated, sequential
Repetition of first syllables	— Fast or slow, intonated

Moog (1976, pp. 39-40) observed that between the ages of four and six months is the stage at which infants begin to respond to music with overt movement. He noted that the infants do not move in disorganized clumsy ways; rather they use clear repetitive movements which are related to the rhythmic aspects of the musical stimulus. As the child develops, the movements increasingly are coordinated with both musical rhythm and dynamics. The movements of the four– to six-month-old infant involve movements with the whole body, but as the child develops the movement responses to rhythm also change, particularly to include more movements with individual body parts. Moog reports that by the age of eighteen months about 10 percent of children are able, for short stretches of time, to match their movements to the rhythm of the music.

Studies of rhythmic behavior in early childhood, childhood, and into adolescence also show a general refinement in rhythmic skills with increasing age. Jersild and Bienstock (1935) examined two– to five-year-old children's ability to beat time to music. Seventy-four children's responses were analyzed, and a large increase in scores was evident between two– and five-year-olds. Of 400 possible beats (administered in smaller segments), the number of correct beats for the two-year-olds was 84.5, three-year-olds, 109.4, four-year-olds, 159.8, and five-year-olds, 192.8.

Rosenbusch and Gardner (1968, pp. 1271-1276) studied five– to thirteen-year-olds' ability to reproduce four different rhythm patterns. Responses were compared for four age groups: five to seven, seven to nine, nine to eleven, and eleven to thirteen. Results showed a significant decrease in errors with increase in age.

Gardner (1971, pp. 335-360) also studied children's ability to reproduce given rhythm patterns. Subjects were twenty first graders, twenty third graders, and twenty sixth graders. Each child was asked to duplicate twenty rhythm patterns which included from four to eight taps each. The mean numbers of correctly tapped patterns for the three groups were 7.35, 13.00, and 16.00 respectively. These differences were statistically significant at the .01 level.

Petzold (1966, pp. 184-251) conducted a one-year pilot study of elementary school children's rhythmic abilities. Children were asked to reproduce common rhythm patterns found most frequently in seven elementary basal series published between 1953 and 1959.

Patterns were about two measures in length and were in three common meters: $\frac{2}{4}$, $\frac{3}{4}$, and $\frac{6}{8}$. The most frequently used patterns in $\frac{2}{4}$ meter were

In addition, children were asked to respond to a "Periodic Beat Test" which involved series of beats at four different tempi. Each beat was presented twice and arranged so that the respondent moved from a fast tempo through three successively slower tempi; the order was reversed for the second part of the test. Usable test data were obtained for 331 children on the "Rhythmic Patterns Test" and for 241 on the "Periodic Beat Test." Petzold summarized his results with respect to differences in grade level responses:

> The ability to respond accurately to the aural presentation of rhythmic patterns does not change substantially after the child has attained third grade. The same plateau is reached by third grade when children are expected to maintain a steady tempo that is provided by a metronome.

Taylor's (1973, pp. 44-49) study of the musical development of children aged seven to eleven also revealed increases in rhythm responsiveness for younger children and a lack of increase with age for the older children in his study. He reports statistically significant differences between the mean rhythm scores of the younger age groups but no significant difference between the means of his two oldest age groups.

Igaga and Versey (1977, pp. 23-27) employed a rhythmic perception test devised by Thackray (1968) to study the rhythmic behaviors of 655 Ugandan and 573 English school children aged between ten and fifteen years. The test battery allowed for administration in groups and included six types of responses to recorded stimuli: (1) counting the number of notes in an item, (2) after being given the tempo, counting the number of beats in a period of silence, (3) matching a given pattern with one of four series of long and short dashes (an elementary aural-visual test), (4) marking in a row of dots the pattern of strong and weak beats heard, (5) comparing rhythm patterns (same or different), and (6) counting the number of notes in a melodic phrase. Although no statistical tests of significance were made between the groups or age levels, means were reported for each cultural group and age level. The mean scores for the Ugandan children increased with each age level between ten and fifteen, although some of these increases would appear negligible. The mean scores for the English school children, while higher at the first four age levels than those for the Ugandan children, showed increases only between ages eleven and twelve and twelve and thirteen. Mean scores for the fourteen– and fifteen-year-old English children were lower than those for the comparable Ugandan children. Although some subtests showed considerable increase with age, the data as presented are inconclusive regarding cross-cultural comparative increases in rhythmic abilities with age.

An examination of norms for children on some standardized rhythm aptitude tests provides another perspective on the development of rhythmic behaviors with age. Bentley (1966b, p. 116) reports a "fairly steady increase from year to year" on the rhythm memory portion of his *Measures of Musical Ability*. The normative data for some 2,000 boys and girls aged seven through fourteen support his statement. There is a mean yearly increase from 3.9 for seven-year-olds to 8.8 for fourteen-year-olds. Normative data for the *Seashore Measures of Musical Talents* (1939) and Gordon's *Musical Aptitude Profile* (1965) also reflect increases in scores with age level, even though both tests purport to measure factors which are influenced little by training.

A series of studies by Pflederer and Sechrest (1968, pp. 19-36) testing Piagetian theories of conservation* tend to support the position that rhythm behaviors (meter and rhythm) are a function of development. More recently, however, Foley (1975, pp.

---

*Conservation refers to the invariance of a particular dimension of empirical objects even though changes occur in other dimensions. Piaget views concept development in terms of conservation, which is nothing more than the stabilizing of a particular concept in the childs thinking (Zimmerman, 1971, pp. 16-17). More material on conservation appears in Chapter Ten.

240-248) reports that conservation can be expedited through training.

In studying the development of rhythmic behaviors, it is apparent that developmental research does not provide any clear-cut answers. The issues are confounded by variables in research design and the type of rhythmic behaviors studied, not to mention the validity and reliability of the various measures of rhythmic behavior. At best, it may be concluded that rhythmic behaviors generally increase with age, although there tends to be a leveling of abilities in older children. To accept unquestioningly, however, that increases in rhythmic abilities are solely a function of age or developmental level, is to disregard both the body of research concerning the development of rhythmic behaviors through experimental tasks and the empirical knowledge of music teachers who "know" that rhythmic behaviors can be developed or improved through instruction. The next section examines the research literature regarding the development of rhythmic behaviors through learning tasks.

Experimental Research

The research discussed herein is "experimental" because it seeks to examine the effects of some learning task on the development of rhythmic behaviors. Much of it, however, lacks the rigorous control of the variables which would enable it to meet contemporary standards for research design in the behavioral sciences (Campbell and Stanley, 1963) and therefore interpretations must be made with great caution.

The scope and variety of experimental research regarding the development of rhythmic behaviors also make it difficult to reach definitive conclusions. While some studies are concerned with behaviors reflecting discriminations among rhythmic stimuli, many others involve complex motor behaviors. Some study the development of rhythmic behaviors in young children whereas others are concerned with older children, adolescents, or adults.

Jersild and Bienstock (1935) studied the effects of practice on young children's ability to keep time with music. Fourteen subjects, ranging in age from twenty-five to forty-four months, participated in a training program distributed over a ten-week period. The training program used a variety of means to direct their attention to the act of keeping time; these included bodily movements, vocalizations, and hand clapping. Although the fourteen children receiving practice obtained a mean score higher than a matched control group, the difference was not statistically significant. Neither were their post-test scores significantly higher than their pretest scores.

Coffman (1949), however, in a study of the effects of training on junior high and college students' scores on the Seashore rhythm discrimination tests, found that trained subjects made statistically significant gains in rhythm discrimination scores while control group subjects did not. The training tasks involved a variety of rhythmic activities, including eurhythmics.

Dittemore (1970) examined the effects of a one-week rote teaching program of chanting and clapping melodic rhythm patterns on first through sixth graders' ability to chant melodic rhythm patterns. For two of the four criterion exercises, there were no significant differences among the six grade levels; for the two exercises involving more complex patterns, however, statistically significant differences were found. Because of the study's nature, it is difficult to draw definitive conclusions regarding either the effects of the training or abilities at the different grade levels.

DeYarmin (1972) compared the effects of training in singing songs in usual, mixed, and unusual meters with the effects of training in singing songs only in usual meter on kindergarten and first-grade children's ability to chant melodic rhythm patterns. As in the Dittemore study, children were taught the songs by rote, and chanting and clapping were part of the learning activities. Five minutes of five successive music classes were used for instruction for each song; a sixth music period was used for recording each child's chanting of the melodic rhythm of the song. Results showed no significant differences in the scores of children receiving instruction with songs in usual meters and scores of children receiving instruction with songs in usual, mixed, and unusual meters. DeYarmin concluded that music programs for young children should include more songs in mixed and unusual meters.

Zimmerman's (1971) recognition that Piaget's developmental sequence applies to the development of musical behaviors has led to some research testing the hypothesis that conservation is a function of developmental level and cannot be influenced by training. Recent research by Foley (1975) and Perney (1976) suggests that training can facilitate conservation in certain musical tasks.

Foley's study dealt with the improvement of conservation in two areas: (1) conservation of tonal patterns under the deformation of rhythmic patterns and (2) conservation of rhythmic patterns under the deformation of tonal patterns. Six intact second-grade classes were subjects, three classes randomly designated as experimental, the others as control. The experimental training used a variety of musical activities to foster the development of conservation. The experimental group made a statistically significant increase in their scores on the test for conservation of tonal and rhythmic patterns; the increase was significantly greater than that of the control group. The investigator concluded that improvements in the conservation of tonal and rhythmic patterns can be accelerated through training. Further, the training program was believed to have much practical significance in that expenses, equipment needs, and training required of teachers were quite minimal.

Perney (1976) examined the relation of musical training, verbal ability, and the combination of sex and grade on second and third graders' development of conservation of metric time. Results indicate no difference in performance of children who played musical instruments and those who did not. The mean performance of the second graders was higher, though not significantly higher, than that of the third graders. The most important finding, however, was that the second graders had greater verbal ability than the third graders, and there was a statistically significant correlation between children's verbal ability and their ability to perform the musical tasks. Perney concluded that performance on the musical tasks is not determined by age alone; rather it is more closely related to verbal ability.

Although there is a clear need for more research before

definite conclusions can be drawn regarding whether rhythmic development is a function of age or development or whether it can be fostered through training, there is sufficient reason to question the hypothesis that rhythmic development is solely a function of age.

Groves (1969) studied the effects of rhythmic training on first, second, and third graders' ability to synchronize body movements with rhythmic stimuli. The study also examined the effects of home musical background, motor ability, sex, and personal social adjustment. The experimental group received two thirty-minute lessons of basic rhythm patterns each week for twenty-four weeks. However, no significant difference was found in the ability to synchronize body movements with rhythmic stimuli between children who had and those who had not received rhythmic training. The study further shows the need for more research in order to gain a clearer understanding of the relationship between developmental factors and training on the development of rhythmic behaviors.

Reading rhythms also is an important rhythmic behavior and the balance of the research discussed in this section focuses on ways of developing such behaviors.

Palmer (1976) compared the approaches to rhythm reading advocated by Richards (1967) and Gordon (1971). Subjects were 136 fourth-grade children, forty-eight in the two Richards experimental classes, fifty in the two Gordon experimental classes, and thirty-eight in two control classes. In addition to an investigator-constructed measure of rhythmic performance achievement, written achievement was measured via the rhythm portions of three standardized music achievement tests. Results showed a statistically significant difference between the control and aggregated experimental classes in terms of rhythm reading achievement. However, no clear-cut differences were found between the achievement of the classes using the Richards approach and the classes using the Gordon approach.

The tachistoscope was employed in two studies concerned with the reading of rhythm notation. In a study using freshman music theory students as subjects, Christ (1953) devised a series of exercises which were flashed on a screen to be tapped, *en masse,* by the eleven students of his experimental group who had been selected randomly from a class of twenty-nine. The remaining eighteen students served as a control group. After ten hours of training, spread over a seven and one-half week period, both experimental and control groups were tested on an individual rhythm performance test in which the task was to tap the notated rhythm pattern. Scores of the experimental group were significantly higher (.002 level) than were the scores of the control group.

Wiley (1962) attempted to determine the relative effectiveness of the tachistoscope and conventional techniques in developing the ability of fifth grade students to sight-read rhythms. He exposed two groups of fifth graders to the same material. One group used conventional methods of learning while the other incorporated tachistoscopic drill. The criterion measure was a specially constructed performance test. He found that, while both groups made significant gains in their scores during the training period, scores of students in the experimental group were not statistically superior to scores of students in the control group. He concluded that tachistoscopic techniques were not superior to conventional techniques in developing rhythm sight-reading ability at the fifth grade level.

Two approaches to the teaching of instrumental music reading to beginners were compared in Skornicka's (1958) study. The experimental approach emphasized time and rhythm by requiring playing of quarter notes at the beginning of training (rather than the traditional whole notes), tapping the foot to mark the beat, and counting time mentally. The control groups used conventional band method books and no bodily movements. At the conclusion of the study, the experimental group achieved significantly higher sight-reading scores on the *Watkins-Farnum Performance Scale* than did the control group.

In a study designed to examine the effects of bodily movement, notably foot tapping the beat and clapping the melodic rhythm, on junior high school bandsmen's ability to sight read rhythms both in isolation and in context with other aspects of notation,

Boyle (1968) found that subjects using movement made significantly (.01 level) greater increases in both rhythm reading scores and music reading scores than did subjects who did not employ movement while reading rhythms. Results were based on individual performance tests given to 191 subjects representing a proportional random sample of the students in twenty-four junior high school training bands. The *Watkins-Farnum Performance Scale* was the measure of music reading ability and the rhythm patterns of it, notated on a single pitch, served as the measure of rhythm reading ability. A high degree of relationship ($r = .81$) was found between subjects' scores on the two measures.

Research employing principles of programmed instruction as the experimental variable in teaching rhythm reading also has been conducted. An important aspect of this approach is the provision of feedback to the subjects regarding their performance. Ihrke (1969), the first to report research of this nature, developed a rhythm monitor which accepted tape recorder impulses and triggered an "error" light unless responses were properly timed. He compared the performances of university students, in a course called "Music for the Classroom Teacher," who used the monitor with performances of students who did not use it. Students using the rhythm monitor system made significantly greater gains (.001 level) in their scores on a rhythm reading test than did students who did not use the system.

Shrader (1970) also developed a program for teaching rhythm reading. He utilized a stereotape teaching machine, with one tape channel activating a counter which indicated the number of correct responses made on a given exercise. He administered ten forty-five minute lessons to thirty-four high school students. Results showed that students using the teaching machine made significantly greater gains in rhythm reading scores than did a control group. Shrader's teaching machine is available commercially and appears to be receiving acceptance as a teaching device.*

Swope (1977) used Shrader's teaching machine with college

---

*For complete information on Shrader's teaching machine, now called the TAP Rhythm System, write Temporal Acuity Products, Inc., P.O. Box 5399, Seattle, Washington, 98105.

freshmen music theory students and found similar results. Students made statistically significant gains between pre– and post-testing. After the six-week training program, their scores were compared to a group of students who were completing a two-year music theory sequence, but without the use of the rhythm teaching machine. No statistically significant difference was found.

Placek (1974) employed computer-assisted instruction as a means for providing learning feedback in a series of rhythm lessons. While the study was essentially a feasibility study and did not provide any comparative data regarding the effectiveness of the lessons, the investigator reported that the system did function as a teaching device for basic rhythm notation and that such teaching systems for rhythm should be developed and utilized in the future.

Teaching Practices for Rhythmic Development

Practitioners' views regarding ways to develop rhythmic behaviors are generally the result of trial and error techniques; once approaches are found "successful," however, they are passed from teacher to student, and many have become tradition. Most appear to work for their proponents, although, as Horner (1965, pp. 140-141) has noted, there is little or no experimental evidence to provide a basis for comparison of the various methods. They are summarized here to provide the reader with an overview of teaching practices.

Jackson (1963) summarizes devices and techniques commonly used in rhythm training. They are (1) counting aloud, (2) tapping the underlying beat, (3) the metronome, (4) tapping or clapping the phrase rhythm, (5) use of words, (6) ensemble experience, and (7) conducting.

The advantage of counting aloud is that it clearly outlines the beat. Its danger, she contends, is that it emphasizes the beat's mathematical rather than rhythmic aspects. Tapping the underlying beat has two advantages over counting: (1) it involves more extensive muscular action and (2) it does not emphasize arithmetic.

The metronome is valuable for setting the tempo and preventing tempo vacillation. Because it is an entirely external criterion its usefulness is limited. Certainly, the use of such a device while reading music with varying tempi is impractical.

Tapping or clapping the phrase rhythm and the use of words as a system of mnemonics are both helpful techniques in the learning of phrase rhythms. Conducting aids in making students aware of the underlying beat.

Ensemble experience is one method of making students conform to the underlying beat. However, Revelli (1955) maintains that ensemble has been a staff for students to lean upon, and that their ability to read suffers from the lack of a systematic procedure for analyzing the various rhythm patterns.

Basic to most of the rhythm teaching devices mentioned above is muscular involvement. That rhythm is best approached through bodily movement which has indeed become the byword of the elementary school music program. Few references to elementary school music fail to support this view.

Jaques-Dalcroze (1921) was one of the first to explore the possibilities of bodily movement as an aid in developing a sense of rhythm. In his system, which is generally referred to as the Dalcroze Eurhythmics, students learned specific movements to different rhythm patterns. After the movements were learned, the students were to realize, i.e. express by movements of the body, the rhythms of music. Much stress was placed upon the ability to improvise movements to music.

An especially pertinent aspect of the Jaques-Dalcroze (1915, p. 33) method is the use of separate limbs of the body to mark the underlying beat and the phrase of rhythms. Coordinated movements to music constitute the essence of the system.

The use of rhythmic syllables also has received a great deal of emphasis in recent years, perhaps because of the emphasis on the application of the various adaptations of the Kodaly approach (Richards, 1967; Bachman, 1969; Lewis, 1972). All of these approaches make extensive use of rhythm syllables as an aid in developing elementary aged children's rhythm reading skills.

Gordon (1971, pp. 72-75) also is an advocate of rhythm syllables in developing rhythm readiness as a prerequisite to rhythm reading, but he also recognizes that the development of rhythmic understanding has its basis in the feeling of rhythm patterns through movement.

In his final publication regarding the teaching of rhythm, Mursell (1956, pp. 265-278) summarized three essential approaches to the development of rhythmic behaviors. He believed the first and most essential approach to rhythm is by way of bodily movement. Secondly, he believed that rhythm instruments are extremely valuable tools. Their value is that they tend to sharpen rhythm behaviors by requiring more precise, more definite, and more discriminating responses. Finally, he believed that the study of rhythm symbols allows children a new, deeper, more generalized understanding of rhythmic experience. Because of Mursell's extensive work in the psychology of teaching music, his recommendations should not be taken lightly.

A recent publication on the teaching of rhythm (Hood, 1970) reflects essentially the type of activities advocated by Mursell. Moving to music, study of rhythm notation, and the use of rhythm instruments are used as approaches for teaching rhythm.

Teachers of instrumental music tend to focus on the teaching of rhythm reading. Magnell's (1968) summary of systems for reading rhythm at sight generally parallel Jackson's. He does, however, elaborate on some approaches. He views foot tapping as basic to counting, chanting, clapping, and conducting. He also advocates the "down-up" principle as a means of organizing rhythm patterns in relation to the beat. Another principle he notes is that of the "time unit." The eighth note is usually the time unit maintained throughout the piece being counted. The student must mark the beat with hand movement (it could be with the foot) and count the number of time units in each note. Many other teachers advocate the use of foot tapping, e.g. Hoover, 1968; D'Angelo, 1968; Pizer, 1969; Kohut, 1973, pp. 19-23; Hoffer, 1973, p. 377.

In summary, there are commonalities among the approaches to rhythm development advocated by practitioners. Most teachers advocate more than one approach. The relative merits of the respective approaches, however, have not all been verified under controlled conditions. Perhaps the most important issue is, as

Palmer (1976) has noted, that teachers at least employ some systematic approach to rhythmic development rather than leaving it to incidental learning as part of a total curriculum.

EVALUATION OF RHYTHMIC BEHAVIORS

Evaluations of rhythmic behaviors generally involve one of three basic types of behavior: (1) behaviors reflecting discriminations between aurally presented stimuli, (2) movement behaviors demonstrating an ability to keep time with the beat or to reproduce an aurally presented rhythm pattern, and (3) behaviors reflecting an ability to associate visual rhythm symbols with aurally presented rhythm patterns. The last category includes all music reading behaviors, although it could be argued that reproduction of rhythm patterns from notated rhythm patterns constitutes a fourth type of behavior. In addition, there are several rhythm tests that require behaviors which at best are only peripherally related to the three basic types of behaviors. This discussion, however, will be limited primarily to the rhythm tests employing the three basic types of behaviors.

Several issues are involved in the evaluation of rhythmic behaviors. One noted previously in this chapter was whether *reproduction* of patterns or steady beats was a legitimate indication of rhythmic perception. Research has provided no clear-cut answers regarding the question. Researchers and test designers usually select the response mode on some philosophical basis or else they follow precedents in test design.

In selecting or developing a test of rhythmic perception or ability, the primary concern is to select a response modality which best demonstrates what one is concerned with measuring. Pilot testing should always be done to ascertain the test's validity and reliability, as well as its appropriateness for the group being tested. If the concern is for measuring discrimination, the response mode should not require movements which may introduce problems for some respondees. If the concern is for aural-visual discrimination, musical performance should not be involved, but if the concern is for reading music, performance should be involved.

Andrews and Deihl (1967) found that several response modes

might be necessary for gaining a clear understanding of children's musical abilities. Their *Battery of Musical Concept Measures,* which unfortunately is not generally available, employed two written group measures (verbal and listening) and two non-written individual measures (manipulative and overt).

The question of group versus individual measure is of practical significance to both researchers and music teachers. While individual testing may be desirable, it is often prohibitive in terms of time and cost. Group measures often must serve as a compromise, although certain performance situations necessarily cannot be so assessed.

The issue of whether to evaluate rhythmic behaviors in isolation from a total musical context has concerned music psychologists since testing became of interest. Seashore's (1938) view, reflecting what has been termed "the theory of specifics" approach, was that given traits or abilities should be isolated for study under controlled situations. Mursell's (1937) view, termed the omnibus approach, reflected the view that musical behavior should be evaluated as a totality rather than breaking it into subparts. Most contemporary approaches to evaluating rhythmic behaviors attempt to incorporate at least some rhythmic behavior in a total music context, although many measures also include some breakdown of rhythmic behaviors. Older tests usually reflect one or the other philosophical viewpoints. The authors see merit in both approaches, depending on the purpose for which the evaluation is made. The purpose of the evaluation and the nature of the data sought should determine the nature of the evaluation approach to be used.

While it is recognized that technological developments have resulted in several ways of objectively evaluating rhythmic behaviors, e.g. Shrader, 1970; Petzold, 1966; Ihrke, 1969; Thackray, 1968; Gutsch, 1964, this discussion is limited to a brief review of approaches which can be used without special equipment. Most of the approaches discussed are published standardized tests. They normally are designed for children above the age of eight, adolescents, and adults. That no standardized tests are generally available for preschool and primary school children perhaps is a contributing factor to the confusion regarding rhythmic abilities of young children.

Test Four of Bentley's (1966a) *Measures of Musical Ability* is a ten-item rhythm test which requires subjects to indicate on which of four beats a second rhythm pattern differs from a first. The rhythm test is an aural discrimination task and is designed for children aged seven to eleven. Although normative data are available for the rhythm test, reliability and validity are available only for the four measures as a whole.

The *Seashore Measures of Musical Talents* (Seashore, Lewis, and Saetveit, 1960) include two tests related to rhythm, both of which are aural discrimination tasks. The "rhythm test" presents two tapped rhythm patterns and asks the respondent to indicate whether they are the *same* or *different;* the other, called the "time test," presents two tones and asks the respondent to indicate whether the second tone is of *longer* or *shorter* duration than the first tone. Although Mursell and other proponents of the omnibus theory question whether these are valid measures of musical talent, there seems little question that they are valid measures of the two particular discrimination tasks. Reliability coefficients for the tests range from .63 to .72.

The "rhythm test" of the *Drake Musical Aptitude Tests* (Drake, 1957), really a measure of the ability to silently maintain a given tempo, has two nonequivalent forms. Reliabilities range from .83 to .95 for form A and .69 to .96 for form B. Validity coefficients, based on comparisons with teachers' ratings of rhythm aptitude, range from .31 to .85.

Gordon's (1965) *Musical Aptitude Profile* includes as one of its three basic parts a "rhythm imagery" test. This test has two subtests, each of which requires respondents to discriminate between two hearings of a musical example performed on a string instrument. The tempo test requires an indication of whether the second presentation of a melody has the same tempo as the first or whether it was changed. The meter test asks the respondent to indicate whether a second statement of a melody is like the first statement or whether it differs from it with respect to *accents* which determine the meter. Split-half reliabilities for the subtests range from .66 to .85; for the "rhythm imagery" portion as a whole they range from .82 to .91. Validity coefficients, based on teachers' estimates of musical talent, range from .64 to .74.

The *Iowa Tests of Music Literacy* (Gordon, 1970) is comprised of two divisions, "Tonal Concepts" and "Rhythmic Concepts." Each division has three subtests, (1) "aural perception," (2) "reading recognition," and (3) "notational understanding." The subtests of the "rhythmic concepts" division require the following types of responses:

"Aural Perception": differentiation between rhythmic patterns on which beats are subdivided into duplets and triplets.

"Reading Recognition": determining whether given aural patterns match given notated patterns.

"Notational Understanding": filling in noteheads, flags, and rests to make a notated pattern match an aurally presented pattern.

Reliability coefficients for the subtests generally are in the .70's and .80's. The author maintains the test has rational and content validity. Concurrent validity coefficients, based on comparisons with sight singing and dictation scores, for the "rhythmic concepts" division range from .44 to .52. The tests have six levels and provide normative data for grades four through twelve.

Colwell's (1969-1970) *Music Achievement Tests* provide measures of rhythm behaviors within a musical context. A "meter discrimination" subtest asks respondents to indicate whether a musical example moves in two's or three's, i.e. is it in duple or triple meter. An "auditory-visual discrimination" subtest asks respondents to indicate measures in which the rhythm of notated melodies differs from the rhythm presented aurally. The test-retest reliability coefficient for the rhythm items is .80. The tests are claimed to possess content validity in that they reflect the objectives of several basal music series.

Several measures of aural discrimination also include rhythm as a part of the total test, but most do not include separate scores for the rhythm portions, e.g. Knuth, 1966; Farnum, 1953. Rhythm also is one of the criteria for scoring *The Watkins-Farnum Performance Scale* (1954), but neither does it provide a separate rhythm score.

Finally, Thackray's (1968) *Tests of Rhythmic Perception* and *Tests of Rhythmic Performance*, discussed previously, should be mentioned here, particularly since they represent a recent effort to gain greater understanding of rhythmic abilities. Although, to the authors' knowledge, the tests are not yet standardized or available commercially, they represent a major contribution to the evaluation of rhythmic behaviors.

Researchers and teachers concerned with selecting or developing measures of rhythmic behaviors should first and foremost consider the nature of the rhythmic task they wish to evaluate and be certain that any measure selected or developed indeed measures that task in a manner appropriate for the level of students being evaluated.

SUMMARY

The major points in this chapter include the following:

1. Rhythm provides structure to music and serves as its dynamic energizing force.
2. Rhythmic structure in music has several basic aspects: (1) meter, (2) tempo, (3) beat, and (4) melodic or phrase pattern.
3. Theories regarding human response to music are of four basic types: (1) instinctive, (2) physiological, (3) motor, and (4) learning.
4. Initial development of rhythmic behaviors is inextricably related to movement.
5. Underlying rhythmic behaviors is the ability to perceive rhythmic structures and perform rhythmic movements.
6. Although developmental research is inconclusive, rhythmic behaviors generally increase with age for younger children but level out for older children.
7. The development of rhythmic behaviors can be expedited through training.
8. Although the development of skills in rhythm reading is a major concern to both researchers and teachers, neither research nor practice has provided any consensus regarding a "best" way to facilitate rhythm reading.
9. Evaluation of rhythmic behaviors usually involves assessment of one of three basic types of behavior: (1) behaviors requir-

ing discriminations between aurally presented stimuli, (2) movement behaviors demonstrating an ability to keep time with the beat or to reproduce an aurally presented rhythm pattern, and (3) behaviors reflecting an ability to associate visual rhythm symbols with aurally presented rhythm patterns.

REFERENCES

Allport, F. H. *Theories of Perception and the Concept of Structure.* New York: Wiley, 1955.

Andrews, F. M., & Deihl, N. C. *Development of a Technique for Identifying Elementary School Children's Musical Concepts.* Cooperative Research Project 5-0233, The Pennsylvania State University, 1967.

Apel, W. *Harvard Dictionary of Music.* Cambridge: Harvard University Press, 1944.

Bachman, T. *Reading and Writing Music* (Books 1 & 2). Elizabethtown, Pa.: The Continental Press, 1969.

Bentley, A. *Measures of Musical Ability.* New York: October House, 1966. (a)

Bentley, A. *Musical Ability in Children and Its Measurement.* London: George G. Harrap & Company, 1966 (b).

Boring, E. G. *Sensation and Perception in the History of Experimental Psychology.* New York: D. Appleton-Century Company, 1942.

Boyle, J. D. The effects of prescribed rhythmical movements on the ability to sight-read music (Doctoral dissertation, University of Kansas, 1968). *Dissertation Abstracts,* 1968, *29,* 2290-2291. (University Microfilms No. 68-17, 359)

Bregman, A. S., & Campbell, J. Primary auditory stream segregation and perception of order in rapid sequences of tones. *Journal of Experimental Psychology,* 1971, *89,* 244-249.

Bregman, A. S., & Dannenbring, G.L. The effect of continuity on auditory stream segregation. *Perception and Psychophysics,* 1973, *13,* 308-312.

Campbell, D. T., & Stanley, J. C. *Experimental and Quasi-experimental Designs for Research.* Chicago: Rand McNally, 1963.

Christ, W. B. The reading of rhythm notation approached experimentally according to techniques and principles of word reading (Doctoral dissertation, Indiana University, 1954). *Dissertation Abstracts,* 1954, *14,* 684. (University Microfilms No. A54-986)

Coffman, A. R. *The Effects of Training on Rhythm Discrimination and Rhythmic Action.* Unpublished doctoral dissertation, Northwestern University, 1949.

Colwell, R. *Music Achievement Tests.* Chicago: Follett, 1969-70.

Cooper, G., & Meyer, L. B. *The Rhythmic Structure of Music.* Chicago: The University of Chicago Press, 1960.

Creston, P. *Principles of Rhythm.* New York: Franco Colombo, 1964.

D'Angelo, D. A new twist to teaching rhythm. *The Instrumentalist,* 1968, *23* (2), 64-65.

DeYarmin, R. M. An experimental analysis of the development of rhythmic and tonal capabilities of kindergarten and first grade children. In E. Gordon (Ed.), *Experimental Research in the Psychology of Music* (Vol. 8). Iowa City: University of Iowa Press, 1972.

Dittemore, E. E. An investigation of some musical capabilities of elementary school students. In E. Gordon (Ed.), *Experimental Research in the Psychology of Music* (Vol. 6). Iowa City: University of Iowa Press, 1970.

Dowling, W. J. Rhythmic fission and perceptual organization. *Journal of the Acoustical Society of America,* 1968, *44,* 369.

Dowling, W. J. The perception of interleaved melodies. *Cognitive Psychology,* 1973, *5,* 322-337.

Drake, R.M. *Drake Musical Aptitude Tests.* Chicago: Science Research Associates, 1957.

Farnsworth, P. R. *The Social Psychology of Music* (2nd ed.). Ames: The Iowa State University Press, 1969.

Farnum, S. E. *Farnum Music Notation Test.* New York: The Psychological Corporation, 1953.

Flavell, J. H. *The Developmental Psychology of Jean Piaget.* Princeton: Van Nostrand, 1963.

Foley, E. A. Effects of training in conservation of tonal and rhythmic patterns on second grade children. *Journal of Research in Music Education,* 1975, *23,* 240-248.

Fridman, R. The first cry of the newborn: basis for the child's future musical development. *Journal of Research in Music Education,* 1973, *21,* 264-269.

Gardner, H. Children's duplication of rhythmic patterns. *Journal of Research in Music Education,* 1971, *19,* 355-360.

Gaston, E. T. Man and music. In E. T. Gaston (Ed.), *Music in Therapy.* New York: MacMillan, 1968.

Gordon, E. *Musical Aptitude Profile.* Boston: Houghton Mifflin, 1965.

Gordon, E. *Iowa Tests of Music Literacy.* Iowa City: The Bureau of Educational Research and Service, The University of Iowa, 1970.

Gordon, E. *The Psychology of Music Teaching.* Englewood Cliffs, N.J.: Prentice-Hall, 1971.

Gordon, E. E. *Tonal and Rhythm Patterns: an Objective Analysis.* Albany N.Y.: State University of New York Press, 1976.

Groves, W. C. Rhythmic training and its relationship to the synchronization of motor-rhythmic responses. *Journal of Research in Music Education,* 1969, *17,* 408-415.

Gutsch, K. U. One approach toward the development of an individual test for assessing one aspect of instrumental music achievement. *Council for Research in Music Education,* 1964, *2,* 1-5.

Hebb, D. O. *Organization of Behavior.* New York: Wiley, 1949.

Hebb, D. O. *A Textbook of Psychology.* Philadelphia: Saunders, 1958.

Hoffer, C. R. *Teaching Music in Secondary Schools* (2nd ed.). Belmont, California: Wadsworth, 1973.

Hood, M. V. *Teaching Rhythm and Using Classroom Instruments.* Englewood Cliffs, N.J.: Prentice-Hall, 1970.

Hoover, W. An approach to rhythm. *The Instrumentalist,* 1968, *23* (2), 59-62.

Horner, V. *Music Education, the Background of Research and Opinion.* Hawthorn, Victoria, Australia: Australian Council for Educational Research, 1965.

Igaga, J. M., & Versey, J. Cultural differences in rhythmic perception. *Psychology of Music,* 1977, *5* (1), 23-27.

Ihrke, W. R. *An Experimental Study of the Effectiveness and Validity of an Automated Rhythm Training Program.* Storrs, Conn.: University of Connecticut, 1969. (ERIC Document Reproduction Service No. ED 032 790)

Jackson, S. L. Ear and rhythm training. *Music Educators Journal,* 1963, *50* (1), 133-135.

Jaques-Dalcroze, E. *The Eurhythmics of Jaques-Dalcroze.* Boston: Small Maynard and Company, 1915.

Jaques-Dalcroze, E. *Rhythm, Music and Education.* London: Chatto and Windus, 1921.

Jersild, A. T., & Bienstock, S. F. *Development of Rhythm in Young Children.* New York: Bureau of Publications, Teachers College, Columbia University, 1935.

Knuth, W. E. *Knuth Achievement Tests in Music.* San Francisco: Creative Arts Research Associates, 1966.

Kohut, D. L. *Instrumental Music Pedagogy.* Englewood Cliffs, N.J.: Prentice-Hall, 1973.

Lewis, A. G. *Listen, Look and Sing.* Morristown, N.J.: Silver Burdett, 1972.

Lund, M. W. *An Analysis of the "True Beat" in Music.* Unpublished doctoral dissertation, Stanford University, 1939.

Lundin, R. W. *An Objective Psychology of Music* (2nd ed.). New York: Ronald Press, 1967.

Magnell, E. Systems for reading rhythms at sight. *The Instrumentalist,* 1968, *23* (2), 68-70.

McDougall, R. The relation of auditory rhythm to nervous discharge. *Psychological Review,* 1902, *9,* 460-480.

McNally, K. A., & Handel, S. Effect of element composition on streaming and the ordering of repeating sequences. *Journal of Experimental Psychology: Human Perception and Performance,* 1977, *3* 451-460.

Moog, H. The development of musical experience in children of pre-school age. *Psychology of Music,* 1976, *4* (2), 38-47.

Morgan, C. T. *Physiological Psychology* (3rd ed.). New York: McGraw-Hill, 1965.

Mursell, J. L. *Psychology of Music.* New York: W. W. Norton and Company, 1937.

Mursell, J. L. *Music Education, Principles and Programs.* Morristown, N.J.: Silver Burdett, 1956.

Nielsen, J. F. A study of the Seashore motor-rhythm test. *Psychological Monographs,* 1930, *40,* 74-84.

Osgood, C. E. *Method and Theory in Experimental Psychology.* New York: Oxford University Press, 1953.

Palmer, M. Relative effectiveness of two approaches to rhythm reading for fourth-grade students. *Journal of Research in Music Education,* 1976, *24,* 110-118.

Perney, J. Musical tasks related to the development of the conservation of metric time. *Journal of Research in Music Education,* 1976, *24,* 159-168.

Petzold, R. G. *Auditory Perception of Musical Sounds by Children in the First Six Grades.* Madison: University of Wisconsin, 1966. (ERIC Document Reproduction Service No. ED 010 297)

Pflederer, M., & Sechrest, L. Conservation-type responses of children to musical stimuli. *Council for Research in Music Education,* 1968, *13,* 19-36.

Pizer, R. Toward more accurate rhythm. *The Instrumentalist,* 1968, *23* (2), 75-76.

Placek, R. W. Design and trial of a computer-assisted lesson in rhythm. *Journal of Research in Music Education,* 1974, *22,* 13-23.

Rainbow, E. A longitudinal investigation of the rhythmic abilities of pre-school aged children. *Council for Research in Music Education,* 1977, *50,* 55-61.

Regelski, T. A. *Principles and Problems of Music Education.* Englewood Cliffs, N.J.: Prentice-Hall, 1975.

Revelli, W. D. To beat or not to beat? *Etude,* 1955, *73* (6), 19; 48.

Richards, M. H. *Threshold to Music.* New York: Harper and Row, 1967.

Rosenbusch, M. H., & Gardner, D. B. Reproduction of visual and auditory rhythm patterns by children. *Perceptual and Motor Skills,* 1968, *26,* 1271-1276.

Ruckmick, C. A. The role of kinaesthesis in the perception of rhythm. *The American Journal of Psychology,* 1913, *24,* 305-359.

Ruckmick, C. A. The nature of the rhythmic experience. *Proceedings of the Music Teachers National Association,* 1945, *39,* 79-89.

Sachs, C. *Rhythm and Tempo.* New York: W. W. Norton, 1953.

Schoen, M. *The Psychology of Music.* New York: Ronald Press, 1940.

Seashore, C. E. *Psychology of Music.* New York: McGraw-Hill, 1938.

Seashore, C. E., Lewis, D. L., & Saetveit, J. G. *Seashore Measure of Musical Talents* (revised). New York: The Psychological Corporation, 1960.

Shrader, D. L. An aural approach to rhythmic sight-reading, based upon principles of programmed learning, utilizing a stereo-tape teaching machine (Doctoral dissertation, University of Oregon, 1970). *Dissertation Abstracts International,* 1970, *31,* 2426. (University Microfilm No. 70-21, 576)

Skornicka, J. E.   The function of time and rhythm in instrumental music reading competency (Doctoral dissertation, Oregon State College, 1958). *Dissertation Abstracts,* 1958, *19,* 1406-1407.

Sperry, R. W.   Neurology and the mind-brain problem. In R. Issacson (Ed.), *Basic Readings in Neuropsychology.*   New York: Harper and Row, 1964.

Swope, R. L.   Improvement of rhythm sight reading ability through use of the tap system.   *PMEA Bulletin of Research in Music Education,* 1977, *8* (1), 23-26.

Taylor, S. Musical development of children aged seven to eleven. *Psychology of Music,* 1973, *1* (1), 44-49.

Thackray, R.   *An Investigation into Rhythmic Abilities.*   London: Novello & Company Limited, 1968.

Watkins, J. G., & Farnum, S. E.   *The Watkins-Farnum Performance Scale.* Winona, Minn.: Hal Leonard Music, 1954.

Wiley, C. A.   An experimental study of tachistoscopic techniques in teaching rhythmic sight reading in music (Doctoral dissertation, University of Colorado, 1962). *Dissertation Abstracts,* 1962, *23,* 3925.

Winick, S.   *Rhythm: an Annotated Bibliography.*   Metuchen, N.J.: The Scarecrow Press, 1974.

Woodrow, H.   Time perception. In S. S. Stevens (Ed.), *Handbook of Experimental Psychology.*   New York: Wiley, 1951.

Woodruff, A. D.   How music concepts are developed. *Music Educators Journal,* 1970, *56* (6), 51-54.

Whitson, T. C.   *A Study of Rhythm Perception at the Junior High School Level.*   Unpublished master's thesis, University of Texas, 1951.

Yeston, M.   *The Stratification of Musical Rhythm.*   New Haven, Conn.: Yale University Press, 1976.

Zimmerman, M. P.   *Musical Characteristics of Children.*   Washington: Music Educators National Conference, 1971.

Chapter Four

MELODIC AND HARMONIC FOUNDATIONS

A**N** UNDERSTANDING of music's pitch structure has interested people since the beginnings of recorded history. Weber (1958) maintains that Western musical development has been shaped to a large degree by this drive to rationalize its structure. This chapter examines music's pitch structure and behaviors related to understanding the structure.

Pitch structure in Western music is unique: It has both horizontal and vertical dimensions. While other music has evolved with elaborate developments of the horizontal dimension, melody, none has approached the sophistication of Western music's vertical dimension, harmony.

The horizontal dimension involves pitch sequences, while the vertical dimension involves structuring simultaneous pitches. Music theorists have been concerned primarily with deriving systems for codifying and explaining practices with respect to these structures. Systems of scales and harmony are outgrowths of theorists' efforts.

Because music is a social phenomenon, and therefore a changing phenomenon, theorists' work is never complete. Scales and harmonic systems based on melodic and harmonic practices of the eighteenth and nineteenth centuries are inadequate for explaining all pitch structure of twentieth century music; no doubt they will be even less adequate for music of the twenty-first century.

An understanding of the melodic and harmonic foundations of musical behavior requires an understanding of melody and harmony. The definitions of melody and harmony which follow are intended to be of sufficient breadth to provide a basis for under-

standing the melodic and harmonic foundations of musical behavior in relation to most, if not all, Western music.

EXTENDED DEFINITIONS

For most people melody is inseparable from harmony and
rhythm. The overwhelming majority of melodies we hear are
couched in tonal harmonic frameworks utilizing chord structures
built in thirds and progressing toward somewhat predictable
"resolutions." Mursell (1937, p. 102) and Smits Van Waesberghe
(1955, p. 19), however, insist that melody should be studied independently of harmonies.

Melody

Whether constructed within a tonal harmonic framework or
not, two factors contribute to the individuality of each melody:
the *pitch relationships* and *durational relationships* (rhythm)
among the tones. As noted in Chapter Two, pitch is a relative
phenomenon concerning the placement of tones on a high-low
continuum.

Constructing a melody involves selecting tones from this continuum and placing them in temporal sequence. Because pitch is
a continuous variable, any pitch can conceivably be used in a
melody. *Portamenti* and *glissandi* are examples of melodies in
which minute pitch differences are used. Electronic music makes
considerable use of these "sliding" pitches; most melodies, Western and non-Western, however, utilize fixed pitches. Particular
fixed pitches for use in melodies usually are selected from within
conventions and traditions of a given musical culture. In non-
Western cultures, most of which have not developed a tonal
system based on a tertian harmonic framework, the octave is
divided in different ways. Some cultures use microtonic scales,
dividing the octave into a greater number of pitches than the
seven tones of the Western diatonic scale. Other cultures utilize
fewer pitches per octave, and their scales are classified as *macro-
tonic* scales. Most Western melodies utilize the tones of scales
within the diatonic scale system and have an implied, if not ac-

companying, harmonic framework.* Regardless of the scale system used in selecting pitches for a melody or whether the melody uses sliding or fixed pitches, the sequence of pitch relationships contributes to a given melody's individuality.

As long as the relative pitch positions and rhythm of the tonal sequence remain constant, a melody remains the same. Changing either the relative pitch positions, (i.e. any tones), or the rhythm, therefore, changes the melody *structurally* and may or may not change it *perceptually*. The melody notated in Figure 4-1 has the pitch relationships of "America" (also "God Save the Queen"), but the rhythm makes it an entirely different melody.

Figure 4-1. "America."

Composers and some performers change tones and pitches of melodies for aesthetic or artistic purposes. The degree to which the tonal or rhythmic structure of a melody can be changed while still evoking a response of "sameness," naturally, is subject to many variables. Farnsworth (1969, p. 49) believes that once a melody is learned it can be changed considerably and still be recognized. The degree to which it can be changed and still be recognized appears to be a function of the *expectations* developed by the listener as a result of familiarity with the melody.

As Lundin (1967, p. 76) has noted, melody can be defined in

---

*Twelve-tone, or serial, melodies should be noted as a major exception to this practice. Such melodies essentially involve the use of each of the twelve tones in any order chosen by the composer, and each tone must be used before another can be repeated.

terms of either its structural characteristics or people's response to it. Music theorists traditionally have examined melody in terms of structural characteristics while psychologists have been more interested in response to or perception of melody. Melody also has been examined from a philosophical perspective, although Hickman (1976) questions whether "aesthetics of melody" has any meaning today. The present discussion examines melody only from structural and psychological perspectives.

Farnsworth (1969, p. 48) classifies descriptions of melody in terms of structural characteristics as *formalistic* and those involving perceptual or psychological variables as *relativistic*.

STRUCTURAL CHARACTERISTICS OF MELODY. In its broadest sense, melody means any succession of single tones (Ortmann, 1926). As noted above, the pitch and durational relationships among the tones contribute to each melody's individuality. A particular tonal and temporal structure creates a constant *melodic contour* that we perceive and to which we respond. The melodic contour is a *Gestalt* or holistic pattern to which a listener responds.

Responses to melody certainly may be influenced by many factors other than its structural characteristic *per se,* but some standard characteristics appear prominent enough to warrant discussion.

Lundin (1967, pp. 77-79) sees three particular melodic attributes: (1) *propinquity,* (2) *repetition,* and (3) *finality.* The tones of most Western melodies generally are *propinquous,* that is, close together. Analyses of intervals in melodies by Ortmann (1937) and Radocy (1977) both revealed a preponderance of smaller successive intervals (conjunct) over larger intervals (disjunct).

Melodies are *repetitious* in that certain tones tend to be repeated with considerable frequency. Radocy's examination of randomly selected melodies from *The Norton Scores* (Kamien, 1972) and from *357 Songs We Love to Sing* (1938) supports Lundin's view. In the *Norton* sample, the tones *do, mi,* and *so* accounted for 45 percent of all the tones; when *ti* and *re* were added the percentage increased to 69. The corresponding songbook percentages were 67 and 81. Clearly there is a tendency in most melodies to return to certain tones with great frequency.

Lundin's third attribute, *finality,* refers to a tendency for melodies to end according to certain conventions of *cadence* which convey an impression of momentary or permanent conclusion. Cadences in melodies constructed within a Western tonal framework often have an implied harmonic accompaniment, although not necessarily. Final tones of melodies often are ones which have been repeated frequently or emphasized in the body of the melody.

Ortmann (1926) believed that melody's structural characteristics could be understood best by examining the pitch relationships of the melodic contour in isolation from harmony and rhythm. His analysis revealed several *static* (his term) attributes of melody which are inherent in all melodies and tend to attract a listener's attention. Such melodic attributes include: (1) *first and last tones,* (2) *highest and lowest tones,* (3) *repeated tones,* (4) *interval,* (5) *pitch direction,* (6) *pitch proximity,* (7) *emphasis in tone groups,* (8) *interval relationship,* and (9) *degree of emphasis. First and last* and *highest and lowest* tones attract attention because of their places in the temporal sequence and pitch continuum respectively. *Repetition* of tones strengthens their impressions upon a listener; the degree to which repetition gives emphasis to a tone depends at least in part on the number of repetitions.

While the first three melodic attributes are termed *absolute,* the balance is considered to be *relative.* Ortmann (1926), maintains that the relative attributes are more important than the absolute attributes. Melodic memory, which involves *relative pitch* recall, is frequently found among Western listeners, while tone memory *per se,* absolute pitch, is relatively rare.

Melodic *interval* results when two tones are heard in succession. A series of tones results in a series of intervals which are much more easily recalled than the particular pitches. Most readers can readily hum the melody of "America" with proper intervals, although most cannot hum it on request in any particular key.

Pitch direction, or melodic direction, can move in three ways: (1) ascending, (2) descending, or (3) horizontally. Naturally combinations of these directions also are used. In thus moving, a *melodic contour* is created. The fewer changes in direction, the more unified is the melody.

Pitch proximity refers essentially to the same phenomenon that Lundin calls propinquity. The nearer the pitches of two tones, the stronger their melodic association.

Emphasis in tone group refers to the absolute placement of a tone within a smaller group of tones in a melody. The first and last, highest and lowest, and any repeated tones within the group become accentuated in relation to the other tones.

Interval relationship refers to the emphasis of tones adjoining first and last, highest and lowest, and any repeated tones because of the relationship via the contiguous intervals. Ortmann notes that this is perhaps the weakest manner of emphasizing a tone within a melody.

When the pitch proximity of a given tone varies greatly from other tones of a melody, it is emphasized. The more a tone varies from the general contour or tessitura of a melody, the greater the *degree of emphasis.*

That melodic attributes can be emphasized in ways which are not inherently melodic also must be noted. Changes in loudness, timbre, harmony, texture, and rhythm also can serve to emphasize particular tones of a melody. However, an examination of inter-actions among these musical attributes is beyond the scope of the present discussion.

As may be apparent, the above discussion does little to delimit the type of tone sequences which can be called melody and is con-sistent with Mursell's (1937, p. 103) view that "melody need have no definite unified structure." The discussion does, however, sug-gest that Western melodies frequently use small intervals between tones, repeat some tones with great frequency, and incorporate some type of convention for finality. Further, the emphasis a tone receives in a melody is dependent on its structural relationship to other tones in the melody.

The answer to "What constitutes a melody?" is not solely a function of its structural characteristics; the answer also must be considered in terms of the psychological attributes of melody.

PSYCHOLOGICAL CHARACTERISTICS OF MELODY. Mursell's (1937, p. 104) statement best characterizes the authors' view with respect to the question, "What constitutes a melody?": *"A sequence of tones constitutes a melody when it is apprehended in terms of a unified and single response."* The more important question that must be considered, however, is, "What psychological factors influence an individual's perception and apprehension of a sequence of tones as a melody?"

Perception of a tonal sequence as a melody involves essentially the same processes which Gestalt psychologists observed in the perception of visual patterns, or Gestalten. A melody is perceived as a Gestalt or a sequence of Gestalten and as such is perceived according to some fundamental organizational laws derived from the study of perceptual processes, the laws of proximity, similarity, common direction, and simplicity (Hilgard and Bower, 1975, pp. 256-263). Tones which are close together are more likely to be perceived as a whole than tones which are not close together. Similar or repeated tones tend to be perceived together. Perceptions proceed in a common direction toward completion, and the tendency is to perceive the Gestalt or tonal pattern in its simplest form.

The organizational laws of Gestalt psychology are reflected in the structural characteristics discussed above. Tone series tend to be perceived and remembered more readily as melodies if their tones are close together, involve a certain amount of repetition, and proceed toward finality in a somewhat direct manner.

The authors do not, however, intend to suggest, as do some proponents of Gestalt psychology, that the capacity to perceive patterns in melody is an inborn capacity which requires no learning. As Hebb (1949, pp. 17-59) both argues and carefully documents, the perception of *relative* phenomena, of which melody is one, involves the ability to perceive patterns and develops only as the result of prolonged experience (learning), whether formal or informal, with the particular phenomenon. Thus, to be able to perceive a given tone series as a melody requires experience with tone series of a similar style.

With this perspective it is no surprise that nearly all writers concerned with melodic perception (e.g. Farnsworth, 1969, p. 67; Lundin, 1967, p. 84; Mainwaring, 1951, p. 115; Mursell, 1937, p. 104) view *familiarity* with a melody or melodic style as the most important variable in influencing what an individual perceives as melody. As an individual interacts with the music of his or her culture, he or she comes to accept the conventions used in melodies. Experience with melodies in a given scale system enables an individual to develop certain expectations. When new tone series in similar style are encountered, the individual recognizes the new series as conforming or not conforming to expectations for that which he or she has learned to call melody.

An individual maturing in a Western culture, therefore, most likely has developed expectations (usually unstated) that melody is couched in a tonal harmonic framework, utilizes tones of the diatonic scale, generally has small intervals between the tones, returns with considerable frequency to certain tones, and usually ends with some conventional cadence.

When an individual is confronted with a melody in an unfamiliar style, the probability of responding to it as a melodic entity is greatly lessened (Meyer, 1967, p. 277). The failure of total serial music to achieve wide acceptance is in part because listeners have not learned the structural premises of the style. Meyer also maintains that the nature of serial melodies, which requires each chromatic tone within the octave to appear before another can be repeated, does not allow sufficient repetition or *redundancy* for listeners to perceive them as a whole. The melodic pattern, while structurally logical, lacks sufficient psychological unity for perception by the casual listener. Further, Meyer suggests that there is no homogeneous core of style to serve as a reference point for serial music; the stylistic diversity within the idiom is too great.

In conclusion, Lundin's (1967, p. 84) position that melody is a function of both the previous experience of a listener and certain characteristics of the tone series appears to provide the most viable basis for defining melody. An individual learns the melodic idioms of his or her culture. Familiarity with the idioms provides a basis for developing expectations in unfamiliar tone series, thus enabling response to the new series as a melodic entity. However, the melodic idioms used in a culture are the product of a musical development which has recognized that melodies must incorporate some unifying structural attributes which will enable listeners to perceive and remember melodies. Tone series which provide bases for perceptual organization according to the Gestalt laws of organization appear to be the most readily accepted, and therefore are perceived as melodies.

Harmony

The development of harmony is a particular achievement of Western music. It has become such an important aspect of Western music that people often respond to isolated melodies in terms of harmonic expectations as much as in terms of melodic expectations. Apel (1969, p. 372) maintains that "from the beginning of the eighteenth century on, the beauty of melodic lines depended largely on the effective arrangement of the harmonies underlying them."

In its broadest sense, harmony refers to music's vertical pitch structures as opposed to its horizontal pitch structure, melody. Apel (1969, pp. 371-374) has summarized its development. Early combinations of melodies, *organum*, generally involved parallel motion between two or three melodies, but as judgments developed that certain intervals between the melodies "sounded better" simultaneously than others, there was increased concern for the resultant sounds of the multiple voices. It was not until about the mid-sixteenth century that harmony, the vertical dimension of sound, gained acceptance as a primary structural concern in music. Apel categorizes the era between 900 and 1450 as the period of *pre-tertian harmony*. (Music prior to this era was essentially melodic.) Harmony of this era is characterized by much parallel motion, open spacing among voices, and some use of triads at the beginning and ending of phrases.

The years between 1450 and 1900 are considered the era of *tertian harmony*.* Western music of this era resulted in the development of triadic harmony from triadic movement in essentially modal sequence, through the strong tonic, subdominant, domi-

---

*"Tonal harmonic framework" as used in the previous section refers to the tertian harmonic system which utilizes vertical structures in intervals of thirds. As will be noted in the discussion of tonality, the tertian harmony system elicits a strong feeling for a tonal center; hence, the expression "tonal harmonic framework" applies to tertian harmony.

nant music of the late baroque and classical periods, to harmonies of the romantic period which exploited the triadic system to its extremes with extensive use of chromatic alterations and distant modulations.

While the preponderance of twentieth century music still is constructed within a tertian harmonic framework, Apel considers the era beginning in 1900 through the present day as the period of *posttertian harmony* because it has seen the development of vertical structures which deliberately violate the triadic harmony system. Debussy's "parallel chords," Scriabin's quartal harmony, Schoenberg's serial techniques, aleatoric music, *musique concrete*, and many of the developments in electronic music reflect efforts to organize the vertical dimension of pitch in manners different than tertian harmony.*

Because harmony in its various forms is such an integral component of most Western music, and therefore a factor to be considered when examining musical behavior, it should be examined in terms of both its structural and psychological characteristics.

STRUCTURAL CHARACTERISTICS OF HARMONY. Simultaneous pitch combinations generally are classified as one of two basic textures, *polyphonic* or *homophonic*. (Melody alone is classified as *monophonic*, i.e. it involves a single pitch at a time.) *Polyphonic* texture involves combining two or more melodies and may or may not be concerned with "how good" the resultant simultaneous pitch combinations sound. The extent to which polyphonic music is concerned with "how good" (the consonance-dissonance character) the simultaneous pitches sound varies to a large degree with the era in which it was composed. Generally, polyphonic music of the pre– and post-tertian eras reflects less concern for the character of the simultaneous sounds than polyphonic music of the tertian harmony era. *Homophonic* texture combines melody with a tertian harmonic framework and considers *both* the resultant horizonal and vertical dimensions of the musical sound.

---

*Readers unfamiliar with structural techniques should see W. Apel, *Harvard Dictionary of Music* (2nd ed., revised and enlarged), Cambridge: The Belknap Press of Harvard University Press, 1969.

Most references to harmony in music are to homophonic music constructed in a tertian harmonic framework.* Harmony in this narrower and more common sense refers to the highly developed system of triadic chords and relations between chords that characterizes most Western music, notably that of the baroque, classical, and romantic periods. While differences in harmonic practices of the three periods are evident, there is a common structural base to the harmony of the three periods.

Music of these periods, which comprises the predominant styles of "classical" music performed today, is constructed around a key center, or tonic. Music constructed around a key center possesses *tonality*, or "loyalty to a tonic" (Apel, p. 855). (The next section provides a more detailed discussion of tonality.) The triads or chords constructed on the first, fourth, and fifth degree of the scale, respectively called the tonic, subdominant, and dominant, served as the primary structural mechanism for maintaining emphasis on the tonal center. Once this mechanism became firmly established as the vehicle for focusing attention on the tonal center, thus providing harmonic unity or repetition, composers then could develop departures from the harmonic framework and then return to the tonic. Harmonic conventions developed through which functional chord progressions, structured around the tonic, subdominant, and dominant but also extending through chords built on other scale tones as well as through modulations into other keys, served as a primary unifying force in music. Harmonic practices of the romantic period carried this system to its extremes.

Twentieth century developments in ways for combining pitches simultaneously have resulted in a variety of styles which will be discussed later. This is not to suggest, however, that tertian harmony no longer is used as a compositional device. To the contrary, it is still the primary structural mechanism for combining pitches simultaneously, particularly in popular music.

PSYCHOLOGICAL CHARACTERISTICS OF HARMONY. Music's harmonic structure has been studied and analyzed by theorists since

---

*Readers unfamiliar with the triadic structure of music should consult a basic harmony text such as A. Forte, *Tonal Harmony in Concept and Practice*. New York: Holt, Rinehart and Winston, 1962.

its inception, and harmony continues to be a major area of study for students preparing for musical careers. On the other hand, there has been relatively little study of harmony in terms of peoples' responses to it or their ability to comprehend it.

Traditionally, attempts to explain response to harmony have been in terms of mathematics. Beginning with the work of the Greek philosopher Pythagoras in the sixth century B.C., and promulgated by the medieval church scholars, music (which was melodic during those times) has been examined and explained in terms of simple mathematical ratios. With the development of music constructed in a tonal harmonic framework, mathematical explanation continued to be offered, the most prominent of which appears to be the "Lipps-Meyer Law."* However, an examination of the ratios of the equal tempered scale,† the standard tuning system for Western harmonic music, reveals no simple mathematical ratios between any intervals except the octave.

Therefore, any attempt to explain harmony in terms of its psychological characteristics must look beyond music's "scientific" or mathematical aspects. The authors' view, which coincides with the position advocated and substantiated by Farnsworth (1969, pp. 37-41) and Lundin (1967, pp. 88-89), is that *harmony* (as all of music) *is a cultural phenomenon.* Just as individuals' experiences with music of their culture enable them to develop melodic expectations, the experiences also foster harmonic expectations. Music for which the harmony does not conform at least in a general way to the harmonic practices with which a listener is familiar sounds "strange" or "different." Even though most listen-

---

*The Lipps-Meyer Law attempts to explain preferences for melodic phrase endings in terms of the "power of two." This law holds that the *ratio* of the interval between two tones determines which will be the preferred ending tone; e.g. of the tones *do* and *re*, *do* will be the preferred ending because the ratio between *do* and *re* is 8:9, similarly the tones *so* and *do* (or *do* and *so*) would resolve to *do* because the interval of a fourth (*so* to *do*) has the ratio 3:4 and would resolve to the tone whose ratio number is reducible to two; the interval *do* to *so* (a fifth), whose ratio is 2:3, would likewise resolve to *do*. Farnsworth (1969, p. 38) and Lundin (1967, pp. 80-85), while recognizing that the phenomenon exists, have discounted the mathematical ratios as a viable explanation for ending preferences. Their views, as well as the present authors', are that experiences with music of a culture are the predominant variables in influencing ending preferences.

†The equal tempered scale is discussed later in this chapter.

ers cannot verbalize *what* sounds strange or different, the effect is disturbing because the listener's general expectations are unfulfilled.

Harmony, just as melody and rhythm, also is comprised of patterns and is perceived in terms of "wholes" (Mainwaring, 1951). Individuals respond to harmony in terms of its totality rather than its individual tones or chords. (It is only during formal musical training that most individuals attempt to analyze harmony into its constituent parts.)

There are three primary "holistic" attributes of harmonic structure toward which individuals respond and develop expectations: (1) tonality, (2) harmonic movement, and (3) finality. The perceptual laws of Gestalt psychology noted under the discussion of melody also appear to be basic to the perception of harmonic attributes. Tonality, or tonal center, provides an underlying repetition or redundancy which helps a listener respond to a complex sequential series of multiple sounds bombarding the central nervous system via the auditory sensory mechanisms. As Meyer (1967, pp. 288-293) has noted, experience with music constructed in a tonal harmonic framework provides the basis for perceiving the redundancy, in this case the tonality, which enables a listener to "make sense" of music heard in relation to expectations.

Response to harmonic movement is in a manner similar to the response to melodic contour. Harmonic movement or progression is a *relative* phenomenon, as is melody. We respond to harmonic movement in *relation* to tonality. Practices in functional harmony become a standard or model for listeners' harmonic expectations. As harmonic practices change, listeners learn the new harmonic style and develop expectations accordingly. Meyer (1967, p. 292) believes that a primary difficulty composers face in having contemporary music, particularly serial music, accepted by a large number of listeners is that it lacks the unifying harmonic attributes which provide the redundancy necessary for meaningful perception. Music constructed in a tonal harmony framework has an inherent redundancy through its tonal center and harmonic movement in relation to that center.

Finality has been examined more in terms of melody than

harmony, but the authors believe that finality effects are rooted in harmony as well as melody. The direction of the melodic line at cadence points is readily predictable only for melodies constructed in relation to a tonal harmonic framework. The conventions of cadence used during the eighteenth and nineteenth centuries still provide the basis for finality expectations. Few individuals in a Western culture would not expect a dominant-seventh chord to resolve to a tonic chord (although few could label the chords). Experience in hearing harmony provides the basis for such expectations even without formal training in harmony. As harmonic conventions change, individuals develop expectations accordingly.

In summary, harmony's psychological characteristics, just as those of melody, generally reflect the organizational laws of Gestalt psychology. Melodies and harmonies which have gained acceptance provide the unifying attributes which enable listeners to perceive and remember them in terms of previous experiences with music.

Tonality

Implicit in the discussion of harmony has been the recognition of tonality as a unifying device. Melodies of Western music constructed in a tonal harmonic framework also utilize tonality as a unifying device. Many developments in twentieth century music, however, are not constructed in a tonal harmonic framework; some specifically are designed to be atonal. Yet Temko's (1971, p. 33) study of pitch predominance in twenty avant-garde compositions revealed a statistically significant agreement among subjects concerning a predominant pitch in each of the compositions. Apparently atonal and electronic music not designed with an *a priori* tonality evoke listener response in terms of tonality. Because of its centrality to musical pitch structure, tonality warrants further discussion. It is examined in terms of its definition, the effects of tonal chroma, and its relationship to melodic and harmonic movement.

TONAL CENTER. In its broadest sense tonality refers to the fact that most musical compositions, whether Western or non-Western, primitive or avant garde, melodic or harmonic, have a primary pitch about which they are structured. This pitch is the *tonal center* and serves as the tone to which other tones ultimately return. It comes to serve as the ultimate musical expectation within the piece, both melodically and harmonically.

Mursell (1937, p. 122) notes that *"the function of tonality in music is to add to the subtlety and decisiveness of its expressive power."* Meyer's (1967, pp. 22-41) theory of value in music appears to be based on recognition of this function. The subtlety with which a melody progresses toward its resolution is a measure of its value. Meyer's theory reflects an information theory perspective.*

Taylor (1976), examining the *perception* of tonality in terms of information theory, sought to ascertain the *strength* of tonality in short melodies. Variables which he examined were melodic length, melodic contour, pitch structure, presentation condition, and perception ability. He concluded that perception of tonality in melodies is a learned phenomenon.

Taylor's conclusion supports Lundin's (1967) and Farnsworth's (1969) views that tonality, as all of music, is a cultural phenomenon. The learning of a culture's musical style, therefore, fosters the development of expectations when listening to other compositions in the same style. Western listeners apparently have developed expectations regarding tonality.

Before leaving the discussion of tonal center it should be noted that tonality unfortunately has meaning other than tonal center. Sessions (1951, p. 29) views the tonal system, or tonal harmonic framework, in which composers of the seventeenth, eighteenth, and nineteenth centuries organized pitch structure as "tonality." Apel (1969, p. 855) notes that another contemporary usage of the

---

*Information theory, in its simplest terms, is a technique for analyzing the amount of uncertainty involved in a sensory stimulus or *message.* The greater the amount of information *conveyed* via the sensory *message,* the greater the *uncertainty* of meaning or response. Under controlled conditions, mathematical formulae can be used to predict the probability of a response. The complex nature of melodic and harmonic movement in music makes accurate prediction virtually impossible; however, information theory still provides a useful and convenient tool for discussion of expectation in music. Although information theory will be discussed later in this chapter, the reader desiring an in-depth discussion of information theory should see A. Moles, *Information Theory and Esthetic Perception,* Urbana: University of Illinois Press, 1966.

term views "tonality" as referring to music written in a major or minor "key" as opposed to modality.

TONAL CHROMA. Roederer (1975, pp. 151-152) calls attention to the little understood phenomenon of tonal *chroma*. The *chroma* of musical tones refers to cyclical pitch properties. Essentially, responses to intervals greater than an octave take on the characteristics "equivalent" to that which they would have if they were within an octave, e.g. an octave *plus* a third is similar to a third. Roederer suggests that this phenomenon is related to the key property of the octave: All its harmonics are coincident with upper harmonics of the fundamental. The implications of this phenomenon are unclear, but one might speculate that it pervades much of musical responsiveness, particularly in light of the fact that listeners appear to respond to harmony with its underlying tonality, regardless of a composition's orchestration. Obviously, tonal chroma need further examination.

MELODIC MOVEMENT. Melodic movement in tonal music includes both conjunct and disjunct motion. Conjunct motion is essentially scalar, although chromatic and/or altered scale tones may be used. Disjunct motion involves skips or leaps, usually on tones outlining chords underlying the implied harmony framework. Melodies of the baroque and classical eras tend to outline scale and chord patterns more clearly than music of the romantic period, much of which involves chromaticism and frequent modulations.

Taylor (1976) reports that pitch structure, or melodic movement, is one determinant of tonal strength. The more the melodic movement conforms to the scale and chord structure of the key within which the melody is constructed, the greater the tonal strength, or tonality, of the melody. Melodies not using the scale and chord patterns of the key have less tonal strength. Melodic contour, on the other hand, does not appear to be a significant factor in the determination of the tonal strength of a melody.

Melodies of the baroque and classical periods, therefore, tend to have greater tonal strength than romantic melodies. In turn romantic melodies elicit a stronger feeling for tonality than melodies which are not written within an implied tonal harmonic framework. The psychological expectations elicited by melodic movement constructed within a tonal harmonic framework apparently facilitate perception.

HARMONIC MOVEMENT. As noted above, harmonic movement is a relative phenomenon perceived in relation to tonality. With the development of functional harmony in the seventeenth and eighteenth centuries, the basic principles of harmonic movement through relationships among chord roots were established. The basic tonic to dominant to tonic root movement was established. The consistency of harmonic progressions in eighteenth century music provides sufficient redundancy for listeners to maintain strong feelings for tonality.

Music of the romantic period, while still constructed within a tonal harmonic framework, extends harmonic functions far beyond the relatively consistent harmonic practices of the baroque and classical periods. Romantic harmonic functions are far more ambiguous than those of baroque and classical music. Although no research was found related to the perception of tonality as a function of harmonic movement, it appears that the harmonic characteristics of romantic music, with its frequent modulations and use of complex chords (often sequenced in ways which do not conform to traditional harmonic movement), detract from the perception of tonality.

MODAL ORGANIZATION

Definitions of *mode* and *scale* are many and varied. In a narrow sense each has a particular meaning, but in a broad sense they both refer to the same phenomenon: the basic tones of a composition arranged in order of pitch from lowest to highest (or highest to lowest). Most Western music divides the octave into a basic number of discrete fixed pitches. The number and particular arrangement of pitches in a mode or scale may vary, although convention suggests that only a limited number of pitch arrangements have gained widespread acceptance.

Acceptance implies usage. The authors agree with Farnsworth's (1969, p. 17) view that usage of pitch arrangements is a sociocultural phenomenon. Particular pitch arrangements must at least be acceptable to some cultural or subcultural group for continued usage. If a particular pitch arrangement does not meet with approval of some group, it simply will not continue to be used.

Conventional practice in today's Western music divides the octave into twelve equal semitones, i.e. a *chromatic* scale. Virtually all standard musical instruments have the capability for producing the chromatic scale. However, the chromatic scale is not the predominant scale; the *diatonic* scale, which preceded the chromatic scale historically, remains the predominant scale pattern. Even though chromaticism was recognized by scholars of ancient Greece and the medieval church, the division of the octave into twelve equal semitones did not occur until the development of equal temperament.* Chromaticism is very much evident in romantic and some contemporary music, but the chromatic scale *per se* has not become a predominant pitch arrangement in Western music.

Essentially a scale is diatonic if the octave includes seven fixed pitches, with an eighth pitch doubling the lowest in frequency and eliciting functional response "equivalent" to the lowest. The seven intervals within the octave usually include five whole tones and two semitones.

In common usage, the arrangement of tones and semitones within the octave determines whether the pitch arrangement is considered a scale or a mode. Two particular pitch arrangements have become the predominant patterns for Western tonal music and generally are called *major* and *minor* scales, although theorists hasten to indicate that these patterns also are considered modes.

Following is discussion of the function of scales, scale tuning systems, the major scale, the minor scale, and other modal and scale structures.

Function of Scales

According to Mursell (1937, p. 107), a musical scale has a two-fold significance: (1) it is a social phenomenon and (2) it makes possible attention to and exploitation of definite tonal relationships. Scales are *not* a manifestation of some mathematical ideal. Mursell maintains that all attempts to rationalize scales in terms

---

*Equal temperament will be discussed later in this chapter.

of clearcut mathematical ratios or logic eventually fall short. *There is no "natural" scale;* if there were, all cultures would use it. "There is nothing in the entire theory of music upon which more perverse quasi-mathematical ingenuity has been wasted than the scale" (Mursell, p. 108).

Musical systems are the creation of man's musical efforts. As the system is developed, changes are made in terms of human feelings and perceptions rather than to fulfill any order of goodness in terms of frequency ratios. Evolved scale systems reflect attempts to codify and make the system available for use by others. If music were not a sociocultural phenomenon, there would be no need for musical scales. Each person could develop a private scale system.

The tempered diatonic scale system is probably the most far-reaching and authoritative standardization of music for social purposes the world has ever known (Mursell, p. 107). Musical instruments, notation, and practices of Western cultures are so integrally bound to this system that new systems which are incompatible with the diatonic scale system appear unlikely to gain widespread acceptance. Even in electronic music, the type of compositions which are meeting with greatest acceptance generally involve the use of some traditional instruments and some melodies and harmonies based on the diatonic scale system.

Musical scales also provide a basis for establishing definite tonal relationships. Together with rhythm they provide the consistency needed for people to deal with the infinite range of sounds which is called music. Without a predominant scale system, it is unlikely that music ever would have become the potent force it is today. Scales make it possible for man to create from sounds a construct (music) which has a certain degree of functional and aesthetic value for significant proportions of given cultural or subcultural groups. The tempered diatonic scale system is the basis for the tonal harmonic framework of most Western music. This tonal harmonic framework allows for the development of perceptual, and as is discussed in Chapters Five, Six, and Eight, functional, and affective responses to music.

Scale Tuning Systems

Throughout the history of music there have been changes in both the frequency standard, an absolute phenomenon, and the tuning of scales, a relative phenomenon. Backus (1969, pp. 131-133) notes that the frequency of A_4 (the present A-440) has varied from somewhere in the range 415 to 428 Hz during the mid-eighteenth century to as high as 461 Hz in the late nineteenth century. Standards also have varied from country to country. Although various attempts to establish a frequency standard had been made previously and a degree of informal and practical consensus had resulted in a narrowing of the range of frequencies for A_4, it was not until 1953 that A-440 officially was recognized by the International Standards Organization as the frequency standard for music.

Scale tuning systems have been subject to much debate by mathematicians, acousticians, and music theorists since the time of the ancient Greeks. While the tempered diatonic scale is today's standard for Western music, there is still much controversy regarding performance practices with respect to it and other tuning systems (Barbour, 1951, pp. 196-201; Farnsworth, 1969, pp. 26-27; Ostling, 1974).

Tempered means that the scale has tones which have been changed so that with the exception of the octave, intervals resulting from simultaneous combinations of tones within the scale are not simple, i.e. whole number, mathematical ratios among the frequencies of the respective tones as are the intervals in some other tuning systems. *Equal temperament* is the name given to the tuning system which divides the octave into twelve equal semitones.

Equal temperament was developed along with, and indeed made possible, the development of Western tonal harmony. Tuning systems developed prior to equal temperament were adequate for monophonic music and to a degree for polyphonic music, but as polyphony developed and there became increased emphasis on the sonorities resulting from the vertical structure of music, previous tuning systems proved inadequate. While discussion of the various tuning systems is perhaps more appropriately a concern of musical acoustics or history books, a brief discussion of the most prominent tuning systems is necessary here, particularly since there still is controversy regarding tunings used in performance today.*

The diatonic scale has its roots in the tetrachords which were the basis of the ancient Greeks' "Greater Perfect System." Tetrachords were series of four descending tones, the range of which was a perfect fourth. Depending on the arrangement of the two inner tones, the tetrachords were one of the three *genera: diatonic* (two tones and one semitone), *chromatic* (a minor third and two semitones), or *enharmonic* (a major third and two quartertones). The *diatonic genus* apparently was the most popular among theorists of the time. Combinations of tetrachords, primarily in conjunct arrangement and with an added tone at the bottom, formed the Greater Perfect System from which the present day diatonic scale evolved. The pattern *do, re, mi, fa, so, la, ti, do,* although originally conceived *do, ti, la, so, fa, mi, re, do,* has been basic to Western music ever since.

Tuning of Greek scale intervals apparently was based on the system developed by Pythagoras (c. 550 B.C.). His tuning system, now called the Pythagorean scale, derived the frequency of all tones from the interval of a pure, i.e. beatless, fifth which has the simple ratio of 3:2 between the respective upper and lower frequencies of the two tones. Theoretically, the Pythagorean diatonic scale frequencies are obtained by forming a series of successive ascending fifths which then are lowered to the correct octave to form the scale. In practice, as Backus (pp. 118-120) and Roederer (1975, pp. 155-156) have described, the tuning of the scale is derived by tuning a beatless ascending fifth, a beatless descending fourth, a beatless ascending fifth, etc. The result is the same, a scale which has beatless perfect fourths, fifths, and octaves. (See Table 4-I).

As long as melodic music is performed without transposing, modulating, or using chromatic tones, the Pythagorean scale works well. However, its small semitone is a problem for instrument makers. Further, when the tuning system is extended to include chromatic tones, it results in nonequivalent enharmonic tones,

---

*Readers interested in studying tuning systems in greater depth should consult J. Backus, *The Acoustical Foundations of Music,* New York: Norton, 1969 or J. M. Barbour, *Tuning and Temperament,* East Lansing: Michigan State Press, 1951.

Table 4-I

RATIOS AMONG INTERVALS OF THE PYTHAGOREAN DIATONIC
SCALE ON C

Freq. ratios from *do*		$\frac{9}{8}$		$\frac{81}{64}$		$\frac{4}{3}$		$\frac{3}{2}$		$\frac{27}{16}$		$\frac{243}{128}$		$\frac{2}{1}$
Freq. ratios adjacent tone	$\frac{9}{8}$		$\frac{9}{8}$		$\frac{256}{243}$		$\frac{9}{8}$		$\frac{9}{8}$		$\frac{9}{8}$		$\frac{256}{243}$	
Frequency*	256		248		324		341.3		384		432		486	512
Pitch name	*do*		*re*		*mi*		*fa*		*so*		*la*		*ti*	*do*

*Scientific pitch, which has middle C = 256 Hz, as opposed to standard pitch, which has middle C = 261.3 Hz, is used for convenience.

thereby yielding different sizes of semitones. Clearly, the Pythagorean scale is inadequate for Western tonal harmony.

Just intonation, according to Barbour (pp. 89, 105), appears to have evolved during the fifteenth and sixteenth centuries as theorists sought to improve upon Pythagorean tuning. Just intonation has some advantages over Pythagorean tuning in that it used more simple ratios between tones and accommodated the building of triads using simple ratios among the tones. Just intonation is so named because its intervals conform to ratios between the tones of the overtone series; i.e. the fifth has a 3:2 ratio, the fourth a 4:3, the major third a 5:4, and the minor third a 6:5. Table 4-II shows the frequency ratios among adjacent intervals and in relation to *do.*

Although having the advantage of simple ratios, just intonation also has a number of disadvantages which for all practical

Table 4-II

RATIOS AMONG INTERVALS IN JUST INTONATION

Freq. ratios from *do*		$\frac{9}{8}$		$\frac{5}{4}$		$\frac{4}{3}$		$\frac{3}{2}$		$\frac{5}{3}$		$\frac{15}{8}$		$\frac{2}{1}$
Freq. ratios adjacent tones	$\frac{9}{8}$		$\frac{10}{9}$		$\frac{16}{15}$		$\frac{9}{8}$		$\frac{10}{9}$		$\frac{9}{8}$		$\frac{16}{15}$	
Frequency	256		288		320		341.3		384		426.6		480	512
Pitch name	*do*		*re*		*mi*		*fa*		*so*		*la*		*ti*	*do*

purposes render it useless in Western tonal music: (1) the scale has two different ratios for whole tones (8:9 and 9:10), (2) the fifth D-A (in reference to the key of C) is not the same as the other fifths (27:40 as opposed to 2:3), and (3) it does not accommodate modulation to other keys. The farther away from the reference key and the more use of accidentals, the more untenable the system becomes. In short, it is of little value for instruments of fixed pitch such as keyboard and wind instruments which must accommodate chromaticism and modulation or transposition to all keys. It has been claimed, however, that instruments of variable pitch (string and voice) can accommodate the difficulties of modulation by adjustment and hence plays thirds "better in tune," i.e. with "purer" or beatless intervals.

As efforts were made to accommodate harmony and modulation in Western music, two other systems evolved: *meantone temperament* and *equal temperament*. Both involved the altering or tempering of some tones. It is not clear when meantone temperament was first used, although Barbour (p. 25) suggests that it was being used as early as the beginning of the sixteenth century. There are several variations of meantone tuning, but the essential aspect of the system is that it alters (flats) some of the fifths of the Pythagorean scale, thus allowing a limited degree of modulation. Its name was derived from the fact that the whole tone C-D was half the size of the major third resulting from the alterations of the fifth. Meantone temperatment was used extensively in Europe throughout the seventeenth century and well into the eighteenth century until the acceptance of equal temperament.

Equal temperament, as is undoubtedly apparent to the reader, is so named because it divides the octave into twelve equal semitones. (Other divisions are possible; technically, division of the octave into any number of equivalent units is "equal temperament.") Each adjacent pair of tones has the same ratio of frequencies, 1:1.05946. Although the octave is the only simple ratio (2:1), there is a consistency among each of the other intervals regardless of key. Equal temperament overcomes the limitations on transposition, modulation, and use of chromaticism which are inherent with Pythagorean, just, and meantone tuning.

The equal tempered semitone has been divided into 100 equal parts called *cents*. A semitone therefore equals 100 cents, a whole tone 200 cents. An equal tempered fifth is 700 cents, i.e. it encompasses seven semitones, while the octave, made up of twelve semitones, equals 1200 cents. Cents for a given interval may be computed with the formula $n = 3986.31$ $[\log (\frac{f_2}{f_1})]$ in which n = number of cents, f_1 = lower tone frequency, and f_2 = upper tone frequency.

Cents are a convenient way for comparing the size of intervals in the various tuning systems. Table 4-III, adapted from Farnsworth (p. 25), compares the size of intervals in the four tuning systems discussed above. As is apparent, the equal tempered fifth is slightly (two one-hundredths of a semitone) smaller than the beatless Pythagorean and just fifths; conversely, the equal tempered fourth is slightly larger than the Pythagorean and just fourths.

Table 4-III

COMPARISON OF PYTHAGOREAN, JUST, MEANTONE, AND EQUAL
TEMPERED TUNINGS

	do	re	mi	fa	so	la	ti	do
Pythagorean	0	204	408	498	702	906	1110	1200
Just	0	204	386	498	702	884	1088	1200
Meantone*	0	204	386	503	697	890	1083	1200
Equal	0	200	400	500	700	900	1100	1200

*This is the tuning used by Pietro Aron around 1523.

The major discussions regarding tuning tendencies in contemporary performances, however, center on the tuning of the major third, *do — mi*, and the size of the interval between the leading tone *(ti)* and *do*. Although equal temperament is the recognized standard, some performers insist that triads are "better in tune" if they approach the tuning of the just triad which has a major third 14 cents lower than the equal tempered major third. This would be possible for performances of a cappella choirs and string quartets which are not bound by the constraints of keyboard or wind instruments. It is also claimed and supported by research (Greene, 1937 and Nickerson, 1949) that soloists on string instruments which can adjust intonation tend to approximate Pythagorean tuning when performing leading tones.

Barbour (pp. 192-202) and Ostling (1974) review much of the rhetoric regarding the issue and in addition cite the limited research on the matter. Apparently no research has been conducted regarding the tuning tendencies of choirs, but Barbour suggests that even if choirs did attempt to adjust to just intonation, the overall pitch probably would fall if the harmonic progressions are traditional diatonic progressions. He does concede, though, that such adjustments might be possible in modal progressions such as used by Palestrina. He maintains, however, that choirs singing with instruments quickly adapt to the intonation of the accompanying instrument.

Perhaps the classic study of intonation tendencies in performance is by Nickerson (1949), who analyzed performances of individual members of string quartets, both in isolation and ensemble. From his analysis he concluded that (1) performances do not conform completely to just, Pythagorean, or equal temperament, (2) performances of melodies both in solo and ensemble approach Pythagorean tuning, and (3) factors which cause this pattern appear to dominate both ensemble demands and presumed experience with equal temperament.

Roederer (1975, p. 159), however, cautions against concluding that soloists have a particular preference for Pythagorean intonation. He notes that other studies (Terhardt and Zick, 1975) have shown a tendency for performers to play or sing sharp the upper tone of all successive intervals.

While research is inconclusive regarding intonation practices in contemporary performances, it is apparent that much deviation from equal temperament does occur and is still perceived as "acceptable." Perhaps Ostling (p. 18) best summarizes the current state of the matter:

> Research agrees that good intonation is not any one basic tuning system used exclusively. Beyond that, it seems to this writer that a basic minimum standard of at least equal temperament should be expected —the norm—from which artist--performers will depart for melodic gravitation and/or harmonic reinforcement, as the situation requires, and that is about all one can conclude, at least to date.

Meanwhile, we still have directors of a cappella choirs who insist that their choirs are able to sing in just intonation; further, string players consistently report that they must adjust their intonation differently when playing in a string quartet and when performing with (an equal tempered) piano accompaniment. Clearly there is need for much more research on the matter.

Major and Minor Modes

Major and *minor* are terms used to describe size of intervals and type of scales, triads, or keys. With intervals the terms simply denote differences in intervals of a second, third, sixth, or seventh; minor intervals in each class contain one less semitone than the major interval in the class.

When used to distinguish between types of scales, triads, and keys, the basic distinction between major and minor is in the size of the third: the third of the major scale (key, triad) is four semitones while the third in the minor scale (key, triad) contains only three semitones.

The basic interval pattern of the major scale is TTSTTTS, where T stands for a whole tone and S stands for a semitone. The minor scale has three variations: natural, melodic, and harmonic. All three forms have the lowered third tone, thus beginning TS for the intervals between the first three tones but vary in the highest three tones. The natural minor also has a semitone between the fifth and sixth tones, resulting in the following pattern: TSTTSTT. The melodic minor raises the sixth and seventh tones when ascending (TSTTTTS) but is the same as the natural minor when descending. The harmonic minor has a raised leading tone both ascending and descending, thus creating an augmented second (A), i.e. three semitones, between the sixth and seventh tones (TSTTSAS).

The establishment of major and minor as the tonal bases of Western music appeared to evolve with the establishment of equal temperament and the development of harmony. Major and minor scales then could be constructed on each of the twelve tones within the chromatic octave, and the interval and chordal relationships within the scale built on each degree of the octave, i.e. in each key, were functionally identical. The fact that music built on major and minor scales (and their harmonic patterns) has dominated Western music of the past three hundred years so completely suggests that major and minor scales and their concomitant systems of tonality and harmony have, as Mursell (p. 108) has noted, provided an intelligible system for the perceptual organization of music.

Other Modes

While major and minor scales have become predominant patterns for Western music, many other scales have been developed both within Western cultures and in other cultures. No other scale system, however, has been developed into a harmonic system which in any way approaches that of Western tonal harmony based on the major and minor scales, although some systems are in many respects compatible with Western tonal harmony.

The traditional narrow sense of the term *mode* refers to the *church modes* devised by scholars of the medieval church. They consist of eight diatonic scales, using the same names of earlier Greek modes but different in organization and structure, which are the tonal basis of Gregorian chant. Apel (1969, p. 165) describes the system as follows:

> Each [consists] of the tones of the C-major scale (white keys) but starting and closing on d, e, f, or g and limited to the range of an octave. For each of these four notes, called a final *(finalis)*, there exists two modes distinguished by the different position of the octave range *(ambitus)* and called respectively authentic and plagal. In the *authentic modes* the ambitus extends from the final to the upper octave; in the *plagal modes,* from the fourth below the final to the fifth above it.

In the sixteenth century two scales on A and two on C, which essentially were the natural minor and major scales, were added to the system, bringing the total to twelve. The four authentic modes are the Dorian, Phrygian, Lydian, and Mixolydian. The plagal modes use the same four names but with the prefix "hypo," and the added minor and major modes are called the Aeolian and Ionian respectively. Some also recognize a Locrian mode. Following are the church modes, their range, and final note, in reference to the white keys. (In actuality, each mode is found by its characteristic interval relationship; a modal scale could start on any tone.)

Mode	Final	Range
Dorian	D	D-D
Hypodorian	D	A-A
Phrygian	E	E-E
Hypophrygian	E	B-B
Lydian	F	F-F
Hypolydian	F	C-C
Mixolydian	G	G-G
Hypomixolydian	G	D-D
Aeolian	A	A-A
Hypoaeolian	A	E-E
Locrian	B	B-B
Hypolocrian	B	F-F
Ionian	C	C-C
Hypoionian	C	G-G

While some of the church modes still are used in the traditional chants in the liturgy of the Catholic Church, there appears to be relatively little interest in the church modes outside of music history and theory classes, although some folk songs and folk-like popular songs of the 1960s and 1970s are modal rather than major or minor.

Within Western cultures many other modes have been developed but only a few have gained any degree of acceptance. Perhaps Debussy's *whole-tone* scale is one of the most successful. It divides the octave into six whole tones, and there are only two basic scales: C,D,E,F-sharp, G-sharp, Bb, C and C-sharp, D-sharp, F,G,A,B,C-sharp.   The purpose of the whole-tone scale was to break away from the strong feeling for the tonic which traditional tonal harmony elicits.   The omission of the three fundamental intervals of tonal harmony—perfect fourth, perfect fifth, and leading tone—was designed to accomplish this.

Pentatonic scales have five tones to the octave and have been developed in other cultures as well as in Western cultures.   The pentatonic scale commonly used in Western Cultures has no semitones and in the key of C uses the following tones: C,D,E,G,A,C. Pentatonic scales can be built on any tone of the chromatic scale;

within each pattern they also can use any of the five tones as a tonic, thus having five different modes in a manner similar to the church modes. In practice, however, only two modes are used to any extent: the authentic mode, using C as the tonic, and the plagal mode, using F as the tonic.

The *chromatic scale* represents another modal system which has received a certain amount of use in Western cultures. It has been most used in terms of serial music. *Quarter-tone* scales also have been developed. They divided each semitone in half, hence, dividing the octave into twenty-four parts.

Backus (1969, p. 129) notes three other scales which have been suggested; these scales divide the octave in nineteen, thirty-one, and fifty-three equal parts respectively. He notes that some combinations of the resulting small intervals closely approximate the semitones, thirds, and fifths of just intervals. Von Hoerner (1976) has developed an elaborate scheme of the chords, intervals, and chromatic properties of the nineteen and thirty-one tone scales.

With developments in synthesizers, computers, and other electronic equipment it is possible to develop many other varieties of scales. The scales, sometimes called *synthetic* scales, however, are intended to be unique and therefore are of little general interest.

Modal organization in music of other cultures offers a great variety of additional modal patterns. Description of even the most common ones is beyond the scope of this discussion, but some are cited as examples.

Farnsworth (1969, pp. 23-25) notes that equally tempered scales also developed in the Orient. The Siamese divided the octave into seven equal steps while the Japanese divided one of their scales into five equal parts. Pentatonic scales, somewhat approximating the authentic mode of the Western pentatonic, have been used in nearly all ancient cultures—China, Polynesia, Africa, and American Indian (Apel, p. 653). Chinese music also uses six-tone (sexatonic) and seven-tone (heptatonic) scales, while scales of India and the Middle East are characterized by the use of microtones, i.e. intervals smaller than a semitone.

The possibilities of modal organization in music are infinite, but it is apparent that only a few modal systems have gained any wide-spread acceptance. The authors agree that the reasons for this are primarily cultural, although the compatibility of the structure of a system with perceptual laws also appears to influence its acceptance. This will be examined further later in this chapter.

OTHER TYPES OF PITCH ORGANIZATION

Earlier in this chapter it was mentioned that the twentieth-century has given rise to new ways for organizing the pitch structure of music. Lest other discussions in this chapter suggest that pitches in music can be organized only within certain conventional frameworks, the present discussion seeks to provide a brief overview of twentieth-century developments in pitch organization of Western music.

The use of chromaticism and the resultant dissonance of the late romantic composers, particularly Wagner, led to a search for pitch organization beyond that which could be provided by triadic harmony. Chromaticism and modulation had evolved to the point that many composers no longer ended compositions in the original tonic key as had been the practice during the baroque, classical, and early romantic periods of music history.

Three distinct developments regarding harmonic practices evolved during the late nineteenth and early twentieth centuries. The development some composers followed was to continue composing within the broad outline of a tonal harmonic framework while at the same time utilizing chords of far greater complexity than traditional triads. A second group of composers continued to use chords from earlier harmonic practices, but sequenced them in such ways that expected progressions and resolutions were not forthcoming. Whole tone music and polytonality were two results of this development. The third development was the abandoning of tonality for Schoenberg's serial techniques which are intended to disrupt any feeling for tonality. Serial techniques, often called twelve-tone techniques because each of the twelve semitones in the octave must be used before another can be repeated, have provided the impetus for renewed interest in structuring the vertical dimension of pitch polyphonically, i.e. in terms of combinations of independent melodic lines. Twentieth century polyphony, however, differs from the contrapuntal writing of the baroque, classical, and romantic periods in that there is little or no concern for the vertical sonorities of traditional tertian harmony.

Three other developments of twentieth century pitch organization also deviate from the practices of tertian harmony. *Aleatoric* or *chance* music introduces an unpredictability regarding either its composition or performance. Such music leaves the pitch, duration, and loudness structure to chance, thus making it very difficult for listeners to develop any melodic or harmonic expectations other than uncertainty itself.

Musique concrete is the name given to the development in which traditional musical sound sources (instruments and voices) are replaced by sounds of various kinds—environmental noises, sounds of nature, or any conceivable sound source. These sounds can be recorded, combined, and modified at the composer's will. It may utilize fixed or changing pitches as well as sounds of indefinite pitches to create a collage of sounds. As might be expected, the pitch structure has no confining framework such as tertian harmony.

A final and perhaps most important development in pitch organization in twentieth century music is electronic music, which has given composers a new vista for organizing pitches. Composers can combine electronically generated pitches in an almost infinite variety of manners, just as in *musique concrete*. No longer do fixed divisions of an octave serve as the basis for all music. The implications of electronic developments are staggering for a listener.

Developments in serial music, aleatoric music, *musique concrete*, and electronic music have created ambiguities for listeners accustomed to hearing music constructed in a tonal harmonic framework. At present, the acceptance of such developments appears to be only among a relatively narrow musical subculture; the general population of Western cultures, including many people who profess to have a "considerable interest" in music, is not flocking to the concert halls or buying recordings of such music. Whether this is just the normal slowness of acceptance of new musical styles or whether it is because the music of these new developments lacks an organizational structure that allows listeners to perceive the unity or Gestalten of it is subject to conjecture. The authors believe the latter is at least partially responsible for the slowness of acceptance of these styles. (See also Chapter Seven.)

PSYCHOLOGICAL PROCESSES AND PITCH-RELATED BEHAVIORS

While the processing of individual pure and complex pitches was examined in Chapter Two, this section examines the psychological processes underlying interactions with the pitch organization of *music*. The concern is with understanding responses to melody and harmony in Western music, i.e. melody and harmony constructed within a tonal harmonic framework. While this may appear to be a limitation in approach, the authors believe that an understanding of the processing of melody and harmony in a tonal harmonic framework reveals much with respect to why some contemporary music, as well as some music of other cultures, is difficult for Western listeners to "understand."

Information Theory and Melodic and Harmonic Expectations

The mass of aural stimuli called melody and harmony, which also have attributes of duration (with its extensions into rhythmic structure), timbre, and loudness, presents listeners with a complexity of stimuli that, without some mechanism for rendering a sense of order in an individual's perceptual system, would appear to be unintelligible cacophony. Indeed, to some individuals, much of what is called music by others is unintelligible cacophony. The question under consideration here, therefore, is "How do individuals create musical meaning out of the mass of sounds called melody and harmony?"

From a psychological perspective melody and harmony are highly complex phenomena, but it appears that most individuals are able to receive a certain amount of musical *meaning* from them.* Many of these individuals who appear to gain meaning from music, however, do not have any extensive or intensive

---

*As used in the present discussion musical meaning refers to perceptual and conceptual meaning; Chapter Six examines musical meaning as aesthetic meaning.

formal musical training. On the other hand, even some highly trained musicians apparently perceive little meaning in some avant garde music. Members of a Western culture also can listen to a given Oriental melody and have great difficulty in recognizing any semblance of organizational structure. Still, some individuals within a Western culture can listen to Brahms's *D Major Symphony* and marvel at its structure while others perceive it as unintelligible cacophony. Such observations beg the question, "Why does some of the music hold meaning for some individuals and not for others?"

Psychologists who have examined perception in terms of information theory, e.g. Broadbent, 1958; Moles, 1966; Meyer, 1956, 1967, have recognized that a central problem in dealing with complexity is an individual's *capacity* for such. Capacity for perception and cognition of complex stimuli is limited for everyone, although each individual's limits are not the same. We do not know how to assess the limits of perceptual capacity except under somewhat artificial conditions for some isolated tasks. While a thorough understanding of individuals' capacities for perception and cognition of music is not available, information theory does provide a construct for examining perceptual capacity for music.

Information theory basically is a system for quantifying the amount of *uncertainty* involved in a sensory stimulus or *message*. "A message is a finite, ordered set of elements of perception drawn from a repertoire and assembled in a structure" (Moles, 1966, p. 9). Messages may be *spatial* or *temporal;* music, like dance, is a time art and provides temporal messages, whereas painting, sculpture, and photography provide spatial messages.

> If the circumstances surrounding the reception of a particular sensory event are such that only one possible symbol *could* have been transmitted, then the amount of information conveyed by the correct identification of that symbol (or message) is zero. If the message is one chosen from two equally likely alternatives then the amount of information acquired through a correct reception of it is one *bit,* or one binary decision's worth. (Watson, 1973, p. 293)

The greater the amount of *information* conveyed via the sensory *message,* the greater the *uncertainty* of *meaning* or response. In theory, a mathematical formula can be used to predict the probability of a response, but the complex nature of melody and harmony, coupled with the human variable in terms of previous experience with melody and harmony, makes absolutely accurate prediction virtually impossible. The authors concur with Meyer (1967, p. 20) that our inability to measure precisely the amount of information in a musical message does not weaken or invalidate information theory as a basis for examining musical meaning; the theory still provides a useful construct for discussion of musical expectation as well as a framework for study of musical perception.

The amount of *information* an individual receives when listening to melody and harmony, and hence *his or her expectations* regarding them, is a function of two basic variables: (1) the extent to which the *structural* characteristics of melody and harmony conform to the fundamental organizational laws of Gestalt psychology and (2) the individual's previous experience with the given style of melody and harmony. As noted previously, melodies and harmonies constructed in a tonal harmonic framework generally conform to the fundamental organizational laws of Gestalt psychology; the tonal harmonic framework provides the structural unity, and the melody or harmony is received as a Gestalt or pattern. Meyer (1956, chapters 3,4,5) provides an extensive discussion of pattern perception in music.

The expectations an individual develops from melody or harmony are related to the *perceptual* redundancy of the message. While information theory *per se* holds that the redundancy in a message is characteristic of the stimulus alone, Meyer (1967, pp. 277-279) maintains that redundancy in a musical message depends on both the extent to which structural characteristics conform to the Gestalt organizational laws of pattern perception and the degree to which the individual has learned the syntactic-formal premises of the musical style.

Redundancy is never total, even in a musical style with which an individual is familiar; melody and harmony in Western tonal music have disorder, ambiguity, and unpredictability.

Were a composition totally redundant, the result would be completely predictable and, consequently, total tedium . . . . The relative disorder or randomness that necessarily complements redundancy may be called *perceptual information.* (Meyer, 1967, p. 278)

If redundancy is too low, the perceptual information is too great for the melody or harmony to be understood. Perceptual redundancy, which will vary with the individual listener, relies heavily on memory of previous experiences with the style and allows the individual listener to create psychological order out of the melody or harmony, thus developing expectations and meaning or understanding.

As may be apparent to the reader, the harmonic framework of Western music, with its melodies and harmonies using a familiar scale system and constructed in such ways that tonality and melodic and harmonic movement are built in, provides the stimulus for redundancy. Regardless of the historical period and its stylistic peculiarities, tonality and scales provide strong *structural redundancy.*

When an individual with his or her lifetime of experience with Western tonal music, which Meyer calls cultural redundancy, listens to unfamiliar tonal music which has structural redundancy built in through its tonal harmonic framework, the *perceptual redundancy* is high, thus delimiting the amount of new or extraneous *information* in the music. Hence, the individual more readily can make "more sense" of the unfamiliar music than he or she could if it were in a style which did not have structural redundancy and for which he or she had developed no cultural redundancy.

This does not mean, however, that everyone maturing in a Western culture automatically will be able to understand all tonal music, because within Western culture the variety of musical styles is great; further, the range of experiences individuals within a Western culture have with music also is great. It does suggest, however, that if given adequate experiences with tonal harmonic music, an individual should have a strong psychological basis for interacting with it.

To recapitulate, perceptual redundancy limits the amount of information a listener receives from a musical message. The greater the redundancy, the more accurate the listener's expectations. Perceptual redundancy enables a listener to conceive melody and harmony as patterns or Gestalten even though he or she obviously may not perceive and remember each constituent tone or chord of the pattern. The expectations complement the tones and chords actually perceived to create the musical pattern.

When a listener encounters melodies or harmonies which do not have structural redundancy built in and with which they have not developed cultural redundancy, there is increased information. With increased information, the accuracy of the individual's expectations decreases. When information is so great that the individual cannot develop expectations regarding the melodic or harmonic patterns, the music holds little meaning. Meyer (1967, pp. 283-293) suggests that the *lack* of perceptual redundancy, with its constituent aspects of structural and cultural redundancy, is most likely the reason serialism has failed to gain widespread acceptance. The authors also submit that avant garde electronic music which does not provide structural redundancy to facilitate the perception of patterns or Gestalten will be unlikely to gain widespread acceptance, particularly since few individuals are developing any cultural redundancy for such music.

In concluding this discussion, it also should be noted that Roederer (1975, p. 163), while concerned more with a description of the psychophysical processes in musical perception, also recognizes the role of expectation in musical perception. He notes that *"the nervous system tries to use whatever information is available from previous experiences to facilitate and even anticipate the identification processes of new incoming information"* (p. 163). He goes on to cite evidence (electrophysiological measurements) that cortical activity is evoked even when a previously learned succession of stimuli is expected but does not occur.

Pitch-related Behaviors

Expectations are fundamental to both receptive and production behaviors. While their role in receptive behaviors should be apparent from the preceding discussion, their role is perhaps less clear regarding production behaviors. In reception of melody and harmony, expectations are essentially a function of memory of previous experiences with melody and harmony which facilitate perception of new melodies and harmonies. Woodruff (1970) calls these memories of previous experiences *concepts* (see also Chapter Ten) and suggests that they provide the basis for musical behavior. Regelski (1975, p. 11) has elaborated on the view that concepts are general thought tendencies and suggests that they result from (1) perception and cognition of many particular personal experiences with the learning or skill to be mastered, (2) the transfer of certain learnings from these particular personal experiences to other particular but somewhat different situations, and (3) a gradually evolving tendency toward increased frequency of the behavior.

Expectations, therefore, are basic to the conceptualization of music. Musical concepts, recognized as cumulative tendencies toward response, are the product of memories of previous experiences with musical stimuli. While musical concepts are essentially covert cognitive activity, they form the basis for both receptive and production behaviors. Receptive behaviors are essentially perceptual and therefore covert in nature; productive behaviors involve production of pitches in music.

RECEPTIVE BEHAVIORS. The basic problem in studying receptive behaviors is that they are essentially covert, and to gain some understanding of them, investigators must devise some overt manifestation of them, a task which often creates as many questions as it answers. Investigators do not always agree regarding the appropriateness of certain overt behaviors as reflections of certain covert perceptual or conceptual activity. For example, investigators concerned with studying "perception of melodies" might devise musical tasks to serve as evidence of melodic perception, which range from simply recognizing a melody or discriminating between two melodies to singing or notating an aurally presented melody. While many investigators operationally define their terms, others apply vague labels to their studies, thereby leaving the general reader with a mass of seemingly contradictory information regarding receptive behaviors. Unfortunately, the present discussion offers no neat and tidy solution to the problem.

The reader should keep in mind, however, that receptive behaviors are essentially perceptual and involve *recognition of,* and *discrimination between,* musical stimuli. Both processes are fundamental to reception of melody and harmony. While listening to music an individual is constantly, and usually without any particular awareness, separating the familiar from the unfamiliar and comparing new patterns with memories of previous patterns. The better the new melodies and harmonies match the expectations based on memories of previous experiences, the more comprehensible they are.

Two additional classes of receptive behaviors also should be noted: *analytical* and *aural-visual discrimination*. Essentially these are extensions of recognition and discrimination, but each goes beyond the basic receptive processes. Analytical behaviors reflect efforts to consciously categorize melodic and harmonic patterns into their constituent parts. Aural-visual discrimination involves associating aural stimuli, melodic and harmonic patterns, with their symbolic (notational) representations.

As may be apparent to the reader, receptive behaviors are difficult to isolate entirely from performance behaviors; there is always an element of "performance" in any overt manifestation of receptive behaviors.

PRODUCTION BEHAVIORS. Production behaviors are of three basic types: singing, performing music with an instrument, and creating music. It is recognized that the ability to make musical discriminations underlies all production behaviors. Without the ability to discriminate among pitch patterns, an individual would be unable to produce his or her musical intentions in any tonal manner. While the concern of the present discussion is production of melodies and harmonies, the principle is the same for all aspects of music, be they dynamics, rhythm, or timbre. If the individual cannot discriminate among the tonal attributes, the production efforts are hindered.

Each of the three types of production behaviors are subdivided according to whether the behavior is a *re*production or *pro*duction of music. Singing and instrumental performance may involve production of musical patterns not previously produced, i.e. improvisation. In improvisation, the performer is combining new melodic and harmonic patterns within a given conceptual framework. Most improvising today, be it by the jazz musician or church organist, is conceived within a tonal harmonic framework. Singers and instrumentalists also are involved in the reproduction of melodies and harmonies. They may reproduce pitch patterns learned "by ear," i.e. by rote procedures, and patterns read or memorized from notation. At the risk of an over-generalization, it appears that most music performed in Western cultures involves reproduction rather than production.

Creation behaviors also can involve either production or re-production of musical patterns. The apparent favorite pastime of music theory teachers, melodic and harmonic dictation, requires music students to reproduce in notation aurally given melodic and harmonic patterns. Production of musical notation, however, involves what some consider to be the ultimate musical behavior, composition.

DEVELOPMENT OF MELODIC AND HARMONIC BEHAVIORS

As may be apparent, the types of receptive and production behaviors are sufficiently broad that they could be divided into many sublevels or categories of musical behavior. While it might appear that a developmental taxonomy of melodic and harmonic behaviors could be developed, the uniqueness of each child's musical experiences is such that any attempt to set forth such a taxonomy would immediately encounter difficulties. Each child's developmental sequence, while subject to general laws of matura-tion, is necessarily unique because musical development is greatly influenced by environment (Phillips, 1976; Sergeant and Thatch-er, 1974). This section, therefore, will examine musical develop-ment from two perspectives: research-based findings and music teachers' views.

Research-based Findings

Research related to development of melodic and harmonic behaviors is primarily developmental research, i.e. studies of chil-dren's ability to accomplish certain musical tasks at various age or developmental levels. A major problem with this approach is the separation of the various musical tasks children are asked to do and interpretation of the implications thereof. Many varieties of tasks, including ones requiring performance, loosely are labeled as melodic perception even though it is obvious that performance tasks involve production behaviors in addition to receptive behaviors. Loose application of labels to measurement of receptive and production tasks is a particular difficulty in studying musical development. When examining research related to musical development, the reader is cautioned to examine the nature of the behavioral tasks required in the study and draw any conclusions only with due consideration of the tasks.

Another difficulty in drawing conclusions from studies of young children is the notorious *un*reliability of the measuring instruments. Often conclusions are drawn on the basis of investigators' observations of a very limited number of cases or on the basis of responses to tests of questionable validity and reliability. These difficulties, coupled with the uniqueness of each child's musical experiences, make sweeping generalizations about children's musical development extremely hazardous.

Zimmerman's (1971, pp. 6-11) review of children's aural discrimination skills reveals that melodic perception precedes harmonic perception. She cites two possible reasons for this:

> One is that the children's perceptions center upon the dominating melodic line making it difficult for them to consider simultaneously both the melodic and harmonic aspects of the song. A second reason is simply that young children might not be completely conditioned to the harmonic cliches of the common practice period of Western music. (pp. 8-9)

She also notes that an ability to discriminate among loudness levels usually precedes pitch discrimination ability, which appears to develop somewhat concurrently with rhythmic discrimination.

Nearly all research on young children's development of melodic discrimination reveals an increase in skills with an increase in age. Shuter (1968, pp. 61-71) summarizes the work of a number of researchers' findings regarding the development of melodic skills. She cites some case studies in which children recognized melodies between the ages of one and two years. These same studies also revealed that some children at this age could reproduce notes or intervals and sing a tune correctly. More recent research by Moog (1976) generally supports Shuter's findings. Moog also reports that there is remarkable improvement in children's singing between the ages of two and four.

Zimmerman (1971, pp. 12-14) notes that responses to melody and harmony are more than a function of perception; they also reflect conceptual development. Her review of studies of children's musical concept formation reveals a dependency relationship between perceptual and conceptual behavior. This is particularly important in dealing within melody and harmony.

While most studies of children's melodic abilities are concerned with response to melodic pattern, Sergeant and Roche (1973) also studied children's ability to sing melodies on a specific pitch level. Over a three-week period they taught thirty-six children (thirteen three– to four-year-olds, ten five-year-olds, and thirteen six-year-olds) to vocalize three melodies. Each melody was taught on an invariant pitch level. One week after the completion of the study, each child's singing of the melodies was recorded. Results revealed an inverse relationship between accuracy of pitch level and accuracy of the melodic pattern. The youngest group sang at the most accurate pitch level, but the oldest group sang the melodic pattern most accurately. The results supported the investigators' hypothesis that younger children tend to focus on pitch *per se,* while with increased age and conceptual development they focus more on the attributes of melodic pattern. They suggest that three– to four-year-olds reflect an absolute pitch ability which decreases with age; further, they suggest that absolute pitch skills could be developed if children were given training on fixed pitch instruments during a critical period, common to all children, before their preconceptual perception of pitch has been transcended by higher-order conceptual thinking (p. 47).

Michel (1973) also notes a critical period in musical development. The critical period he observed is between the ages of five and six, whereas Sergeant and Roche's data suggest the critical period might come earlier. Wherever the critical period lies, there is need for further research on the matter.

Zimmerman (1971, p. 28) notes the ages of six to eight are marked by rapid development in melodic perception. Petzold (1966, p. 254) and some other researchers, however, reported a leveling effect following the third grade, or around the age of nine. Taylor (1973) notes that there is a marked development of harmonic perception around the age of nine; however, Thackray

(1973) maintains that results of his harmonic perception test provide positive evidence that many children develop a considerable degree of harmonic awareness well before the age of nine. Bridges' (1965) study of harmonic discrimination ability of children in kindergarten through grade three also suggests a gradual development in harmonic discrimination ability. Moog (1976), however, maintains that his research shows unequivocally that preschool-aged children cannot yet experience any sort of harmony at all.

In summary, there is a general development of melodic discrimination skills from infancy through about the age of eight, with a critical period for development somewhere around the age of five or six. Harmonic discrimination skills appear to develop later, with earliest awareness of harmony appearing around age five or six and with a marked increase in harmonic discrimination skills developing around age nine. Whether the leveling in melodic skills around age nine is due to increased harmonic awareness, however, is subject to conjecture.

Music Teachers' Views

Music teachers are concerned with much more than the development of melodic and harmonic behaviors, but the present discussion is limited to a discussion of some commonly used methods for developing melodic and harmonic behaviors. A general sequence for emphasis at the various levels of the elementary school appears to be that rhythm is emphasized at the earliest levels, nursery school, kindergarten, and early primary grades; melody appears to receive greater attention in grades two through four, and harmony begins receiving greater attention in grades four through six. Nye and Nye (1970, p. 371) note that this also is the general order in which children develop musical concepts.

The major musical activities through which melodic and harmonic behaviors are developed include singing, listening, and playing instruments. While movement sometimes is used to reinforce melodic behavior, it primarily is used to develop rhythmic behaviors.

Music teachers also recognize that much development of musical behaviors occurs outside of school, but for most children school music represents the first formal learning experiences with music. The initial pitch-related concept that teachers try to develop is that of *high* and *low* pitch, or more properly, *higher* and *lower* pitch, since pitch is a relative phenomenon.

Aronoff (1969, p. 42) notes that behaviors related to melodic direction and shape should be developed by young children. Melodic direction and shape are developed and reinforced through musical activities—singing, listening, and playing instruments. Children learn that melodies move up, move down, or repeat tones; once direction is established, children's discrimination can be refined to the point that they can describe how a melody moves —by steps or skips, repeated tones, sequences, etc.

While music reading is recognized as a developmental process ranging from the following of simple line notation to reading of actual notation, music teachers do not all agree as to how best to teach music reading. Many, of whom Mursell is a particularly strong advocate, maintain that reading is best facilitated through instrumental experiences in which the visual symbol stands for a particular sound and set of movements. Others advocate a system to foster *relative* pitch reading within a scale or key. The predominant system of this type is the movable *do* syllables, although some teachers use a number system for the eight tones of the major scales. A fixed *do* system is used primarily in Europe. Gordon (1971, pp. 100-103) cites the advantages and disadvantages of syllables and numbers and concludes that the movable *do* is best.

Just as research showed that harmonic behaviors develop following melodic behaviors, music teachers have determined empirically that the teaching of harmony should follow the teaching of melody. Whether there is any cause and effect relationship here is unsettled. Nye and Nye (pp. 371-440) provide an extensive discussion of procedures used to develop children's harmonic behaviors.

While this brief sketch of music teachers' views on the development of melodic and harmonic behaviors is limited both in scope and depth, it does indicate that the teaching sequence generally recognizes and follows the hierarchy of development found by researchers.

EVALUATING MELODIES AND HARMONIES

While an examination of "goodness" of melody or "appropriateness" of harmony perhaps is more appropriate in a chapter on aesthetics, it also is relevant to the psychological foundations of melodic and harmonic behaviors. The present discussion, while recognizing that "good" and "appropriate" can reflect value judgements and thereby are legitimate concerns from an aesthetic perspective, focuses on "goodness" and "appropriateness" from a perceptual frame of reference.

Earlier discussions in this chapter suggest that melodies and harmonies can be considered in terms of both their structural and psychological characteristics. Perception necessarily involves both structural and psychological characteristics.

What is "Good" Melody?

The fundamental problem in determining goodness of a melody rests with the relative emphasis one places on its structural and psychological characteristics. If one evaluates solely on structure, such characteristics as propinquity, repetition, and finality might be important evaluative criteria, or one might turn to some quasi-mathematical explanation such as the Lipps-Meyer Law.

On the other hand, explanations in terms of psychological characteristics might concern the extent to which melodies are perceived as Gestalten or the degree to which the melody was perceived as being within a familiar style. Obviously, neither approach is adequate.

Mursell (1937, pp. 105-106) notes that essentially all that is needed for an authentic melodic experience is "a tonal sequence held together and unified by a unity of response." He notes that "inferior" melodies lack unity in both structure and response.

Hickman (1976) reviewed a number of discussions of melody, including ones which variously treated melody from technical, educational, musicological, and sociological perspectives among others, and concluded that order and pattern are essential constituents of good melodies. He then offered a model which has four criteria against which melodies can be evaluated: (1) the melody must manifest a pattern of elements, (2) it must be a product of a person or persons, (3) the melody must do more than adhere to specifications previously laid down, and (4) the melody must be worth having in itself apart from any purpose it may serve.

Lundin (1967, pp. 84-85) offers a behavioral or cultural interpretation of melody in which melody is viewed as a function of both the previous experience of the listener and certain characteristics of its structure. He maintains that what have come to be perceived as melodies are a result of many centuries of musical development. As scales changed, the new patterns were accepted gradually as people became familiar with them.

Reimer (1971, pp. 103-105), while concerned with musical goodness rather than just melodic goodness, cites two aspects of goodness: *excellence*, which has to do with syntactic or structural refinement in the music, and *greatness*, which has to do with the level of profundity of the music's expressive content. The two aspects are based respectively on Leonard Meyer's (1967, pp. 22-41) theories of value and greatness in music which are discussed in Chapter Six. While the criterion *greatness* is more properly discussed under aesthetics, the criterion *excellence* has its roots in the meanings of musical messages an individual receives while listening to music.

The meaning an individual receives when listening to a melody is a function of the uncertainty reflected in the information present in the melody. The amount of information an individual receives is dependent on both the structural and cultural redundancy of the melody, i.e. the extent to which the melody reflects a particular melodic style and the degree to which the individual is familiar with and has developed expectations within that style. The greater the perceptual redundancy, the combined effect of structural and cultural redundancy, the more likely the melody is meaningful, and hence good, for the individual.

Goodness in terms of meaning implies that goodness of a melody varies from individual to individual. A good melody for kindergarten children is different than what is good to an adolescent. Similarly, a good melody for the musically sophisticated is different than that which is good for an untrained listener. A melody in unfamiliar style also would lack goodness for an individual. However, the greater the number of individuals who find meaning in a melody, the more it would appear that the goodness status of the melody should be elevated in some manner.

What is "Acceptable" Harmony?

"Acceptableness" of harmony *per se* has received considerably less attention than either melody or music as a whole. What attention there has been is related to one of two basic approaches: (1) studies of the age at which children become cognizant of harmony, e.g. Bridges, 1965, and (2) individuals' preferences for harmony of traditional tonal compositions (Wing, 1961; Long, 1965). (Wing has a separate test for harmony whereas Long asks individuals to select the "better" of two musical renditions and tell whether it was better in terms of melody, harmony, or rhythm.)

The latter approach is particularly relevant to our discussion because in essence it seeks to assess individuals' preferences in terms of appropriateness of the harmony for given examples of Western tonal music in what we loosely call classical style. To the extent that an individual's preferences conform to what musically trained judges agree is appropriate, the individual exhibits knowledge of harmonic style for Western music. While the "agreements with the experts" approach can be criticized as somewhat snobbish, the particular mode for evaluating has merit and offers many possibilities for examining views of "acceptable" harmony.

Ultimately the acceptableness of harmony, just as the goodness of melody, is an individual matter and is a function of an individual's experiences with harmonic styles. The meaning an individual receives from harmony is related to the expectancies he or she has developed for the given style. The information theory framework noted in the discussion of goodness of melody also can be applied in the discussion of harmony. Appropriateness of harmony, therefore, also is an individual matter; the degree to which groups of individuals find given harmonies acceptable reflects a cultural or subcultural acceptance.

EVALUATION OF MELODIC AND HARMONIC BEHAVIORS

Evaluations of melodic and harmonic behaviors generally involve one of three basic types of behavior: (1) behaviors reflecting discriminations between aurally presented tonal patterns, (2) behaviors reflecting recognition of tonal patterns, (3) production behaviors. The preference tests described above conceivably could be considered a fourth type of behavior, although the authors view them as essentially requiring discriminations between tonal patterns. Also, the production behaviors possibly could be subdivided into notation and performance behaviors.

Some of the same concerns noted under the discussion of the evaluation of rhythmic behaviors also are apparent in the evaluation of melodic and harmonic behaviors. The nature of the response mode selected for measuring discrimination could affect the assessment; group versus individual measurement also is an important consideration, both in terms of economy and accuracy. Finally, the specifics versus omnibus question is reflected in the approaches used in some of the tests. The value of a particular approach depends ultimately on the purpose of the evaluation and the nature of the data sought.

While the bulk of this discussion is devoted to selected published standardized music tests, it should be recognized that the most commonly used measures of melodic and harmonic behaviors involve performance, usually from notation. Performance of both prepared pieces and sight-read pieces is used for evaluative purposes at all levels ranging from primary school through professional levels. Melodic and harmonic dictation also are much used, particularly in high school and college music theory classes. The evaluative criteria for performances are usually in terms of a teacher's or panel of judges' perceptions of what is "correct" performance. While the pitfalls of this are many, the system apparently works to the satisfaction of many musicians; otherwise there would be greater demands for refinements in the system.

Common to many published music tests is a *tonal memory* test, of which there are two basic approaches. One plays a melody or series of tones as a model and then in subsequent hearings, which range from two to six in number, the testee is asked to indicate how the melody was changed, usually to be selected from options such as key, rhythm, or pitch of some individual tone. The (Gaston) *Test of Musicality* (1957) and the *Drake Musical Aptitude Tests* (1957) use this type of tonal memory test.

The other type of tonal memory test also provides a model, but in subsequent hearings the testee is required to indicate which tone has been changed. The number of subsequent hearings also varies, usually from two to six. Tests using this type of tonal memory include *Seashore Measures of Music Talents* (1960), (Wing) *Standardised Tests of Musical Intelligence* (1961), and (Bentley) *Measures of Musical Ability* (1966).

Gordon's *Musical Aptitude Profile* (1965) measures tonal memory, or imagery as it is labeled in the test, by providing a model melody and then a second melody which is either an embellished rendition of the model or an entirely different melody. The testee must determine whether the second would be like the model if the embellished notes were not present. The "harmony" portion of the Gordon test also is unique. It involves essentially the same process although the changes are in a bass line. The upper part remains the same for both the model and the second hearing.

Thackray (1973, 1976) has devised measures of tonality and harmonic perception which appear to be useful. The tonality test measures tonality in melodies. The test has four subtests. Part I introduces modulations in some familiar melodies and asks respondents to indicate whether the melodies sound "right" or "wrong." Part II uses short unfamiliar melodies, some of which are diatonic and adhere clearly to tonality while others do not. Testees are asked to determine whether the melody is "ordinary" or "peculiar." Part III asks testees to determine whether the melodies sound "finished" or "not finished," and Part IV asks testees to determine whether the concluding tone is the same as the beginning tone of the melody. Although this test is not yet standardized, it appears to be potentially very useful in assessing tonality.

Thackray's harmonic perception test, also not standardized,

has three parts. Part I presents a series of sounds played on the piano, some of which are single tones and some of which are chords. The testee is asked to indicate which are chords. Part II presents three or four-note harmonized melodies. The testee is asked to indicate which tone (if any) in a second hearing is harmonized differently. Part III presents a chord followed by a pause and then a progression of three, four, or five chords, and the testee is asked to indicate where the given chord appears in the progression.

Two recent standardized tests appear to be potentially very useful in evaluating melodic and harmonic behaviors. Colwell's (1969-1970) *Music Achievement Tests* measure a variety of behaviors related to melody and harmony. Among the behaviors measured are determining whether a pattern or phrase moves scalewise or by leaps, whether chords and/or phrases are in major or minor mode, whether notated melodies match aurally presented melodies, which among three tones following a cadence or phrase is the keytone, and what is the style period of aurally presented melodies.

The *Iowa Tests of Music Literacy* (Gordon, 1970) measure three aspects of tonal concepts: aural perception, reading recognition, and notational understanding. Essentially the aural perception tests measure the ability to discriminate between major and minor modal patterns and some extensions thereof. The reading recognition test asks testees whether given notated melodies match aurally given melodies. The notational test is a type of dictation test.

Several aural-visual discrimination tests measure melodic aural-visual discrimination, but separate scores are not provided for melody, e.g. Knuth, 1966; Farnum, 1953. Melodic performance also is a major criterion in the scoring of the *Watkins-Farnum Performance Scale* (1954), but neither does it provide a separate melody score.

The same recommendation offered at the conclusion of the discussion on rhythm tests applies here. Researchers and teachers concerned with selecting or developing measures of melodic and harmonic behaviors should first and foremost consider the nature of the behaviors they wish to evaluate and be certain that any measures selected or developed indeed measure that behavior in a manner appropriate for the level of students being evaluated.

SUMMARY

Following are the major points discussed in the chapter:

1. The vertical structure of Western music is considerably more highly developed than that of other cultures.
2. Most Western music is constructed within a tonal harmonic framework.
3. Changing either the relative pitch positions of tones or the rhythm of a tonal sequence changes the melody structurally, although not always perceptually.
4. Melodies are perceived as Gestalten.
5. Melodies can be defined both as structural and psychological entities.
6. Harmony in Western music is tertian harmony.
7. There are three primary "holistic" attributes of harmony: (1) tonality, (2) harmonic movement, and (3) finality.
8. Melodic and harmonic movement are relative phenomena.
9. The diatonic scale is the basic scale of Western music.
10. Scale systems are codifications of musical practices.
11. The tempered diatonic scale is the most far-reaching standardization of music in the world.
12. The diatonic scale evolved from the Greek "Greater Perfect System."
13. Equal temperament is the most satisfactory tuning system for Western music.
14. Major and minor scales comprise the basic tonal patterns for most Western music.
15. Other modes include the church modes, the whole tone scale, the pentatonic scale, the chromatic scale, the quarter tone scale, synthetic scales, and scales of other cultures.
16. While most music uses fixed pitches in a tonal harmonic framework, some contemporary music uses sliding and indefinite pitches and is designed without an intention for tonality.

17. Musical meaning is a product of expectations a listener develops.
18. Expectations are a function of the information a musical example provides.
19. Information increases as redundancy decreases.
20. Redundancy is a function of the structural characteristics of the music and a listener's previous experiences with music of that style.
21. The basic receptive behaviors include recognition and discrimination.
22. Production behaviors are of three basic types: singing, performing music with an instrument, and creating music.
23. Children generally develop melodic behaviors before harmonic behaviors.
24. Practices of music teachers generally reflect the sequence in which melodic and harmonic behaviors develop.
25. The "goodness" of a melody and "acceptableness" of harmony in the psychological sense are functions of an individual's previous experiences with melodies and harmony in given styles.
26. Evaluation of melodic and harmonic behaviors involves one of three types of behavior: (1) discriminations between aurally presented tonal patterns, (2) recognition of tonal patterns, and (3) production behaviors.

REFERENCES

Apel, W. *Harvard Dictionary of Music* (2nd ed.). Cambridge, Mass.: Belknap Press, 1969.

Aronoff, F. W. *Music and Young Children.* New York: Holt, Rinehart and Winston, 1969.

Backus, J. *The Acoustical Foundations of Music.* New York: W. W. Norton, 1969.

Barbour, J. M. *Tuning and Temperament.* East Lansing: Michigan State Press, 1953.

Bentley, A. *Measures of Musical Ability.* New York: October House, 1966.

Bridges, V. A. An exploratory study of the harmonic discrimination ability of children in kindergarten through grade three in two selected schools (Doctoral dissertation, The Ohio State University, 1965). *Dissertation Abstracts,* 1965, *26,* 3692, (University Microfilms No. 65-13, 206)

Broadbent, D. E. *Perception and Communication.* New York: Macmillan, 1958.

Colwell, R. *Music Achievement Tests.* Chicago: Follett, 1969-70.

Drake, R. M. *Drake Musical Aptitude Tests.* Chicago: Science Research Associates, 1957.

Farnsworth, P. R. *The Social Psychology of Music* (2nd ed.) Ames: The Iowa State University Press, 1969.

Farnum, S. E. *Farnum Music Notation Test.* New York: The Psychological Corporation, 1953.

Forte, A. *Tonal Harmony in Concept and Practice.* New York: Holt, Rinehart and Winston, 1962.

Gaston, E. T. *Test of Musicality.* Lawrence, Kansas: O'dell's Instrumental Service, 1957.

Gordon, E. *Musical Aptitude Profile.* Boston: Houghton Mifflin, 1965.

Gordon, E. *Iowa Tests of Music Literacy.* Iowa City: The Bureau of Educational Research and Service. The University of Iowa, 1970.

Gordon, E. *The Psychology of Music Teaching.* Englewood Cliffs, N.J.: Prentice-Hall, 1971.

Greene, P. C. Violin intonation. *Journal of the Acoustical Society of America, 1937, 9,* 43-44.

Hebb, D. O. *Organization of Behavior.* New York: Wiley, 1949.

Hickman, A. Some philosophical problems of melody. *Psychology of Music, 1976, 4* (1), 3-11.

Hilgard, E. R., & Bower, G. H. *Theories of Learning* (4th ed.). Englewood Cliffs, N. J.: Prentice-Hall, 1975.

Kamien, R. (ed.). *The Norton Scores* (rev. ed.). New York: Norton, 1972.

Knuth, W. E. *Knuth achievement tests in music.* San Francisco: Creative Arts Research Associates, 1967.

Long, N. H. *The Indiana-Oregon music discrimination test.* Bloomington, Indiana: N. H. Long, 1968 (originally developed as the *Oregon Music Discrimination Test* by K. Hevner in 1935).

Lundin, R. W. *An Objective Psychology of Music* (2nd ed.). New York: Ronald Press, 1967.

Mainwaring, J. Psychological factors in the teaching of music. *British Journal of Educational Psychology, 1951, 21,* 105-121, 199-213.

Meyer, L. B. *Emotion and Meaning in Music.* Chicago: The University of Chicago Press, 1956.

Meyer, L. B. *Music the Arts and Ideas.* Chicago: The University of Chicago Press, 1967.

Michel, P. Optimum development of musical abilities in the first years of life. *Psychology of Music, 1973, 1* (2), 14-20.

Moles, A. *Information Theory and Esthetic Perception* (J. E. Cohen, trans.). Urbana: University of Illinois Press, 1968.

Moog, H. The development of musical experience in children of preschool age. *Psychology of Music, 1976, 4* (2), 38-45.

Mursell, J. L. *Psychology of Music*. New York: W. W. Norton, 1937.

Mursell, J. L. *Music Education, Principles and Programs*. Morristown, N.J.: Silver Burdett, 1956.

Nickerson, J. F. Intonation of solo and ensemble performances of the same melody. *Journal of the Acoustical Society of America*, 1949, *21*, 593-595.

Nye, R. E., and Nye, V. T. *Music in the elementary Schools* (3rd ed.) Englewood Cliffs, N.J.: Prentice-Hall, 1970.

Ortmann, O. On the melodic relativity of tones. *Psychological Monographs*, 1926, *35* (1), 1-35.

Ortmann, O. Interval frequency as a determinant of melodic style. *Peabody Bulletin*, 1937, 3-10.

Ostling, A., Jr. Research in Pythagorean, just temperament, and equal-tempered tunings in performance. *The Journal of Band Research*, 1974, *10* (2), 13-20.

Petzold, R. G. *Auditory Perception of Musical Sounds by Children in the First Six Grades*. Madison: University of Wisconsin, 1966. (ERIC Document Reproduction Service No. ED 010297)

Phillips, D. An investigation of the relationship between musicality and intelligence. *Psychology of Music*, 1976, *4* (2), 16-31.

Radocy, R. E. *Analysis of Three Melodic Properties in Randomly Selected Melodies*. Unpublished research report. The University of Kansas, 1977.

Regelski, T. A. *Principles and Problems of Music Education*. Englewood Cliffs, N. J.: Prentice-Hall, 1975.

Reimer, B. *A Philosophy of Music Education*. Englewood Cliffs, N.J.: Prentice-Hall, 1970.

Roederer, J. G. *Introduction to the Physics and Psychophysics of Music* (2nd ed.). New York: Springer-Verlag, 1975.

Seashore, C. E., Lewis, D. L., & Saetveit, J. G. *Seashore Measures of Musical Talents (revised)*. New York: The Psychological Corporation, 1960.

Sergeant, D., & Roche, S. Perceptual shifts in the auditory information processing of young children. *Psychology of Music*, 1973, *1* (2), 39-48.

Sergeant, D., & Thatcher, G. Intelligence, social status and musical abilities. *Psychology of Music*, 1974, *2* (2), 32-57.

Sessions, R. *Harmonic Practice*. New York: Harcourt Brace, 1951.

Shuter, R. *The Psychology of Musical Ability*. London: Methuen, 1968.

Smits van Waesberge, J. *A Textbook of Melody*. Nijmegen, Netherlands: American Institute of Musicology, 1955.

Taylor, J. A. Perception of tonality in short melodies. *Journal of Research in Music Education*, 1976, *24*, 197-208.

Taylor, S. Musical development of children aged seven to eleven. *Psychology of Music*, 1973, *1* (1), 44-49.

Temko, P. M. The perception of pitch predominance in selected musical examples of avante-garde composers, 1945-1961 (Doctoral dissertation, Florida State University, 1971). *Dissertation Abstracts International*, 1972, *32* (2), 5275. (University Microfilms No. 72-0918)

Terhardt, E., & Zick, M.   Evaluation of the tempered tone scale in normal, stretched and contracted intonation.   *Acustica,* 1975, *32,* 268-274.

Thackray, R.   Tests of harmonic perception.   *Psychology of Music,* 1973, *1* (2), 49-57.

Thackray, R.   Measurement of perception of tonality.   *Psychology of Music,* 1976, *4* (2), 32-37.

357 Songs We Love to Sing.   Minneapolis: Schmitt, Hall, and McCreary, 1938.

Von Hoerner, S.   The definition of major scales, for chromatic scales of 12, 19, and 31 divisions per octave.   *Psychology of Music,* 1975, *4* (1), 12-23.

Watkins, J. G., & Farnum, S. E.   *The Watkins-Farnum Performance Scale.* Winona, Minn.: Hal Leonard Music, 1954.

Watson, C. S.   Psychophysics.   In B. B. Wolman (Ed.), *Handbook of General Psychology.*   Englewood Cliffs, N.J.: Prentice-Hall, 1973.

Weber, M.   *The Rationale and Social Foundations of Music* (D. Martindale, J. Riedel, & G. Neuwirth, Ed. and Trans.).   (n.p.):   Southern Illinois University Press, 1958.

Wing, H. D.   *Standardised Tests of Musical Intelligence.*   The Mere, England: National Foundation for Educational Research, 1961.

Woodruff, A. D.   How music concepts are developed.   *Music Educators Journal,* 1970, 56 (6), 51-54.

Zimmerman, M. P.   *Musical Characteristics of Children.*   Washington: Music Educators National Conference, 1971.

Chapter Five

MUSIC, A PHENOMENON OF MAN

ETHNOMUSICOLOGISTS TELL US that music is present in all cultures, primitive and civilized (Nettl, 1956, p. 6).

> The importance of music, as judged by the sheer ubiquity of its presence, is enormous and when it is considered that music is used both as a summatory mark of many activities and as an integral part of many others which could not be properly executed, or executed at all, without music, its importance is substantially magnified. There is probably no other human cultural activity which is so all-pervasive and which reaches into, shapes and often controls so much of human behavior. (Merriam, 1964, p. 218)

The preceding statement, while made by an individual concerned with the study of music outside Western traditions, accurately reflects the place of music in contemporary society. The ever-presence of music, be it in the concert hall, supermarket, discotheque, home, church, school, radio, television, etc., provides evidence that the statement is equally as true for "sophisticated" as for primitive societies.

While most people would agree that music is important, few stop to consider how it became so important or why. The authors maintain that music's import is more than a philosophical concern. Music serves functions beyond the aesthetic. The present discussion, therefore, examines music from several perspectives; these include its functions, its differences from other sounds, its theories of origin, and its role as a cultural phenomenon.

WHY MUSIC?

Underlying this discussion is Gaston's (1968) advocacy that music is human behavior: "Music is the essence of humanness, not only because man creates it, but because he creates his relationship to it" (p. 15). Gaston maintains that the human brain, which distinguishes man from other animals by making possible speech, communication, and abstract thinking, also enables "significant nonverbal communication in the form of music." Artistic creativity and appreciation are unique to human beings (Roederer, 1975, p. 11).

While most readers probably will agree that music is behavior unique to mankind, there may be less consensus regarding why music exists. While philosophical inquiry has been concerned with music as an art form having aesthetic value, ethnomusicologists have examined music's uses and functions in society. Merriam's (1964, pp. 209-227) insightful discussion of the function of music offers a broader based perspective to the question "Why Music?"

Merriam's Functions of Music

Merriam distinguishes between *uses* and *functions* of music. *Uses* refer to ways or situations in which people employ music; *functions* concern the reasons, particularly the broader purposes, for which it is used. Merriam notes that while nonliterate societies might *use* music in minute and directly applied ways more than do more sophisticated societies, such use is by no means necessarily more *functional*. Music appears to serve essentially the same functions in most cultures. Merriam recognizes ten major musical functions:

1. Emotional expression
2. Aesthetic enjoyment
3. Entertainment
4. Communication
5. Symbolic representation
6. Physical response
7. Enforcing conformity to social norms
8. Validation of social institutions and religious rituals
9. Contribution to the continuity and stability of culture
10. Contributions to the integration of society

Music as *emotional expression* provides a vehicle for expression of ideas and emotions which might not be revealed in ordinary discourse. It can convey either individual or group emotions. The social protest songs of the sixties allowed young people a socially tolerable outlet for expressing displeasure with the world situation. Teenagers with guitar in hand publicly will express feelings toward the opposite sex which otherwise might not be expressed, at least in socially acceptable fashion. By serving as a means for expressing feelings toward subjects which are taboo, music allows the release of otherwise unexpressible thoughts and ideas and provides an opportunity to "let off steam" with respect to social issues.

Music as *aesthetic enjoyment* will be examined in Chapter Six. Suffice it to say here that the creating and contemplating of beauty in music is evident in Western culture as well as many other major cultures including those of China, Japan, Arabia, India, and Indonesia. Gaston (1968) contends that aesthetic experience is ultimately physiological, a function of man's need to create and enrich the sensory environment. Roederer (1975, p. 164) relates musical experience to dispensation of reward and punishment by the limbic system. The making of beauty and sensitivity to beauty presumably comprises a basic need for man's well-being.

Music functions as *entertainment* in all societies. Musselman (1974, p. 140) notes that *entertainment* "engages the attention agreeably" and "amuses or diverts" while *art* is concerned with aesthetic principles. To say that music cannot serve both an entertainment and aesthetic function is difficult and would probably depend on how aesthetic experience is defined. In Western culture, it appears that "popular" music in its broadest sense serves an entertainment function while art music seems to serve an aesthetic function; this is not to say, however, that popular music cannot function as aesthetic nor that art music cannot serve as entertainment. What appears to interest, amuse, or divert one individual might provide an aesthetic experience for another. The crux of the matter, discussed in Chapter Six, is the nature of the response to or involvement with the music. Music as entertainment also can be combined with other functions, particularly in nonliterate societies where the function of music is more directly related to its uses.

Merriam suggests that music's function as *communication* is perhaps the least understood of the ten major functions. He notes that music is *not* a universal language; rather it is shaped in terms of the culture of which it is a part. It may convey emotion or something similar to emotion to those who understand the musical idioms of the culture, although it is doubtful that even individuals within a given culture will receive the same emotional meaning. Farnsworth (1969, p. 80) notes that the mood or emotion conveyed depends on a variety of factors external to the music itself. A listener's personality structure, the mood he or she holds just prior to the listening period, the word meanings of the libretto if there is one, and the listener's attitudes toward music in general and the particular composition in question all affect the mood or emotion perceived. On the other hand, Gaston (1968) maintains that music's ability to provide *nonverbal* communication reflects its potency and value. He maintains that feelings or emotions can be conveyed nonverbally through music and that attempts to express such feelings verbally often are totally inadequate. That which is communicated, however, does not necessarily have common meanings to any large group of people.

Music functions in all societies as a *symbolic representation* of other things, ideas, and behaviors. Merriam cites two essential attributes of a symbol: First, a symbol must be different in kind from that which it symbolizes; otherwise it is an *icon*. Second, a symbol must have ascribed meaning. According to Merriam, symbolism in music can be considered at four levels: (1) the symbolizing evident in song texts, (2) the symbolic reflection of affective or cultural meaning, (3) the reflection of other cultural behavior and values, and (4) the deep symbolism of universal principles.

Music's function as a *physical response* is based on the fact that music does elicit physical response. The use of music with dance is a part of all cultures. Music also elicits, excites, and channels crowd behavior, although the type and extent of the behavior also is shaped culturally.

Enforcing conformity to social norms is one of music's major functions. Merriam notes that songs of social control play an important part in many cultures by providing either direct warnings to erring members of the society or by indirectly indicating what is considered proper behavior. Related to this function is the function of *validation of social institutions and religious rituals.* Social institutions are validated through songs which emphasize the proper and improper in society, as well as through songs which tell people what to do and how to do it. Religious systems are validated through recitation of myth, legend, or doctrine in song.

By providing a construct through which emotion can be expressed, aesthetic experience and entertainment can be received, communication can occur, physical response is elicited, social norms are reinforced, and social institutions and religious rituals are validated, music also *contributes to the continuity and stability of culture.* Merriam maintains that "music is in a sense a summatory activity for the expression of values, a means whereby the heart of the psychology of a culture is exposed" (p. 225).

Perhaps the most important function of music is its *contribution to the integration of society.* Music is truly a social phenomenon, inviting, encouraging, and in some instances almost requiring individuals to participate in group activity. Music is used as a signal to draw people together or as a rallying point around which individuals gather to engage in activities which require group cooperation and coordination.

Music's ability to function in all of the above ways depends, of course, on a commonality of experience with music in the appropriate functional contexts. Emotional expression of taboo subjects is less meaningful to those for whom the subjects never have been taboo. Music with powerful religious significance may lack any validation or ritualistic function for persons who do not practice the religion.

Gaston's Fundamental Considerations of Man in Relation to Music

Gaston's (1968) "fundamental considerations" are in essence another view of music's functions, and while some of these considerations express functions similar to those noted by Merriam, some are sufficiently different to warrant separate discussion. The eight considerations include:

1. Need for aesthetic expression and experience
2. The cultural matrix determines the mode of expression
3. Music and religion are integrally related
4. Music is communication
5. Music is structured reality
6. Music is derived from the tender emotions
7. Music is a source of gratification
8. The potency of music is greatest in the group

Gaston views the *need for aesthetic expression and experience* as essential to the development of humanness. Sensitivity to beauty and the making of beauty are recognized as one of man's most distinguishing characteristics. Individuals who are not sensitive to beauty—whether in music or some other medium—may not be achieving their full potential as human beings; Gaston goes so far as to suggest that they may be handicapped.

While perhaps not a function *per se,* the view that *the cultural matrix determines the mode of expression* is fundamental to all functions of music. While music serves similar functions in nearly all cultures, individuals respond only to functional music within their own culture; i.e. they learn the music of their own culture and generally react to it in terms of the way their particular society reacts to it.

The *integral relationship of music and religion* is evident in virtually every culture. Gaston believes the primary reason for this is that there are some common purposes to religious services and music performances, the greatest of which is their valence for drawing people together. Music and religion go hand in hand to defend against fear and loneliness. Music also seems to be a particularly appropriate mode for reaching for the supernatural, which is a concern of many religious services.

As mentioned above, *music as communication* is viewed by Gaston as nonverbal communication, which provides music its potency and value. Gaston maintains that there would be no need for music if it were possible to communicate verbally that which is easily communicated musically. Even the best verbal descriptions of feelings elicited by music fail to communicate adequately. Perhaps it is because of music's wordless meaning that philosophical explanations of music's meaning are inadequate.

That *music is structured reality* should be evident from discussion in Chapters Three and Four. Just because music is temporal does not suggest that it is any less tangible sensorily than objects which we touch, see, feel, or smell. Gaston maintains that music therefore is a particularly valuable therapeutic medium through which reestablishment of contact with reality can be accomplished for individuals who have withdrawn from society. (This will be discussed further in Chapter Eight.)

Gaston's contention that *music is derived from the tender emotions* is clearly evident in the uses made of today's popular music, as well as in religious music, folk songs, art songs, and patriotic music. All such music reflects a concern for other individuals, and the predominant theme is love in one of its various manifestations—love of one another, love of country, love of God, etc. Music also provides a feeling of belonging, thus providing a sense of closeness to others and the alleviating of loneliness.

> In our culture, as well as in others, *music is nearly always an expression of good will, a reaching out to others,* and is so interpreted. Music, then is a powerful expression of the interdependence of mankind, and from the lullaby to the funeral dirge, an expression of the tender emotions. (Gaston, 1968, p. 25)

The recognition of *music as a source of gratification* is particularly apparent in children and adolescents, although it also is apparent in adults. Gratification is a by-product of achievement per se rather than competition. Music provides opportunities for achievement in noncompetitive situations. The self-esteem which results from musical accomplishment contributes greatly to an individual's state of well-being.

That *the potency of music is greatest in the group* should be self-evident. Music is a social phenomenon which invites and encourages participation. Music provides group activities which bring together individuals who otherwise might not come in contact with one another. It provides them opportunities to interact in intimate yet ordered and socially desirable ways.

In conclusion it should be noted that the functions of music recognized by Merriam and Gaston in many respects are overlapping, but with different labels attached to them. Further, the various functions are not discrete; given musical experiences may serve different functions for different individuals and more than one function for a given individual. The important point is that music is human behavior that serves a variety of functions in virtually every culture. While some cultures, particularly Western ones, place greater emphasis on the aesthetic function, all functions contribute to the importance of music in society.

WHAT MAKES SOME SOUNDS MUSIC?

Studies of the development of musical behavior suggest that differential responses to musical sounds and other sounds become evident during infancy (Michel, 1973; Moog, 1976; Fridman, 1973). Virtually every child and adult "knows" what music is. The enculturation process assures that early in life children develop a concept of music, albeit vague, ill-defined, and nonverbalized. That individuals' concepts reflect cultural bias is readily apparent, although the authors believe that most individuals will recognize another culture's music as music even though it may sound "strange."

Music of all cultures involves the organization of sounds with varying pitches, loudness levels, and timbral qualities within a rhythmic framework. When one considers the range of perceptually just noticeable differences in pitch, loudness, and timbre it would appear that the variety of sounds and sound combinations which could comprise music are infinite.

It also can be argued that all sound has the attributes of pitch (perhaps indefinite and transient), loudness, and timbre and that these sounds are temporal. Further, while the claim is usually made that musical sounds have organization, it also is apparent that many "nonmusical" sounds have discernible organization, e.g. speech, sounds of machinery, and many natural sounds. Also, some contemporary music, *musique concrete*, records and incorporates sounds of nature into a recognized musical style.

The question of why some sounds (but not others) are music has been studied by philosophers, musicologists, psychologists, and theorists, thereby resulting in a variety of explanations, ranging from physical explanations in terms of the harmonic structure of musical sounds, to elaborate metaphysical theories to psychological characteristics. Others (Gaston, 1968, Beament, 1977) even suggest that the basic difference in what is recognized as music is ultimately a function of the physiological or biological nature of man.

Perhaps there is no acceptable answer for everyone, but there appears to be one basic difference in the sounds of nature and the sounds of music. Sounds of nature are "constantly changing from instant to instant in the frequencies present and in the amplitudes of the frequencies" (Beament, 1977, p. 7). Beament notes that music primarily involves sounds with sustained constant frequencies (heard as fixed pitches) without which melodic and harmonic music could not exist. He maintains that fixed pitches "are virtually an *artefact* [sic] *of man.*"

Revesz (1953, p. 219) holds that music should manifest three further characteristics: (1) fixed intervals, (2) their transposition to various pitches, and (3) their use in heterogeneous rhythmically articulated tone combinations. His definition would exclude (as music) emotional outbursts and songs with no graspable and recurrent intervals.

Whether one would want to be as limiting as Revesz in defining musical sounds is doubtful, but the use of fixed pitches in music is virtually universal. Further, psychophysical explanations of the processing of music support the need for using fixed pitches. Roederer (1975, pp. 161-163) maintains that fixed pitches are essential for perception of music. A tone has to last a minimum period of time for it to be processed by the brain. Sounds continually changing in frequency do not allow sufficient processing time. In everyday terms, it is easier to identify pitches of sounds which have a certain duration than pitches of sounds which pass by quickly. Even with music constructed in a tonal harmonic framework, music students find the notating of a given aurally presented melody much more difficult when the tempo is quite fast as opposed to when it is slower.

Roederer (pp. 161-162) suggests that recurring patterns of a relatively small number of fixed pitches have come to be used for music within given cultures because

> it is easier for the brain to process, identify, and store in its memory a melody that is made up of a time sequence of discrete pitch values that bear a certain relationship to each other . . . rather than one that sweeps continuously up and down over all possible frequencies.

While the use of fixed pitches appears to be an attribute of sound which is used in most music, it should be noted that the range of sounds used in music has many additional attributes for which adequate "reasons for being" have not been offered. Apparently, however, since the beginning of mankind sounds have been combined as a construct, music, which has served a variety of functions. The particular combinations of sounds have varied from culture to culture, although the attribute of fixed pitches appears to be present in all. Therefore, any "answer" to the question "What makes some sounds music?" must consider that musical sounds vary from culture to culture. The diversity of sound combinations which various cultures consider music is great.

The ultimate answer to the question under consideration must be in terms of the *function* of the sounds within a given cultural context. If sounds are created or combined by a human being, are recognized as music by some group of people, and serve some function which music has come to serve for mankind, then those sounds are music.

ORIGINS OF MUSIC

If music is viewed as human behavior, explanations of its origins must be in terms of how man came to use sounds for musical functions; metaphysical and etheral explanations, while perhaps of interest to those examining music from a philosophical perspective, are inadequate.

Unfortunately, music's temporal character does not afford anthropologists the same opportunities for studying its beginnings as do many other artifacts of human behavior. While the study of music in primitive societies offers some insights, the origins of music and musical behavior still are primarily a matter of conjecture.

Nettl (1956, pp. 134-137) and Revesz (1953, pp. 224-235) have summarized the prominent theories regarding music's origins; in addition, each has offered another theory. The present discussion reviews the theories they discuss as well as one implicit in the writings of Gaston (1968).

The *Darwinian theory* of music's origins holds that music developed in conjunction with sexual instincts and was originally a mating call. Proponents of this theory cite the mating calls of some animals and bird songs which often serve a sexual function. The song was used in seeking a mate. Although most music today is related to the tender emotions, there is little evidence to support the Darwinian theory. Both Nettl and Revesz criticize the theory, although from different perspectives. Revesz notes that birds "sing" outside of the mating season and suggests that music in primitive cultures today should be preponderantly love songs (which they are not) if the theory were true. Nettl says that perhaps the weightiest argument against the theory is the absence of music-like mating calls among apes.

A *theory of rhythm* suggests that music evolved from its close relationship to dance. That dance is ordinarily accompanied by music in many cultures is indisputable. Revesz acknowledges that dance provides motives or occasions for singing and music-making, but maintains that because they are used together offers little or no support for the argument that music evolved from dance or vice versa. "It does not make us see how man came to combine movements with words and notes, to choose a number of fixed intervals in the continuous tone-series, and to link the intervals together in larger combinations" (Revesz, p. 228).

A *work song theory*, attributed to Karl Buecher, holds that work songs provide the impetus for music. Buecher's study of Western folksongs revealed a number of such songs, and he postulated that primitive people must have devised songs to coordinate their work efforts. Nettl criticizes this theory because the world's simplest cultures do not have work songs, and even when they do work in groups, they do not recognize rhythmic efficiency.

Revesz recognizes a *theory of imitation* which suggests that music originated as a result of man's imitation of bird songs. Support for this theory generally has been because some birds' songs consistently tend to use some fixed pitches and the same relative intervals. Perhaps the strongest argument against this theory is the fact that no primitive cultures have songs which are imitative of bird calls. Revesz also asserts that supporters of this theory have overlooked the fact that the vocal utterances of animals, even when serving as mating calls or alarm cries, are merely direct and automatic reactions of biological states of the animals. Bird songs and animal sounds are dominated by instincts, whereas man's music is guided by purposive, conceptual, and aesthetic behaviors.

The *theory of expression* reflects the view that music evolved from "emotional" speech. The argument made for this theory is that as an individual becomes emotional in his or her speech, the speech patterns acquired the characteristic of fixed pitches. Revesz notes, however, that the speech-sounds manifesting emotion have nothing in common with music or song; neither do they serve a musical function. They are reflexive and invariable expressions of momentary emotion which lack any sort of musical significance.

What Nettl calls a *theory of impassioned speech* appears to be somewhat similar to the above theory of expression and to what Revesz calls the *theory of melodic speech*. The basic view is that music evolved from the accentuation and intonation of human speech. These melodic characteristics arise in excited speech and during recitation, and gradually evolved into music. Revesz recognizes that recitative-like speech is present in most cultures, but questions whether such speech had any formative influence on music's development. He further argues it cannot be assumed that recitative speech developed in advance of the most primitive form of music.

Revesz notes that parallels have been drawn between the beginnings of music and the *lalling melodies of children*. The assumption of this view is that primitive peoples created melodies in a manner similar to the ways young children's earliest melodies are created. However, he quickly discounts this theory on the basis that young children's melodies are conditioned by the singing and other music they have heard in their environment. Obviously, music's originators would have had no such models to condition their efforts.

Several versions of a *communication theory* have been offered. Revesz is a proponent of the communication theory, labeling his the calling signal theory. The basic view is that individuals desiring to communicate a message from a distance use shouting or calling signals. Such signals, maintains Revesz, acquire musical characteristics in that they use fixed pitches and varying loudness levels. Nettl, while noting that Carl Stumpf also advocated this theory, disregards it because his study of primitive cultures reveals that calling signals with fixed pitches are not used.

Nettl also cites Siegfried Nadel's *theory of communication with the supernatural* as one view of music's origins. Nettl recognizes the theory's logic in view of the close connection between music and religion, but suggests that it is supported by little more than circumstantial evidence. Further, he maintains that "the high degree of complexity in many contemporary primitive religious songs discourages assuming that they are survivals of the earliest musical style" (p. 135).

Nettl's theory of music's origins assumes that an undifferentiated method of communication existed in the earliest primitive cultures. Such communication was neither speech nor music, but possessed three attributes common to both: pitch, stress, and duration. There were no fixed pitches nor definite vowels and consonants; rather, the sounds were grunts, cries, and wails which sounded neither like speech nor music. Nettl hypothesizes that through a long, gradual stage of differentiation and specialization in culture language acquired the characteristics of vowels and consonants while music acquired the characteristic of fixed pitches. In summary, there are three stages to Nettl's theory: (1) undifferentiated communication, (2) differentiation between music and language, and (3) differentiation between various musical styles. Nettl acknowledges that it is only for the last stage that any data are available.

Gaston's views on the origin of music hold that music developed along with the beginnings of family and society, thus giving music "a biological as well as a cultural basis" (p. 11). With the development of the brain's cortex, primitive man was able to suppress rage and hostility, a necessity for the development of society. Cortical development also freed the primitive female from blind, instinctive behavior that would cause her to accept a different male at each period of estrus. The cortical became dominant over the endocrine factor. These two factors, both a result of the brain's cortical development, fostered the beginnings of family with its resulting division of labor, modified aggressive behavior between male and female, and increased communication. "All this leads to a uniqueness in humans, among all animals, of the mother-child relationship, without which there would be no culture as we know it" (Gaston, p. 11). The human infant is highly dependent on the mother for a long period of time. While the primitive father provided food and protection, the mother devoted time to the care of her baby. It could be hypothesized that as the primitive mother sought to soothe her child and express feelings for it, her soothing efforts assumed the rhythmic character of lullabies. Further, the kinds of sounds which are most effective in soothing are repetitious, sustained, and legato. (See Chapter Eight.) These early lullabies, developed for functional purposes, could have been one of the earliest forms of music.

Perhaps "the truth" regarding the origins of music never will be known. Whatever its beginnings, the authors submit that the earliest music, just as all music today, including art music, ultimately was functional to the well-being of its creators.

MUSIC IN CULTURE

Whatever its origins, music is human behavior which occurs within a cultural context. Through the enculturation process each social order develops its institutions and artifacts for perpetuation of itself, and music is one of the few things common to all cultures (Nettl, p. 71). Previously in this chapter it has been noted that music serves some common functions in most societies even though the musical styles and forms vary from culture to culture. Through its functionality to society, music has become an integral cultural component, serving both as a cohesive and perpetuating force. On the other hand, music itself also reflects cultural values and temperaments. Max Weber's (1958, p. xxvi) analysis of the rational and social foundations of music even suggests that the difference between Western music and that of other (particularly Eastern) cultures is rooted in Western peoples' temperament and their drives to rationalize and understand environmental phenomena.

Perhaps Lomax (1968, p. 133) best summarizes music's cultural role when he suggests that music is man's vehicle for expressing what is most basic in his relationships with others. Lomax's examination of music in different cultural settings revealed that a culture's favorite music "reflects and reinforces the kinds of behavior essential to its main subsistence efforts and to its central and controlling social institution" (p. 133). Nettl (p. 93) concurs that the character of a society and its quality of life greatly influence the style of its music; although he also notes that other factors, e.g. technological level of the society, types of raw materials available for instrument construction, amount of contact with other cultures, attitudes toward cultural change or continuity, and the development of literacy and musical notation, also influence the development of a culture's music.

Nettl (1975, pp. 71-100), studying music's role in Iranian culture, examined three distinct musical traditions: folk music of rural areas, popular music of the cities, and the traditional classical music. While the three musical traditions reflected different walks of Iranian life, it was apparent that each also reflected the values and attitudes of the respective subculture. For example, a dominant mood of traditional Iranian classical music is sadness. Nettl notes that Iran (Persia) has a long tragic history of warfare, struggle, and divisiveness and that its music reflects the bitterness and other feelings resulting from such a history.

The work of Nettl (1956), Hamm, Nettl, and Byrnside (1975), Merriam (1964), and Lomax (1968) alone supports the hypothesis that music is an integral part of culture.   Lundin (1967) and Farnsworth (1969) premise their psychology of music texts on the view that music is a cultural and social phenomenon.   Many musicologists and music historians concerned with the development of music in traditional Western culture also recognize music as a sociocultural force which must be studied within its societal and cultural framework.

In short, music's role in culture should be apparent.   Study of musical behavior must recognize this.

SUMMARY

Following are the major points of this chapter:
1. Music is present in all cultures.
2. Music is unique to human beings.
3. Merriam's ten functions of music include
   a. emotional expression
   b. aesthetic enjoyment
   c. entertainment
   d. communication
   e. symbolic representation
   f. physical response
   g. enforcing conformity to social norms
   h. validation of social institution and religious rituals
   i. contribution to the continuity and stability of culture
   j. contributions to the integration of society
4. Gaston's fundamental considerations of man in relation to music include:
   a. need for aesthetic expression and experience
   b. the cultural matrix determines the mode of expression
   c. music and religion are integrally related
   d. music is (nonverbal) communication
   e. music is a source of gratification
   f. music is derived from the tender emotions
   g. the potency of music is greatest in the group
5. Music of all cultures involves the organization of sounds with varying pitches, loudness levels, and timbral qualities within a rhythmic framework.

6. Fixed pitches are an attribute of music.
7. Sounds which are created or combined by a human being, are recognized as music by some group of people, and serve some function for man may be considered music.
8. Some theories regarding music's origins include the
   a. Darwinian theory
   b. theory of rhythm
   c. work song theory
   d. theory of imitation
   e. theory of expression
   f. theory of melodic speech
   g. communication theory
   h. Nettl's theory of an undifferentiated method of primitive communication
   i. Gaston's view that music developed with the beginning of family
9. Music reflects the values, attitudes, and temperament of a culture.

REFERENCES

Beament, J. The biology of music. *Psychology of Music,* 1977, *5* (1), 3-18.

Farnsworth, P. R. *The Social Psychology of Music* (2nd ed). Ames: The Iowa State University Press, 1969.

Fridman, R. The first cry of the newborn: Basis for the child's future musical development. *Journal of Research in Music Education,* 1973, *21,* 264-269.

Gaston, E. T. Man and music. In E. T. Gaston (Ed.), *Music in Therapy.* New York: MacMillan, 1968.

Hamm, C., Nettl, B., & Byrnside, R. *Contemporary Music and Music Cultures.* Englewod Cliffs, N. J.: Prentice-Hall, 1975.

Lomax, A., *et al. Folk Song Style and Culture.* Washington, D.C.: American Association for the Advancement of Science, 1968.

Lundin, R. W. *An Objective Psychology of Music* (2nd ed.). New York: Ronald Press, 1967.

Merriam, A. P. *The Anthropology of Music.* (n.p.): Northwestern University Press, 1964.

Michel, P. Optimal development of musical abilities in the first years of life. *Psychology of Music,* 1973, *1* (2), 14-20.

Moog, H. The development of musical experience in children of preschool age. *Psychology of Music,* 1976, *4* (2), 38-45.

Musselman, J. A. *The Uses of Music.* Englewood Cliffs, N.J.: Prentice-Hall, 1974.

Nettl, B. Music in primitive cultures: Iran, a recently developed nation. In Hamm, C., Nettl, B., & Byrnside, R., *Contemporary Music and Music Cultures.* Englewod Cliffs, N.J.: Prentice-Hall, 1975.

Revesz, G. *Introduction to the Psychology of Music* (G. I. C. deCourcy, Trans.) London: Longmans, Green, 1953.

Roederer, J. G. *Introduction to the Physics and Psychophysics of Music* (2nd ed.). New York: Springer-Verlag, 1975.

Weber, M. *The Rational and Social Foundations of Music* (D. Martindale, J. Riedel, G. Neuwirth, trans. and ed.). (n.p.): Southern Illinois University Press, 1958.

Chapter Six

AFFECTIVE BEHAVIORS AND MUSIC

The preceding chapter primarily was concerned with the role
and value of music for groups, whereas affective behaviors are
considered herein primarily in terms of individuals. In recent years
psychologists have become increasingly concerned with affective
behavior in its various manifestations, and with this increased
interest several issues have surfaced. For example: What is
meant by *affect* and *emotion?* Is *aesthetic* behavior the same as
affective behavior? Are changes in physiological rates affective
response? Can the affective and aesthetic be examined from a
behavioral perspective? Are philosophical explanations of the
aesthetic experience sufficient?

The purpose of this chapter therefore is to examine some of
these basic questions. Discussed are extended definitions of central terms, the range of behaviors which are considered affective,
some approaches to the study of the affective responses to music including physiological and mood responses, philosophical and experimental aesthetics, musical meaning, and the variables which
contribute to musical meaning.

EXTENDED DEFINITIONS

Terms essential to the discussion are affect, emotion, and aesthetic. While the terms perhaps are encountered most often in
philosophical discussions, the intent here is to examine them from
a psychological perspective. That the distinction between psychological and philosophical is not clear-cut is evident, particularly
for behaviors which traditionally have been recognized as subjective and personal. However, some of the confusion and contro-

versy appears to be caused by the lack of adequate definitions for the terms.

Affect

For hundreds of years students of human behavior have recognized three basic categories: thinking, feeling, and acting.   Psychologists today refer to these as cognitive, affective, and psychomotor behaviors respectively.   Affective behaviors include those which have a significant *feeling* component.

As used in everyday life, feeling has a variety of meanings, e.g. tactual perception (to *feel* the texture of a piece of cloth), cognitive belief (he *feels* something is true), emotion, or simply whether an experience is pleasant or unpleasant.   Psychologists do not use the term in a consistent way.   To clarify matters, Young (1973) has summarized eight classes of affective processes: (1) *simple feelings* of pleasantness or unpleasantness in response to sensory stimuli, (2) negative and positive *organic feelings* such as hunger, thirst, dietary satisfaction, or physical well-being, (3) *activity feelings* including appetitive states such as hunger or sexual desire and also including activity feelings such as enthusiasm or aversion, (4) moral, *aesthetic,* religious, or social sentiments and attitudes based upon previous experiences, education, and training, (5) persisting *moods* such as cheerfulness, elation, anxiety, or grief, (6) pathological *affects* of deep depression, apathy, or hostility, (7) *emotions* such as fear, anger, laughing, agony, or embarrassment, and (8) *temperaments* such as vivaciousness, cheerfulness, or moodiness.

As should be apparent, affect is a broad term applied to a wide variety of human feeling behaviors.   The problem is further complicated by the fact that affective processes are related to virtually everything that is psychological—perception, memory, learning, reasoning, and action (Young).   Therefore, any discussion of affective behavior in relation to music must be defined in terms more definitive than just whether or not they are affective.

Emotion

One school of thought regarding music's import is that it conveys or expresses emotion.   However, proponents of this position appear to be using the term *emotion* in a broader sense than contemporary psychologists use the term. Today emotion is considered only one type of affect. Young (p. 750) defines emotion as a disturbed affective process or state *"which originates in the psychological situation and which is revealed by marked bodily changes in smooth muscles, glands, and gross behaviors."* This definition suggests that emotional behavior is a relatively temporary state—a departure from the normal state of composure. Emotions involve perception and memory and always include an environmental factor, present or past.

Meyer (1956, pp. 13-32) has theorized how emotion is aroused by music. Central to his theory is the view that emotion is aroused when a tendency to respond is arrested or inhibited. An individual's tendency to respond is a result of previous experience with music of the style to which he or she is listening. From the previous experience the individual has developed expectations (tendencies to respond) regarding what types of patterns might come next in the music. To the degree that the anticipated patterns are not forthcoming, i.e. they are delayed or do not come at all, *tension,* or *emotion,* is aroused.

Listeners to Western music, for example, learn that certain chords or "sound terms" imply certain other musical entities. When the expected musical consequent is delayed, suspense is aroused. However, Meyer maintains that the mere arousal of tension via the inhibition of musical expectations is of little import in itself. To have *aesthetic meaning* the tension must be followed by a fulfillment of the expectation and hence resolution of the tension. More will be said of this later.

The important point is that Meyer's view of how emotion is created in music is consistent with the contemporary psychological viewpoint that emotion is a relatively temporary disruption of a norm. Further, emotion is seen as an essential component of aesthetic meaning, although emotion alone is, in Meyer's words, "aesthetically valueless" (p. 28).

Aesthetic

Aesthetic feeling is a particular type of affective behavior and is the outcome of aesthetic experience. The term *aesthetic* usually is used in relation to art and its value or meaning, although it is recognized that aesthetic feeling could result from interactions with phenomena of nature or from interactions with non-art objects or events. What makes some interactions *aesthetic* and others not has been subject to much discussion by philosophers, even to the point that aesthetics traditionally has been viewed as a branch of philosophy. While it is recognized that philosophical theory and discussion have provided many valuable insights regarding the nature and value of aesthetic feeling and experience, the present discussion also recognizes aesthetic feeling and experience as psychological behaviors which are subject to study via the same methods that are used to examine other forms of human behavior. Unfortunately, psychologists only recently have begun to study aesthetic behavior, while philosophical examination of the aesthetic has a long history. To the extent that psychologists will be able to substantiate philosophical theory regarding aesthetic behaviors, theory will be strengthened. If, however, psychological investigations do not support theory, then the dilemma regarding the aesthetic will continue to exist.

Common to most discussions of aesthetics is the concern for beauty, and it is with definitions of beauty that difficulties arise. When one says something is beautiful, he or she is reflecting a value. What causes this something to be valued as beautiful is subject to much debate. Some would hold that the beauty is inherent in the object or event due to its structure and form. In other words, beauty is a property of the object or event and remains so regardless of what an individual respondent might "feel." The opposite view is that "beauty is in the eyes of the beholder." Perhaps Saint Thomas Aquinas, as cited by Rader and Jessup (1976, p. 20), stated it best: "Let that be called *beauty,* the very perception of which pleases." The statement has two implications: First, beauty gives pleasure, and second, not everything that gives pleasure is beautiful, but only that which gives pleasure in immediate perception. Whether the final truth regarding beauty lies in either of these positions is subject to conjecture. The point here is that beauty is the subject matter and stimulus for aesthetic experience and feeling. However, for an experience to be considered aesthetic experience, it must reflect other characteristics.

Characteristics of aesthetic experience have been described in many ways by many writers, but the present discussion is based primarily on the descriptions offered by two current advocates of aesthetic education, Bennett Reimer (1970, pp. 72-87) and Gerard L. Knieter (1971, pp. 3-20). Both recognize aesthetic experience as human experience, and while they also recognize beauty in nature and other objects or events which are not primarily intended to be art, they generally discuss aesthetic experience in relation to artworks.

Knieter cites five characteristics of an aesthetic experience: (1) focus, (2) perception, (3) affect, (4) cognition, and (5) cultural matrix. *Focus* suggests that an individual must devote his attention to the artwork and respond thereto. *Perception* is viewed as the process through which sensory data are received and through which the individual becomes aware of the artwork. Knieter sees two basic types of *affect* occurring during the aesthetic experience, physiological change and feelingful reaction. Concomitant with the aesthetic experience are changes in blood pressure, respiration, and psychogalvanic response. The feelingful reaction may vary from simple feeling to complex emotional sets. *Cognition* is a particularly important attribute of aesthetic experience which reflects the intellectual processes involved: analysis, synthesis, abstraction, generalization, evaluation. Knowledge and learning regarding the stylistic attributes of a musical work are essential for aesthetic response. Finally, the *cultural matrix* is reflected in the aesthetic experience. Aesthetic values are learned within a cultural context.

Reimer's characteristics of the aesthetic experience differ from those cited by Knieter. He emphasizes that an individual's interest and reactions must be absorbed by or immersed in aesthetic qualities of the music being attended to; the feelingful reaction must be with the expressive aesthetic qualities rather than with any symbolic designation. For Reimer, the aesthetic qualities of music conveyed by melody, harmony, rhythm, tone color, texture, and form are "expressive of or analogous to or isomorphic with the patterns of felt life or subjective reality or the conditions of livingness" (p. 74). The individual must be involved with the *embodied* meaning of the music rather than any symbolic designations it might have.*

Reimer also maintains that the aesthetic experience is valuable in and of itself, is not a means toward non-aesthetic experience, and serves no utilitarian purpose. Taken at face value this might suggest a contradiction to the authors' view that aesthetic experience serves a human function and that music also serves other functions. This is not the case. While the aesthetic experience may appear to have no purpose or *use,* it still serves a valuable *function,* providing an individual an opportunity for feelingful experience above and beyond the meeting of basic human needs. Maslow (1970, p. 51) contends that aesthetic experience is a human need, albeit one with which people become involved only when their physiological, safety, and certain psychological needs have been met. Therefore, an aesthetic experience can be valuable in and of itself to the experiencing individual; however, the very fact that the experience holds value for the individual suggests that it is functional to his well-being.

Reimer's final characteristic of the aesthetic experience is that it must involve the qualities of a perceptible "thing." The "thing" is the sensuous element, the "formed substance," containing the aesthetic qualities which an individual perceives and responds to.

Implict in both of the above descriptions is that aesthetic experience requires psychological *involvement* with the aesthetic stimulus, *perception* of interacting events within the artwork, *cognition* of the interplay among the events within the aesthetic stimulus, and *feeling* reaction thereto. Aesthetic experience differs from most affective experience in that it must involve perception and cognition of an aesthetic stimulus. Without the immediacy of the aesthetic stimulus, the affective behavior cannot be an aesthetic behavior.

By the definition given here, an aesthetic experience is limited

---

Embodied musical meaning results from expectations *within* the music whereas *designative* meaning refers to meaning symbolized by the music. These differences are discussed in more detail later in the chapter.

to that experience which results in feeling reactions to perceived interactions of attributes within an artwork or some other stimulus in which an observer (listener in music) is involved perceptually, perceives beauty therein, and has a feeling reaction thereto. The limiting of aesthetic experience to experiences from which the feeling results from perception of the events within the aesthetic stimulus does not, however, deny that music and other aesthetic stimuli elicit many other significant feelings. Certainly the hearing of a composition with which one has had previous associations can elicit feelings regarding those associations. For example, hearing a theme song of a movie which one has seen generally elicits thoughts and feelings regarding the movie. To say, however, that this feeling is aesthetic feeling is questionable. On the other hand, it does not deny that the feelings thus elicited may be extremely meaningful to the individual. More will be said of this type of feeling response to music in another section of this chapter.

TYPES OF AFFECTIVE RESPONSES TO MUSIC

Aesthetic experience as just described represents but one type of affective response to music. However, to say that aesthetic experience is the only important feeling response elicited by music is to deny a broad spectrum of affective behaviors related to music. The present discussion does not purport to consider the relative value of the respective types of affective behaviors in relation to aesthetic experience per se, but it does recognize that various affective behaviors are important to greater or lesser degrees for many individuals. The relative value of the various affective modes differs for *individuals,* and it is unlikely that any given affective mode, even the aesthetic mode, is of greater or lesser value for all individuals.

The variety of affective responses to music is great. Concomitant with all types are *physiological reactions* of the autonomic nervous system. Hector Berlioz's descriptions of his reactions while listening to a piece of music, as reported by Schoen (1940, p. 103), included increased blood circulation, violent pulse rate, muscle contractions, trembling, numbness of the feet and hands, and partial paralysis of the nerves controlling hearing and vision. While it is doubtful that many individuals' physiological mechanisms are affected to the extent that Berlioz claimed, there is objective evidence to support the view that changes in certain physiological rates do accompany affective behaviors. Whether these changes themselves are affective behaviors is subject to interpretation. The true behaviorist insists that they are because they can be observed (via certain measuring instruments); another view, however, is that they are merely physiological correlates of affective behavior, because feelings by definition are psychological rather than physiological.

A common affective behavior is the *mood* or *character* response. In Western cultures certain musical sound patterns have come to be reflective of different psychological states. Certain music is soothing or relaxing, other music makes an individual feel happy or sad, while still other music may elicit feelings of frustration, agitation. The range of moods which may be characterized by music is as great as the range of moods people can feel. There is no question but what music can elicit mood response; further, within a given cultural context there tends to be agreement among individuals as to the mood elicited by certain types of music. While the variables underlying this are many, it should be noted that whatever mood response is elicited by music is much more than a response to any inherent mood or character of the music. Mood responses to music, just as virtually all other responses to music, are essentially determined by an individual's previous experience with music. *Learning underlies all musical behavior, affective or otherwise.*

Affective responses to music also may be the result of *associations* an individual makes with music. The most common example of this is when an individual responds to the programmatic content of music. Feelings of this type are in relation to an event or story with which they have previously associated the music. The popularity of recordings of movie soundtracks suggests that many people want to re-experience the occasions through listening to the music. The same type of associations are made with opera and musical comedy. The feeling response is to much more than the music itself. Listening to music of one's childhood or adolescence evokes feelings of childhood and adolescent experiences associated with that music. Lovers recall special occasions through "their song." The power of music to elicit strong feelings of experiences associated with it provides individuals with a mechanism for re-experiencing many significant events within their lives.

Another type of association experience is labeled by Reimer (1970, p. 92) as *intrasubjective* experience. Intrasubjective experiences differ from other association experiences in that the associations evoked by the music are imaginary stories or visual scenes. While the type of story or scene imagined is most likely influenced by the individual's previously experienced associations of music with programmatic content, the intrasubjective affective response is to fanciful images rather than direct associations.

While philosophers and aestheticians have been greatly concerned with the wordless meaning of music, there has been relatively little study of the feelings evoked by the words of songs. One only has to listen to the words of folk music, popular music, and art music, however, to realize that the verbal messages of music are primarily affective. Feelings of love, frustration, and virtually every deep-seated and persisting type of human feeling that individuals hold toward one another have been verbalized through song. Feelings expressed or elicited through blues, country-western, and rock music are primary examples of the affective impact of combined word meanings and music.

Words and music also have been combined to express and elicit affective reactions to all types of social, political, and religious issues. Music has been used as a persuasive tool throughout the history of mankind. As noted in Chapter Five, some of the basic functions of music are to sway feelings. There is little doubt that patriotic, social protest, and religious songs can arouse strong affective response. Such songs are symbols, are perceived and reacted to accordingly, and serve a legitimate and important function (Reimer, p. 92).

Many additional human behaviors related to music have affective components in greater or lesser degree. Musical *preferences* (discussed in Chapter Seven), musical *interests*, musical *values*, *attitudes* toward music in general and various styles of music, and *appreciation* of music all reflect affective components. While it is recognized that these behaviors also are dependent in many respects on knowledge, their importance to music educators is great. Appreciations, values, and preferences are of essence to music education. Interests and attitudes are central to both the process and outcomes of music education.

As should be apparent, there is a wide range of affective behaviors related to music. The extent of psychologists' understanding of them, however, is quite limited. Perhaps the limited understanding is due in part to the ways in which affective responses to music have been studied. The next section of this chapter, therefore, examines the primary ways in which affective responses to music have been examined.

APPROACHES TO STUDY OF AFFECTIVE RESPONSES TO MUSIC

Approaches to the study of affective response to music traditionally have been of three types: (1) physiological measures, (2) mood responses, and (3) philosophical inquiry. Lundin (1967, pp. 150-203) categorizes physiological and mood responses as affective and philosophical inquiry as aesthetic, but the present discussion views all three types as approaches to the understanding of affective responses to music. More recently there has been a growing body of research, following the work of Berlyne (1971, 1974), called experimental aesthetics. This section, therefore, discusses approaches to the study of affective responses under four headings: (1) physiological measures, (2) mood responses, (3) philosophical inquiry, and (4) experimental aesthetics.

Physiological Measures

Few musicians or psychologists deny that music can evoke changes in the rates of bodily processes, but there is little or no agreement regarding the degree to which these changes are reflective of affective responses to music. Affective behaviors are *psychological* behaviors whereas measures of the rates of various bodily processes are *physiological* behaviors. The study of the interrelationships between physiological and psychological aspects of behavior is called *psychophsiology* (Sternbach, 1966, p. 3). If one is seeking to understand affective responses to music through study of changes in the rates of certain bodily processes, then one is engaged in psychophysiological research.

With the exception of a few studies, research on physiological responses to music stops short of actually examining interrelationships between the two types of behaviors, hence providing little insight regarding affective responses to music. Generally such studies involve the presentation of a musical stimulus as the independent variable and use polygraph data regarding the various physiological rates as the dependent variable. The most frequently studied dependent measures include heart rate, respiration rate, respiration amplitude, and galvanic skin response.

Schoen (1927, 1940), Diserens and Fine (1939), Lundin (1967), and Farnsworth (1969) have summarized early research on the physiological response to music. A brief chronology of some research conducted prior to 1950 follows:

1880—Dogiel discovered that music influences blood circulation, heart rate, and respiration.

1888—Féré used music as a stimulus in studying galvanic skin response (GSR)

1895—Binet and Courtier measured pulse and respiration rate changes with changes in music.

1900—Féré discovered that isolated tones, scales, and tonal sequences energize muscles.

1906—Foster and Gamble concluded that music generally causes faster and shallower breathing regardless of loudness or mode.

1912—Weld recorded changes in pneumographic (breathing) and plethysmographic (blood supply) responses as a function of listening to music.

1918—Vescelius reported that music without abrupt key changes can relieve high fever, high pulse rate, and hysteria.

1925—Wechsler found that subjects' GSR curves changed when music was played, although he noted that such curve changes were smaller than those elicited by direct sensory stimulation such as the prick of a pin.

1927—Hyde studied the effects of different kinds of musical select-
tions on the cardiovascular responses of individuals fond of
music, those indifferent or insensitive to music, as well as
the effects of music on individuals of different nationality
and training. She reported that people are psychologically
and physiologically affected unfavorably by "tragic mournful tones" and favorably by "gay rhythmical melodies," concluding that music can be effective in physiotherapy as well
as psychotherapy.

1932—Misbach studied the effects of isolated tonal stimuli on
GSR, blood pressure, and pulse changes. He found no
significant pulse rate or blood pressure changes, although
GSR changes were observed for tones of 512 Hz or higher
and increased in magnitude as frequency became higher.

1933—Wascho found that changes in pulse rate and blood pressure
occurred when different types of music were played. More
definite rhythms and melodies yielded more definite physiological changes.

1934—Phares reported a positive relationship between amount of
GSR change and the strength of the verbally reported
pleasantness of music. She also reported, however, that the
GSR results were of little value in her analysis of music
appreciation.

1947—Dreher compared subjects' verbal reports and GSR responses to various types of music. Musically trained subjects showed a relationship between GSR and mood as
measured by adjectives checked on the Hevner Adjective Circle; data for untrained subjects revealed no relationship.

While the bulk of this early research on physiological responses to music has been in terms of heart rate, respiration rate,
and galvanic skin response, it should be noted that a variety of
other physical responses also have been examined in at least one
study. These responses include the patellar (knee-jerk) reflex,
gastric motility, the pilomotor response (movement of hairs on

the skin), electroencephalography (brain wave response), and electromyography (muscle tension). Because most of these approaches reflect isolated studies, the balance of this discussion examines the more frequently studied physiological responses to music. It should be recognized, however, that these studies for the most part are merely descriptions of physiological responses to various musical stimuli and therefore cannot be viewed as true affective responses. They are indicative of the physiological concomitants of affective responses, but with the exception of a very few studies no attempts have been made to examine relationships between these types of responses and affective responses. The balance of this discussion relies heavily on Dainow's (1977) recent review and synthesis of the literature regarding the physiological response to music. His review cites many of the studies noted above as well as the more recent research. Readers are encouraged to examine Dainow's excellent review and bibliography.

For hundreds of years philosophers and musicologists have maintained and sought to substantiate the existence of a relationship between heart rate and music. Most "substantiation," however, has just been rhetoric. Dainow's review of studies of heart rate in response to music provides virtually no support to the hypothesis that heart rate varies with tempo of music. Of eight studies examining the effects of music on heart rate, all but one failed to elicit any statistically significant changes in heart rate. Some other studies suggested that any music will increase heart rate, although it was not clear whether these changes in heart rate were statistically significant for any of the studies. Another group of studies cited by Dainow did not produce any effects on heart rate. Dainow concludes that, "despite considerable research the relationship between HR and music is still unclear" (p. 212). Even if clearcut relationships could be established between heart rate and tempo, it would provide little insight into the affective response.

Dainow notes that summarizing research on respiration rate or amplitude is particularly difficult because of the variety of experimental conditions. Some studies examine rate while others examine amplitude; further, some research has sought to examine

respiration in relation to tempo, while other research has attempted to relate respiration to listener's attention or enjoyment.
Ries (1969), in one of the few studies which actually compared a
physiological response to subjects' indicated enjoyment of musical
examples, reports a .48 *(p* < .01) correlation coefficient between
the two variables. Most of the other studies examined by Dainow,
however, reported no clearcut data regarding the relationship between respiration rate or amplitude and musical stimulus or response. They merely describe the responses to the musical
stimulus. As was apparent for heart research, respiration research to date presents a confusing picture and provides little or
no information regarding the affective response to music.

Dainow maintains that galvanic skin response (GSR) experiments are even more incomplete and inconclusive than those related to heart rate and respiration. He suggests that there is a
general methodological "hodgepodge" in galvanic skin response
research, noting that some studies measure magnitude and direction of response, some the number of deflections, and others observe rising period or latency. Some have attempted to relate
GSR to some ill-defined emotional response to music, while others
have examined it in relation to stimulative vs. sedative music or
dissonant vs. consonant sounds. Despite occasionally well-con-
ceived studies such as Dreher's (1947) study of comparisons of
verbal reports and GSR to different types of music, little can be
concluded regarding GSR and affective response because of the
many methodological problems involved in such research.

A physiological response which has received relatively little
study in relation to music but for which Dainow sees potential is
electromyography, or muscle tension. Western music appears to
organize sounds in which tension-resolution patterns are developed and Dainow suggests that "it might be expected that inherently tense music could induce a corresponding physical or
muscular tension in the listener" (p. 214). He cites research by
Sears (1957, 1960) which provides evidence that muscle tension
can be altered by music. The potential of electromyography for
evaluating affective response to music, however, has yet to be
thoroughly explored.

Clearly, physiological research to date has provided little insight into the affective response to music. Reasons for this are difficult to pinpoint, although Dainow suggests that many methodological issues are involved. Particular concerns which he notes are instructions to subjects, loudness of the musical stimuli, subject attention, and possible suppression of response due to fear of disturbing electrodes. Another major difficulty involves measures of the psychological variable, affect. In addition, the sheer diversity of physiological variables themselves and the many aspects of each creates an overwhelming array of measurement and interpretation problems. Finally, even if all of the measurement and research design problems can be resolved, it may be that responses of the autonomic nervous system are sufficiently unique to each individual, who also brings a unique experiential background to the measurement situation, that making predictions or generalizing about affective response on the basis of physiological responses would be inappropriate. Certainly the present state of physiological research prohibits the making of any predictions or generalizations about the affective response to music. As Hahn (1954, p. 11) has stated, "An investigation of the physiological response may offer a clue but not a solution to the individual's psychological reactions."

Mood Responses

Laymen, musicians, psychologists, and philosophers agree that music can reflect moods and evoke mood responses in listeners. Mood response to music, as other psychological responses to music, involves learning. Individuals within given cultural groups *learn* that music with certain characteristics reflects certain moods while music with different characteristics reflects different moods. A particular concern of research on mood responses to music has been to study the extent to which given groups of subjects reflect similarity of response to given musical excerpts.

Moods have been described in various ways by psychologists and philosophers, but as used in research related to music, *mood* generally refers to "relatively transient states . . . which can be cognized by individuals and designated with words" (Eagle, 1971, p. 19).

Most of the research on mood response has used classical music as the stimulus, although the functional application of music to effect mood change appears to have been most successfully accomplished with "popular" or "easy listening" music. (The functional application of such mood music will be discussed in Chapter Eight.)   Farnsworth (1969, pp. 79-96) and Lundin (1967, pp. 160-172) both summarize research on mood response to music, but perhaps the most extensive review of the literature on mood responses to music is that provided by Eagle (1971, pp. 27-80). These summaries, particularly the one by Eagle, provide the basis for the balance of the discussion on mood response.

Eagle notes that mood response to music has been studied primarily in terms of verbal descriptions of the mood. Three basic methods for gathering verbal descriptions have been used: (1) adjective check lists, (2) the semantic differential, and (3) various types of rating scales. The most commonly used of the three methods has been the adjective checklist. Following is a brief review of the major research using adjective checklists.

1927—Schoen and Gatewood presented ten musical selections to thirty-two female subjects on two separate occasions under similar testing conditions. Although no statistical analysis was made beyond frequency count of the adjectives checked for each selection, the results were sufficiently similar for the researchers to conclude that "a given musical selection will arouse a certain definite reaction and will arouse the same reaction on different occasions." (Schoen and Gatewood, 1927, p. 151).

1927—Gatewood presented a list of twelve adjectives to thirty-five female subjects who were asked to check the moods elicited by each of ten selections. The study sought to examine the influence of rhythm, melody, harmony, and timbre on stated mood effects. Again without statistical evaluation, it was concluded that mood effects are dependent on definite musical elements.

1928—Heinlein studied adjectives checked in response to major and minor chords by 30 musically trained and untrained subjects. Two additional variables studied were intensity and pitch register. He found that mood effects were more a function of intensity than the chord per se. Further, pitch register also made a difference in which adjectives were checked. He concluded that "any fixity of feeling-tone in relation to a given mode is dependent upon training to react in a specific manner to a purely intellectual discrimination" (Heinlein, 1928, p. 140).

1935—Hevner (1935, 1936) developed an adjective checklist which has served as the basis for much subsequent research on mood response to music. She developed an adjective circle grouping 67 adjectives into eight clusters, each cluster containing adjectives of approximately the same meaning. (See Figure 6-1.) Listeners were asked to check the adjectives describing the mood of the music. The intent was that as one progressed around the circle from cluster one to cluster eight there would be eight more-or-less discrete moods, representing a general trend of mood change through the respective clusters. Her results revealed a general consistency among subjects in the adjectives checked. She conducted a series of follow-up studies in the late 1930s to ascertain the effects of various elements of music (modality, rhythm, tempo, harmony, melody, and pitch) on mood response. From her series of studies she concluded that the major mode is "happy, graceful, and playful"; the minor mode is "sad, dreamy, and sentimental"; firm rhythms are "vigorous and dignified"; flowing rhythms are "happy, graceful, dreamy, and tender"; complex, dissonant harmonies are "exciting, agitating, vigorous and inclined toward sadness"; simple consonant harmonies are "happy, graceful, serene, and lyrical"; and differences in expressiveness caused by rising and falling of melodic line are not clear-cut, distinct, or constant (Hevner, 1936, p. 268). Hevner (1937) also reported that slow tempos express "dignity, calmness, and sadness"; fast tempos, "restlessness and happiness." High pitches are "sprightly and humorous," while low pitches reflect "sadness, dignity and majesty." She also found that responses were generally the same for listeners of all kinds, intelligent and less intelligent, trained and untrained (Hevner, 1939).

6

bright
cheerful
gay
happy
joyous
merry

7

agitated
dramatic
exciting
exhilirated
impetuous
passionate
restless
sensational
soaring
triumphant

5

delicate
fanciful
graceful
humorous
light
playful
quaint
sprightly
whimsical

8

emphatic
exalting
majestic
martial
ponderous
robust
vigorous

4

calm
leisurely
lyrical
quiet
satisfying
serene
soothing
tranquil

1

awe-inspiring
dignified
lofty
sacred
serious
sober
solemn
spiritual

3

dreamy
longing
plaintive
pleading
sentimental
tender
yearning
yielding

2

dark
depressing
doleful
frustrated
gloomy
heavy
melancholy
mournful
pathetic
sad
tragic

Figure 6-1. Hevner Adjective Circle.

1952—Capurso (1952) developed a list of 105 musical selections to match six mood categories. He then asked 1,075 "non-musical" subjects to listen to the selections and categorize them according to mood. He found that sixty-one selections had listener agreement at least 50 percent of the time and thus suggested that the resulting list of musical selections may be suitable for creating a "desired emotional effect" on listeners and for selecting background music for television and radio programs.

A	B	C	D	E
cheerful	fanciful	delicate	dreamy	longing
gay	light	graceful	leisurely	pathetic
happy	quaint	lyrical	sentimental	plaintive
joyous	whimsical		serene	pleading
bright			soothing	yearning
merry			tender	
playful			tranquil	
sprightly			quiet	

F	G	H	I	J
dark	sacred	dramatic	agitated	frustrated
depressing	spiritual	emphatic	exalting	
doleful		majestic	exciting	
gloomy		triumphant	exhilarated	
melancholic			impetuous	
mournful			vigorous	
pathetic				
sad				
serious				
sober				
solemn				
tragic				

Figure 6-2. Farnsworth's modification of the Hevner Adjective Circle.

1954—Farnsworth (1954) tested the internal consistency of the clusters of the Hevner Adjective Circle. He found that several of the clusters did not describe internally consistent mood patterns, and therefore did not justify the circle arrangement. He rearranged 50 of Hevner's adjectives into ten more consistent categories. (See Figure 6-2.)

1955—Sopchak (1955) developed a twelve-category adjective checklist which 553 college sophomores used in responding to fifteen compositions, five classical, seven popular, and three folk. Subjects also were asked to classify their own moods on a three-point scale: "cheerful" to "neutral" to "gloomy." It was found that a higher percentage of gloomy subjects responded to sorrow, joy, calm, love, eroticism, jealousy, wonder, and cruelty. Sopchak speculated that gloomy subjects have many tensions and thus more readily project into the music, while cheerful subjects may have less need to project into the music.

1960—Van Stone (1960) sought to ascertain mood differences associated with tone quality of music. Eight musical excerpts representing the eight clusters of the Hevner Adjective Circle were orchestrated and recorded by three ensembles: string, woodwind, and brass. Results indicated no significant differences among adjectival responses to the three types of ensembles. Apparently timbre change had little or no effect on mood response.

While mood response in terms of adjective checklists has been subject to considerable study, the semantic differential technique is a more recently developed technique and therefore has been used less for study of mood response. Essentially the technique attempts to measure subjects' concepts by use of series of bipolar adjectives between which subjects give a response on a five- or seven-point continuum.* For example:

---

*Readers interested in more information of the semantic differential technique should consult Osgood, C. E., Suci, G. J., and Tannenbaum, P. H. *The Measurement of Meaning.* Urbana: Unversity of Illinois Press, 1957.

Concept: Mood

Happy   ___ ___ ___ ___   ___ ___ ___ Sad
Light   ___ ___ ___ ___   ___ ___ ___ Heavy
Humorous   ___ ___ ___ ___   ___ ___ ___ Solemn

Two studies using this technique are summarized briefly below.

Edmonston (1966) sought to evaluate seventy-three subjects' "esthetic evaluations" of ten musical excerpts by means of a fifteen-pair semantic differential. He concluded that rhythm was the primary factor affecting response and that neither sex nor musical training influenced the affective responses.

Eagle (1971) used the semantic differential technique in a study which sought to answer three questions: (1) Does existing stated mood affect rated mood responses to music? (2) Does presentation order of music affect rated mood response to music? (3) Do similarly rated mood responses hold true for both vocal and instrumental music? Subjects were 274 undergraduate and graduate music majors who were asked to rate their own present mood on a ten-step scale and then respond to twenty musical selections in terms of five pairs of bipolar adjectives (good-bad, pleasant-unpleasant, bright-dark, depressed-elated, and happy-sad). The ten vocal excerpts included rock, folk, country-western, popular ballad, and hymns; instrumental excerpts included jazz, march, semiclassical, and classical. Eagle found that existing mood of the listener does influence mood response to music, but order of presentation does not significantly affect mood response to music. In response to his third question, Eagle (p. 171) states that

> Similar rated mood responses do not hold true for both vocal and instrumental music. A person responds differently to vocal music than to instrumental music, although both may seem to reflect the same mood qualities.

Other scales used with some frequency in assessing mood response include ratings on "like-dislike" continua, combination of continua such as "like-dislike" with "happy-sad," and free response, using any word a subject believes appropriate in describing the music.

Eagle's (pp. 70-80) analysis of the literature on mood response revealed a number of research concerns. Only three studies mentioned the reliability of their testing instruments and only two attempted to validate their instruments. Statistical analyses were not reported in more than half of the forty-three studies he reviewed, and of the twenty reporting statistical data, nearly half used only frequency counts; he did note, however, that eight of nine studies conducted since 1960 employ statistical analyses more sophisticated than frequency counts. Findings were not consistent regarding the importance of the elements in eliciting mood, although it was possible to make some broad generalizations:

> Rhythm seems to be the primary element in evaluating mood responses to music. "Happiness" was the term used most often to describe fast tempi, major mode, consonant harmonies, and tunes pitched in high registers. "Excitement" or "agitation" described dissonant harmonies. (p. 79)

The length of the musical excerpts ranged from thirteen seconds to five minutes with the median length about one minute and twenty seconds. Kate Hevner Mueller's (1973) review of Eagle's study raised the question regarding just how transient mood effects are. She suggests that composers often write ten, thirty, or seventy minute compositions to establish a "genuine mood." However, few would deny that most compositions express a variety of different moods, so a question remains regarding optimal length required to establish a mood.

Finally, Eagle's analysis of the literature revealed no consistent relationships between mood response to music and the following: sex, age, intelligence, or musical training. Apparently mood as expressed in music is learned as part of a general enculturation process and does not vary greatly with any of these variables.

As several studies suggested, a number of factors beyond the character of the music itself may contribute to a subject's indicated mood response. An individual's mood at the time of the listening, the meaning of the words, the dynamic level of the music, and the extent to which the excerpt reflects more than one mood are among the variables beyond learning and the musical attributes themselves which may influence mood response to music. Even though a certain amount of research has been conducted on mood response to music, the authors agree with Eagle that there is a "need for many carefully designed and analyzed investigations before generalizations can be made concerning the interaction of mood and music" (p. 172).

Philosophical Inquiry

Philosophical explanations regarding the value or meaning of artistic phenomena and experience have been a part of Western culture since the time of Plato, whom Hofstadter and Kuhns (1964, p. 3) consider to be the founder of philosophical aesthetics. The range and diversity of views which have been offered regarding the value and meaning of art (and music in particular) has resulted in a philosophical quagmire which often engulfs those who are not well schooled in aesthetics. While philosophical inquiry by nature arouses divergent viewpoints, it is believed that at least a cursory examination of some of the classical viewpoints will contribute to the understanding of the affective response to music, particularly since philosophical aesthetics represents the traditional and longest standing approach to the study of man's response to arts phenomena.

Berlyne (1974) suggests that *speculative aesthetics* is the most apt term for disciplines traditionally called philosophical.

> They depend heavily on deduction—from definitions of concepts, from self-evident principles, from generally accepted propositions, from an author's own beliefs, intuitions, and experience. To a large extent, their method is "hermeneutic," to use a term that is currently popular in continental Europe, i.e., they rely heavily on interpretive examination of particular texts, particularly specimens of literary, musical, or visual art. Their ultimate criterion of validity is whether they leave the reader with a feeling of conviction. (p. 2)

Berlyne sees two divisions of speculative aesthetics: traditional *philosophical aesthetics,* usually taught in univeristy departments of philosophy, and *art theory,* which is usually taught in the respective art, music, or literature departments. Philosophical aesthetics includes general statements regarding arts phenomena and their intent, value, or meaning, while art theory involves more examination of individual art works, art styles, and artists.

In music, courses which concern art theory as defined by Berlyne are music history, music appreciation, music literature, and to a degree, form and analysis courses. As should be apparent, there is overlap among the various types of courses. Disciplines concerned with speculative aesthetics generally are viewed as subjective in approach while the other approaches to study of the affective response are considered to be objective, although it is recognized that verbal responses to the mood of music also are subjective. The present discussion, however, examines only philosophical aesthetics.

Readers interested in examining some of the classic aesthetic theories should consult texts such as Morris Weitz's (1970) *Problems in Aesthetics* or Hofstadter and Kuhns' (1964) *Philosophies of Art and Beauty*. However, a sampling of some of the various theories' basic tenets suffices to illuminate the dilemma philosophical aesthetics holds for the uninitiated. Plato viewed art as an *imitation* of an ideal—the beautiful and the good. Aristotle also viewed art as imitation, but in a different sense; for him imitation is the realization of form in a sensory medium and therefore art is a revelation of reality. Rousseau considered art an *expression*. French classicism turned art into arithmetical problems while German romanticism sought explanations in metaphysical terms. Shiller viewed art as the most sublime form of play. Maritain suggests that all art begins for functional reasons and is a value of the practical intellect. Croce maintains that art is intuition. Schopenhauer sees music as the art "par excellence" because it "objectifies the world directly" and is "independent of the phenomenal world." Dewey views art as experience reflecting the tension-release patterns of everyday life. Some other theories, as capsulized by Schwadron (1967, p. 33), are:

> Freud, desire and the unconscious; Santayana, reason; Langer, symbolic transformation; Garvin, feeling response; Stravinsky, speculative volition; Schoenberg, logical clarity; Leichtentritt, logical imagination; and Hindemith, symbolic craftsmanship.

To facilitate a modicum of order in dealing with aesthetic theories related to music, several writers have grouped aesthetic theories according to basic philosophical position (Meyer, 1956, pp. 1-3; Schwadron, 1967, pp. 34-47; Reimer, 1970, pp. 14-24). Brief summarizations of the basic viewpoints are discussed below.

The two basic positions usually are classified as the *absolutist* and *referentialist* viewpoints, or in Schwadron's terminology, the *isolationist* and *contextualist*. Basically absolutist (isolationist) theories view music's value or meaning as the result of the musical sounds themselves and nothing more. For an absolutist, there is no musical meaning beyond that inherent in the sounds *per se*. Meyer (1956, pp. 2-3) sees an additional distinction within the absolutist framework. An absolutist may be a *formalist*, who contends that musical meaning is primarily intellectual based on perception and understanding of the formal structural relationships within a composition, or an *expressionist*, who views these structural relationships as capable of exciting feelings and emotions in the listener. The essential point regarding absolutist theories, however, is that any meaning or value derived from the music must be in terms of the musical sounds and nothing else. Eduard Hanslick (1891) is generally recognized as one of the earliest proponents of the absolutist position. For Hanslick (and other absolute formalists), the value and meaning of music is derived entirely from musical structure.

The opposite viewpoint, i.e. the view that the meaning of music involves more than the sounds themselves—it includes extra-musical ideas, emotions, stories, and even spiritual states (Sullivan, 1927, pp. 27-37), is labelled the *referentialist* or *contextualist* position. Nearly all advocates of the referentialist, or contextualist, position are expressionists; i.e. they view music as expressive of human experiences, although they also recognize that it can have other extramusical connotations.

A third position noted by Schwadron (p. 42) is *relativism*. The relativist position allows for the development of personally derived value criteria which consider that values are relative to and conditioned by cultural groups and historical periods. "For the relativist, musical meaning is a psychological product of expectation, an outgrowth of stylistic experience and cultural orientation" (Schwadron, p. 47).

From this cursory examination of philosophical aesthetics, no clear-cut answers emerge regarding the affective response to music. No position has been substantiated by empirical methods. Any information offered remains purely speculative, and as a result leads many individuals concerned with understanding the affective response to accept some other philosophical positions noted by Schwadron (pp. 34-35): complacency, eclecticism, skepticism, and agnosticism. Such philosophical positions, however, are not conducive even to attempting to understand the affective response to music. The authors encourage those readers who find themselves reflecting one of these latter philosophical positions to examine particularly the section below on meaning in music.

Experimental Aesthetics

In contrast to philosophical aesthetics, experimental aesthetics has a relatively short history. Although Berlyne (1974, p. 5) traces its roots back to the work of Fechner in the 1860s and 1870s, he noted that its products were relatively sparse and not very enlightening prior to 1960. Since about 1960, however, there has been a marked increase of interest in the discipline which has been characterized by some new approaches, techniques, aims, and ideas, thus causing Berlyne and his followers to speak in terms of the *new experimental aesthetics.*

While examinations of art and other aesthetic phenomena from a psychological perceptive have been made for more than a century, little of the early, i.e. prior to 1960, psychological study (and even much being conducted today) truly can be termed experimental aesthetics, although most of it still might be considered *empirical aesthetics,* i.e. study of aesthetic behavior through observation using methods and objectives similar to empirical science. Berlyne, who is recognized as the founder and chief proponent of the new experimental aesthetics, notes that experimental aesthetics is most properly recognized as the branch of empirical aesthetics termed *psychobiological aesthetics,* which "applies the methods of empirical science to the investigation of human and animal behavior and its relations to the observable conditions that can influence behavior" (p. 4). Experimental aesthetics is but one of three basic approaches to psychological aesthetics, the other two being *correlational study* and *content analysis*. While *correlational studies* examine how two or more factors vary in relation to one another and *content analysis* involves measurement of characteristics of artistic and other artifacts of specific social groups or historic periods, *experimental aesthetics* examines aesthetic response via the experimental methods, i.e. through systematically varying some factors to determine their effects on some aspect of behavior. For research to be identifiable with the *new* experimental aesthetics, Berlyne (p. 5) maintains that it must possess one or more of four features: (1) a focus on the collative* properties of stimulus patterns, (2) a concentration on motivational questions, (3) study of nonverbal behavior as well as verbally expressed judgments, and (4) efforts to establish links between aesthetic phenomena and other psychological phenomena.

The work of Berlyne and his followers reflects three basic theoretical premises: First, a work of art is analyzed in information-theoretic terms, i.e. it is comprised of elements, each of which can transmit *information* of four types: (1) semantic, (2) expressive, (3) cultural, and (4) syntactic. Berlyne recognizes some overlap between the four types of information, but notes that the four information sources also emit independent information, thus setting up a competition among them. More information from one generally allows less from other sources.

The second theoretical premise is that artworks are regarded as collections of symbols in accordance with the conception of signs and symbols of the semiotic movement.** Artworks have

---

*Collative properties include structural or formal properties of a stimulus, e.g. variations along such dimensions as simple-complex, familiar-novel, stable-variable.

**The semiotic movement uses the terms *sign* and *symbol* in a broader sense than used by speculative aestheticians. In this movement, a *sign* is anything that "stands for" something else. The movement involves four entities: (1) the *sign*, which is an object or event which serves as the stimulus, (2) the *interpreter*, the human (or animal) whose sense organs are stimulated by the sign, (3) the *interpretant*, which is the effect that the sign has on the interpreter, and (4) the *significate*, the object or event for which the sign stands. Readers interested in more information on the semiotic movement should consult Chapter 6 of D. E. Berlyne's *Aesthetics and Psychobiology* (New York: Appleton-Century-Crofts, 1971).

properties in common with objects or events that they signify, and
they serve as symbols for communication of artists' values regarding which objects or events deserve attention.

The third theoretical premise, elaborated on by Berlyne (1971,
Ch. 8; 1974, pp. 8-12), is that an artwork serves as a stimulus pattern whose collative properties give it a positive intrinsic hedonic
value. Dependent variables for measuring "hedonic value" include degree of pleasure, preference, or utility, which are usually
measured via verbally expressed means, and such nonverbal variables as reward value and incentive value. An artwork that has
"positive intrinsic hedonic value" is pleasureable or rewarding in
itself and not because it serves as a means to the ends. Berlyne
hypothesizes that positive hedonic values are a function of
arousal—through a moderate increase in arousal or through a
decrease in arousal when arousal has reached an uncomfortable
high. The "arousal potential" of an artwork's stimulus pattern
for an individual depends on many factors, including intensity,
association with, or resemblance to, biologically significant events,
and collative properties.

Dependent variables for the new experimental aesthetics include verbal ratings, psychophysiological measures, and behavioral
measures. The seven-point semantic differential has come to be
the predominant framework for verbal ratings. Three basic
classes of scales are used: (1) *descriptive scales,* in reference
to collative properties of stimulus patterns, (2) *evaluative scales,*
reflecting hedonic value, and (3) *internal state scales,* for assessing
subjects' reactions or mood while exposed to a stimulus. Psychophysiological measures generally are used as indicators of "arousal"
rather than as attempts to measure "affect" as in most of the
psychophysiological studies cited earlier in this chapter. Behavioral measures are generally *exploration time* (in music, *listening
time)* or *exploratory choice* (in music, *listening choice).* Exploratory time variously has been interpreted as a measure of the intensity of orientation time, the intensity of attention, or perceptual curiosity, while exploratory choice is viewed as an index of
"incentive value" or "utility." (Berlyne, 1974, pp. 13-14) .

Independent variables in the new experimental aesthetics generally reflect the *approach* to experimentation. The *synthetic* approach involves a more-or-less laboratory approach in which particular variables are isolated for manipulation and study, while the *analytic* approach examines reactions to art and other aesthetic stimuli taken from real life. While there are obvious advantages to the synthetic approach, McMullen (1978) maintains that there is a great need for music psychologists to examine musical behaviors from the latter perspective. He maintains that the psychology of music reflects too much the one-sided position of psycho*acoustics* rather than psycho*music*. Berlyne (1974, p. 18) also notes that both synthetic and analytical approaches are necessary, although he also recognizes that the synthetic approach has dominated both old and new experimental aesthetics. Independent variables generally are structural or formal characterictics, i.e. the collative characteristics of the artwork, and their effects frequently are evaluated within an information theory framework.

Research in music using the theory and methodology of the new experimental aesthetics appears to be spearheaded by J. B. Crozier (1974, pp. 27-90; Bragg and Crozier, 1974, pp. 91-108). In the United States, McMullen seems to be the chief proponent (McMullen, 1976, 1977; McMullen and Arnold, 1976).

Crozier (1974) used a synthetic approach to analyze level of uncertainty in melodic structure. Dependent variables included verbal rating scales for four classes—descriptive, evaluative, internal-state, and stylistic, as well as two behavioral variables—listening time and exploratory (listening) choice. Essentially he examined the effects of selected structural attributes of melody on the respective dependent variables. He found that variations in information, i.e. varying levels of uncertainty, affected subjects' ratings of "pleasingness" and "interestingness." Further, he reported a "remarkably high degree" (p. 86) of interpredictability between mean verbal ratings and nonverbal measures of exploratory behavior.

McMullen and Arnold (1976) examined the effects of distributional redundancy on preference and interest response for rhythmic sequences. Their results suggest that distributional redundancy does influence both preference and interest. Preference tended to increase as redundancy decreased to a point, after which preference began to decrease; interest generally increased as redundancy decreased.

The new experimental aesthetics appears to hold much promise for systematic evaluation of the affective response to music. Clearly, the theoretical and methodological foundations are well defined and systematized so that research findings will not be subject to many of the weaknesses of early psychological aesthetics.

Summary

The four approaches discussed here represent the basic ways used to examine the affective response to music. The traditional philosophical or speculative approach appears to offer many theories or hypotheses regarding what has been termed the aesthetic response to music. While many divergent views have been offered, the essential debate is whether the meaning or value of music comes from the structure of the musical sound or from some nonmusical referent to which it points. A limitation of the philosophical approach is its lack of objectivity .

The traditional psychological approaches, psychophysiological research and mood response, have suffered from a lack of sound theoretical foundation as well as a lack of methodological rigor and consistency, although some of the more recent efforts are clearly superior to some of the earlier work, but the more recent work in the new experimental aesthetics appears to hold the most promise for objective analysis of the affective response to music. If the methodological rigor of the new experimental aesthetics can be applied to current psychophysiological and mood response research, it would appear that psychological approaches to the study of affective responses to music should be able to provide better "answers" to some of the perplexing questions facing musicians, music educators, and music psychologists.

MEANING IN MUSIC

As suggested in the preceding section, there apparently is a broad gap between philosophical and psychological aesthetics.

Philosophers tend to talk to philosophers and psychologists tend to talk to psychologists. Philosophers tend to be concerned with whether music's value and import comes from within the music or its referents, while psychologists studying the affective response have been concerned with psychophysiological, verbal, or behavioral response to music. Some recent psychological approaches have begun to examine responses in terms of information theory and the effects of melodic or rhythmic redundancy on affective response.*

Fortunately, one contemporary writer, Leonard B. Meyer, has bridged the gap between aesthetic theory and information theory. Meyer (1956, pp. 1-42) espoused a theory of musical meaning based on a theory of emotion and expectation. The relationships between his theory of musical meaning and information theory were explored in his more recent publication, *Music, the Arts, and Ideas* (1967). This section examines Meyer's theories of emotion and meaning in music as well as some of the parallels between his theories and information theory. The primary sources for this discussion are the two cited above, although interpretations by Trolio (1976) also have been included.

Meyer's theory of musical meaning is based upon his *theory of emotion* which has the same basic tenets as Dewey's "conflict theory of emotion." "Emotion or affect is aroused when a tendency to respond is arrested or inhibited" (1956, p. 14). Emotional responses are dependent upon the relationship between a stimulus (music) and a responding individual. A musical stimulus must produce a tendency for an individual to respond in a particular way. A stimulus which arouses no tendency or which is satisfied without delay cannot arouse emotion.

Meyer differentiates between emotion *per se* and the emotional experience: the latter includes an awareness and cognition of a stimulus situation which always involves specific stimuli. Thus, affective experiences with music depend upon *musical* stimuli.

---

*Besides the work of Berlyne, Crozier et al., significant work has been reported by Abraham Moles in *Information Theory and Esthetic Perception,* (Urbana: University of Illinois Press, 1968). In addition, much of Roederer's (1975) work in the psychophysics of music, previously noted in Chapters Two and Four, also utilizes information theory as a framework for examining responses to aural stimuli.

Musical affective experience is distinguished from affective experience in everyday life. Tensions created by tendencies to respond in everyday life may go unresolved, whereas in music they are resolved. Further, music can serve as both stimulus and as meaningful resolution to such tendencies; in life a factor which stimulates a tension usually cannot serve to resolve it.

Tensions, which may be either conscious or unconscious, are referred to as expectations. Music arouses expectations in various ways. Listeners to Western music learn (consciously or unconsciously) that certain chords or "sound terms" imply certain other musical entities. When the expected musical consequent is delayed, suspense is aroused. In Meyer's (1956, p. 28) words:

> The greater the buildup of suspense, of tension, the greater the emotional release upon resolution. This observation points up the fact that in aesthetic experience emotional pattern must be considered not only in terms of tension itself but also in terms of the progression from tension to release. And the experience of suspense is aesthetically valueless unless it is followed by a release which is understandable in the given context.

A musical consequent which will fulfill such expectations is dictated by the possibilities and probabilities of the style of the musical composition in question. When seen in this light, the importance of stylistic knowledge becomes essential.

In summary, Meyer's theory of emotion is a theory of expectation which necessarily has certain cultural and stylistic presuppositions. He states his central hypothesis as follows:

> Affect or emotion felt is aroused when an expectation—a tendency to respond—activated by the musical stimulus situation, is temporarily inhibited or permanently blocked. (1956, p. 31)

While the question of musical meaning is centered around the opposing views of the absolutists and the referentialists, much of the confusion concerning it may be attributed to the different views with regard to the definition of meaning. The following definition suffices for Meyer:

> Anything acquires meaning if it is connected with or indicates, or refers to something beyond itself, so that its full nature points to and is revealed in that connection. (1956, p. 34)

Meaning is defined in terms of the relationship between a stimulus and the thing it points to or indicates. Such a relationship must be perceived by an individual. Meaning thus arises out of triadic relationship between (1) a stimulus, (2) that to which it points, and (3) the conscious observer.

Meyer believes that music's meaning has been further muddled by the failure of aestheticians to state explicitly to what musical stimuli point. He recognizes two types of musical meaning: designative and embodied. The designative meaning of a musical stimulus may indicate events or consequents which differ from itself in kind, i.e. nonmusical events. Embodied meaning refers to those in which the stimulus and consequent are of the same kind, i.e. both musical. It is the embodied meaning of music with which Meyer is concerned. For Meyer, one musical event has meaning because it points to and makes the listener expect another musical event. Embodied musical meaning, therefore, is a product of expectation and is a result of past experiences with music of the given style. Music which does not arouse expectations of a subsequent musical consequent is meaningless. Because expectation is largely a product of stylistic experience, music in a style with which an individual is totally unfamiliar is meaningless.

A knowledge of style implies that learning has taken place; thus, the perception of meaning cannot take place without involving cognition. The affective and intellectual responses to music cannot be separated. They both depend upon the same perceptual processes, stylistic habits, and the same mode of mental organization. The same musical processes give rise and shape to both types of experience. Meyer maintains that the formalists' and the expressionists' conception of it appear as complementary rather than contradictory. They are considered, not different processes, but different ways of experiencing the same process. "Whether a piece of music gives rise to affective experience or to intellectual experience depends upon the disposition and training of the listener." (1956, p. 40)

Those people who have been taught that musical experience is primarily emotional will probably experience delay of expectations as affect. The trained musician will probably listen in more technical terms and will tend to make musical processes an object of conscious consideration. Regardless of the way in which one views the delay of expectations, Meyer's theory of expectation will suffice to explain it.

Meyer (1967, pp. 5-21) noted striking parallels between his theory of musical meaning and information theory and hypothesized that "the psychostylistic conditions which give rise to musical meaning, whether affective or intellectual, are the same as those which communicate information" (1967, p. 5). Meyer specifically notes that it is the *embodied* meaning of music which is most consistent with information theory.

As discussed in Chapter Four, information theory is a system for quantifying the amount of uncertainty in a stimulus. The greater the amount of *information,* the greater the *uncertainty* of meaning or response. The amount of information a listener receives from a musical stimulus is a function of two basic variables: (1) the extent to which the structural (collative) characteristics of the music conform to the fundamental organizational laws of Gestalt psychology and (2) the listener's previous experience with the given musical style. The greater the perceptual redundancy of the music, the more predictable the musical response.*

The relationship between Meyer's theory of musical meaning and information theory also has been examined by Trolio (1976). She notes that the uncertainty created by antecedent-consequent relationships provides both meaning and information. The relationships also arouse emotion. The relationship between information and emotion is further clarified with the recognition that uncertainty arising when habit responses have been arrested or delayed is caused by a disturbance in the order and/or timing of a sequence of responses. Information is the measure of uncertainty, which also may arouse emotions.

VARIABLES CONTRIBUTING TO MUSICAL MEANING

Variables contributing to musical meaning can be classed under two broad categories: (1) those related to the structural

---

*The relationship of perceptual redundancy to *structural* and *cultural* redundancy is discussed in Chapter Four.

(collative) characteristics of the musical stimulus and (2) those related to the listener, particularly the experiential variables. McMullen (1978) conveniently has grouped the variables related to musical structure under three headings: *order, complexity,* and *energy.*

He notes that order is closely related to a traditional aesthetic principle of "unity in variety." Order within musical structure appears to be a function of the amount of structural redundancy in a composition, e.g. tonality and rhythmic redundancy appear to contribute greatly to musical meaning, but systematic investigation of the effects of order in musical structure have just begun to be examined.

Complexity of musical structure also has been long recognized as an important variable, but again, little systematic exploration of its effects on musical meaning has been undertaken. Certainly complexity is a factor in musical preferences. McMullen maintains that both order and complexity lend themselves to examination within an information theory framework.

Energy is the musical quality which reflects stimulation or drive. Variables such as tempo and dynamics generally are recognized as primary contributors to energy, but other variables such as melodic and harmonic movement also appear to contribute. Some of the earlier work regarding mood response, as reported by Lundin (1967, pp. 160-177) and Farnsworth (1969, pp. 83-90), examined some of these variables, although it appears that many of the tentative conclusions reached were artifacts of the particular musical examples and evaluative measures employed. There is clearly a need for systematic examination of such variables and their effect on musical meaning.

Variables related to the listener are many and complex. Perhaps of greater importance are the variables related to the listener's previous experiences with music. From infancy on, individuals have many varieties of experiences with music. They develop expectations regarding its structure (embodied meaning) as well as regarding its referents (designative meaning). In addition to expectations, formal musical training and the resultant learning, associations with particular musical examples and styles, as well as all of an individual's informal musical learning are variables which appear to affect musical meaning. Further, an individual's basic personality as well as state of motivation for interacting with music have been receiving increased recognition as potential variables affecting musical meaning. Systematic examination of the effects of these variables on musical meaning, however, is virtually nonexistent.

In conclusion, the efforts of previous researchers in examining the effects of selected variables is acknowledged; they have contributed much to the understanding of musical meaning. However, it also is apparent that research efforts related to musical meaning, or the affective response to music, are still in their infancy, and much effort must be directed toward examining the effects of the variables noted here (as well as many others) before any "final truth" is reached regarding affective responses to music.

SUMMARY

The major points of this chapter are:

1. *Affect* is a broad term referring to a wide variety of human feeling responses.
2. *Emotion* is a particular type of affect reflecting a relatively temporary disturbance from a normal state of composure.
3. *Aesthetic* feeling results from certain types of experiences with artworks, natural phenomena, or other objects or events in which beauty or artistic value may be perceived.
4. *Aesthetic experience* requires perceptual involvement with interacting attributes within artwork (or natural phenomena or other objects or events), perception of beauty therein, and a feeling reaction thereto.
5. Other types of affective responses to musical stimuli (besides the aesthetic) include *mood,* or character responses, *association* responses, *intrasubjective* responses, reaction to word meanings of songs, preferences, interests, attitudes, values, and appreciations.
6. Concomitant with affective responses are physiological reactions of the autonomic nervous system.
7. Although physiological reactions, particularly heart rate, res-

piration rate, and galvanic skin responses, to music have been examined for nearly a century, such research provides little insight into the affective response to music.

8. Mood response to music has been examined most frequently via adjective checklists.

9. While there appears to be a certain consistency among mood responses as indicated by adjective checklists, there is a need for much more carefully designed and analyzed research before generalizations can be made concerning the interaction of mood and music.

10. Speculative aesthetics is of two basic types: *philosophical aesthetics,* which seeks to make general statements regarding arts phenomena and their intent, value, or meaning; *art theory,* which in music includes courses such as music history, literture, and analysis, and which involves examination of individual compositions, styles, and composers.

11. Basic philosophical aesthetic positions include the *absolutist,* which views the value or meaning of music as resulting from the musical sounds themselves, and the *referentialist,* which views music as reflecting more than sounds themselves; it includes extramusical ideas, emotions, stories, and even spiritual states.

12. A more recent approach to study of affective responses to music is through the *new experimental aesthetics* which, utilizing methods of empirical science, focuses on collative properties of aesthetic stimuli, examines motivational questions, studies nonverbal as well as verbal behavior, and seeks to establish links between aesthetic phenomena and other psychological phenomena.

13. There appear to be parallels between Leonard B. Meyer's theory of musical meaning, which views meaning in terms of expectations, and information theory, which appears to be a promising method for examining affect resulting from musical uncertainty.

14. Variables contributing to musical meaning are of two broad classes: (1) those related to the structural (collative) char-

acteristic of a music stimulus and (2) those related to the listener, particularly the experiential variables.

REFERENCES

Berlyne, D. E. *Aesthetics and Psychobiology.* New York: Appleton-Century-Crofts, 1971.

Berlyne, D. E. (Ed.). *Studies in the New Experimental Aesthetics: Steps Toward an Objective Psychology of Aesthetic Appreciation.* New York: Halsted Press, 1974.

Bragg, B. W. E., & Crozier, J. B. The development with age of verbal and exploratory responses to sound sequences varying in uncertainty level. In D. E. Berlyne (Ed.), *Studies in the New Experimental Aesthetics: Steps Toward an Objective Psychology of Aesthetic Appreciation.* New York: Halsted Press, 1974.

Capurso, A. The Capurso study. In *Music and Your Emotions.* New York: Liveright Publishing, 1952.

Crozier, J. B. Verbal and exploratory responses to sound sequences varying in uncertainty level. In D. E. Berlyne (Ed.), *Studies in the New Experimental Aesthetics: Steps Toward an Objective Psychology of Aesthetic Appreciation.* New York: Halsted Press, 1974.

Dainow, E. Physical effects and motor responses to music. *Journal of Research in Music Education,* 1977, *25,* 211-221.

Diserens, C. M., & Fine, H. *A Psychology of Music.* Cincinnati: College of Music, 1939.

Dreher, R.E. *The Relationship between Verbal Reports and Galvanic Skin Response.* Unpublished doctoral dissertation, Indiana University, 1947.

Eagle, C. T., Jr. Effects of existing mood and order presentation of vocal and instrumental music on rated mood responses to that music (Doctoral dissertation, The University of Kansas, 1971). *Dissertation Abstracts International,* 1971, *32,* 2118-A. (University Microfilms No. 71-27, 139)

Edmondston, W. E., Jr. The use of the semantic differential technique in the esthetic evaluation of musical excerpts. *American Journal of Psychology,* 1966, *79,* 650-652.

Farnsworth, P. R. A study of the Hevner adjective list. *Journal of Aesthetics and Art Criticism,* 1954, *13,* 97-103.

Farnsworth, P. R. *The Social Psychology of Music* (2nd ed.). Ames: The Iowa State University Press, 1969.

Gatewood, E. L. An experimental study of the nature of musical enjoyment. In M. Schoen (Ed.), *The Effects of Music.* Freeport, N.Y.: Books for Libraries Press, 1927.

Hahn, M. E. *A Proposed Technique for Investigating the Relationship Between Musical Preferences and Personality Structure.* Unpublished doctoral dissertation, The University of Kansas, 1954.

Hanslick, E. *The Beautiful in Music* (G. Cohen, Trans.) New York: Liberal Arts Press, 1957. Originally published 1854, translation, 1891.

Heinlein, C. P. The affective characters of the major and minor modes in music. *The Journal of Comparative Psychology*, 1928, *8*, 101-142.

Hevner, K. Expression in music: a discussion of experimental studies and theories. *Psychological Review*, 1935, *42*, 186-204.

Hevner, K. Experimental studies of the elements of expression in music. *American Journal of Psychology*, 1936, *48*, 246-268.

Hevner, K. The affective value of pitch and tempo in music. *American Journal of Psychology*, 1937, *49*, 621-630.

Hevner, K. Studies in expressiveness of music. *Proceedings of the Music Teachers National Association*, 1939, 199-217.

Hofstadter, A., & Kuhns, R. (Eds.). *Philosophies of Arts and Beauty.* New York: The Modern Library, 1964.

Knieter, G. L. The nature of aesthetic education. In *Toward an Aesthetic Education.* Washington, D.C.: Music Educators National Conference, 1971.

Lundin, R. W. *An Objective Psychology of Music* (2nd ed.). New York: Ronald Press, 1967.

Maslow, A. H. *Motivation and Personality* (2nd ed.). New York: Harper & Row, 1970.

McMullen, P. T. Influences of distributional redundancy in rhythmic sequences on judged complexity ratings. *Council for Research in Music Education*, 1976, *46*, 23-30.

McMullen, P. T. *Organizational and Technical Dimensions in Musical Stimuli.* Unpublished research paper presented at the MENC Eastern Division Conference, Washington, D.C., February 18, 1977.

McMullen, P. T. *Music and Empirical Aesthetics: Present and Future Directions.* Unpublished paper presented at the Symposium on the Psychology and Acoustics of Music, The University of Kansas, Lawrence, Kansas, February 2, 1978.

McMullen, P. T., & Arnold, M. J. Preference and interest as functions of distributional redundancy in rhythmic sequences. *Journal of Research in Music Education*, 1976, *24*, 22-31.

Meyer, L. B. *Emotion and Meaning in Music.* Chicago: The University of Chicago Press, 1956.

Meyer, L. B. *Music, the Arts, and Ideas.* Chicago: The University of Chicago Press, 1967.

Moles, A. *Information Theory and Esthetic Percepton* (J. E. Cohen, Trans.). Urbana: University of Illinois Press, 1968.

Mueller, K. H. Review of *Effects of Existing Mood and Order of Presentation of Vocal and Instrumental Music on Rated Mood Responses to that Music by C. T. Eagle, Jr. Council for Research in Music Education*, 1973, *32*, 55-59.

Osgood, C. E., Suci, G. J., & Tannenbaum, P. H. *The Measurement of*

Meaning. Urbana: University of Illinois Press, 1957.

Rader, M., & Jessup, B. *Art and Human Values.* Englewood Cliffs, N.J.: Prentice-Hall, 1976.

Reimer, B. *A Philosophy of Music Education.* Englewood Cliffs, N.J.: Prentice Hall, 1970.

Ries, H. A. GSR and breathing amplitude related to emotional reactions to music. *Psychonomic Science,* 1969, *14,* 62-64.

Roederer, J. G. *Introduction to the Physics and Psychophysics of Music* (2nd ed.). New York: Springer-Verlag, 1975.

Schoen, M. (Ed.). *The Effects of Music.* New York: Harcourt, Brace, 1927.

Schoen, M. *The Psychology of Music.* New York: Ronald Press, 1940.

Schoen, M., & Gatewood, E. L. An experimental study of the nature of musical enjoyment. In M. Schoen (Ed.), *The Effects of Music,* New York: Harcourt, Brace, 1927.

Schwadron, A. A. *Aesthetics: Dimensions for Music Education.* Washington, D.C.: Music Educators National Conference, 1967.

Sears, W. W. The effects of music on muscle tones. In E. T. Gaston (Ed.), *Music Therapy 1957.* Lawrence, Kansas: Allen Press, 1958.

Sears, W. W. A Study of some effects of music upon muscle tension as evidenced electromyographic recordings (Doctoral dissertation, The University of Kansas, 1960). *Dissertation Abstracts,* 1960, *21,* 208. (University Microfilms No. 60-2316)

Sopchak, A. L. Individual differences in responses to different types of music in relation to sex, mood, and other variables. *Psychological Monographs,* 1955, *69* (11), 1-20.

Sternbach, R. A. *Principles of Psychophysiology.* New York: Academic Press, 1966.

Sullivan, J. W. N. Music as expression. In J. W. N. Sullivan, *Beethoven, his Spiritual Development.* New York: New American Library, 1927.

Trolio, M. F. Theories of affective response to music. *Contributions to Music Education,* 1976, *4,* 1-20.

Van Stone, J. K. The effects of instrumental tone quality upon mood response to music. In E. Schneider (Ed.), *Music Therapy 1959.* Lawrence, Kansas: Allen Press, 1960.

Weitz, M. (Ed.). *Problems in Aesthetics* (2nd ed). New York: MacMillan, 1970.

Young, P. T. Feeling and emotion. In B. B. Wolman (Ed.), *Handbook of General Psychology.* Englewood Cliffs, N.J.: Prentice-Hall, 1973.

Chapter Seven

MUSICAL PREFERENCES

PEOPLE VARY IN THEIR PREFERENCES for any sensory experience in which they have a choice. Personal preferences for certain foods, paintings, home decor, clothing, and music are rooted in individual biological needs, cultures, training, and experience. Preferences are not always consistent, and they can be modified. What is preferred in one instance is not necessarily preferred in another.

The term "preference," as used herein, means an expressed choice of one musical work or style over other available works or styles. Some writers prefer the term musical taste; Farnsworth (1969) defines musical taste as a person's overall attitude toward collective musical phenomena. Such attitudes require tangible expression in the form of musical choices, which are indications of preferred music in various situations.

A simple preference of one musical work to another may have meaning beyond the obvious musical evaluation. Expressed musical preferences sometimes are used to assess personality via deviations from population trends regarding musical choices. "Illogical" aesthetic reactions are believed to differentiate psychotics and paranoids from normals and alcoholics from other psychotics (Cattell and Anderson, 1953).

Hahn (1954) compared the clinical personality assessments of twelve students, randomly chosen from those seeking help at a university counseling center, with their musical preferences, expressed through musical choices and listening logs. He found that personality was reflected in individual musical choices, which also depended upon aesthetic values and individual needs for sensual pleasure. Aesthetic values in turn depended upon cultural background, musical training, and the general attraction of music. Rhythm, staccato-legato, timbre, loudness level, and tempo influenced preferences. A large degree of idiosyncratic behavior was reflected in expressed preferences, and Hahn believed that musical preferences would continue to require study on an individual basis. Group preference tendencies perhaps are more obvious a quarter-century after Hahn's study, but prediction of individual musical preferences, particularly from personality information, remains tenuous.

This chapter examines the difficulties of determining what is "good" music, existing musical preferences, various societal influences, and alteration of preferences.

WHAT IS "GOOD" MUSIC?

It is difficult to study artistic phenomena, particularly as they relate to preferences, in a scientific manner because of longstanding views of the arts as supernatural events (Berlyne, 1971). There are individuals who believe that music is a gift of (a) divine being(s), and people must hope to understand it through revelation. Others consider art as a personal experience, unopen to analysis.

Reasons for individual musical preferences include musical characteristics, such as tempos, orchestral colors, and lyrics, extra-musical associations ("Darling, our song . . ."), and societal pressures. There are group preference tendencies; they are not solely a matter of individual choices. Group tendencies and differences arouse concern for what good music really is—what *should* be preferred?

One view of "good" music is that that which is good is good because of inherent aspects of the musical stimulus. In such a view there are melodic, harmonic, rhythmic, and formal ideals which are characteristic of good, even great music, and if the listener can be educated in such ideals, his or her preferences will conform to some aesthetic ideal. The view that good music owes its goodness to its structure is a manifestation of a formalistic (Meyer, 1956; Reimer, 1970), or *isolationist* (Schwadron, 1967) position regarding musical aesthetics: The value of music supposedly is inherent in the music itself.

All art has properties which are able to arouse people. The so-called "collative" variables of novelty, surprise, complexity, and ambiguity, related to form and structure, influence the response of one who observes art. Instability can lead to discomfort; incongruity may increase attention (Berlyne). The essence of Meyer's (1956) theory regarding musical enjoyment is that the delay of musical expectancy promotes pleasure through the ultimate dissipation of resulting frustration; complex music thereby is more likely than simple music to be preferred over a longer period. McMullen and Arnold (1976) showed a tentative relationship between rhythmic redundancy and preference: the less the dominance of one rhythmic figure, the less the redundancy and the greater the preference, to a certain point.

Adorno (1976) classified musical listeners on the basis of how accurately they listen to what is in music's objective structure. The listening types, exemplifying various listener behaviors, imply a qualitative continuum of musical taste and preference.

The highest level of listening, for Adorno, is reached by the *expert,* who is able to hear musical structures completely and properly order all the formal nuances. Experts, not numerous, almost always are professionals.

The *good listener* hears beyond musical details but lacks the expert's awareness of musical structure. Adorno suggests that the good listener is like a person able to understand language without understanding grammar and syntax.

For the *culture consumer,* the musical structure is immaterial, although he or she has a considerable amount of musical information and listens extensively. Culture consumers tend to be conservative; Adorno believes that many patrons of the arts are of this type. (Perhaps the fish who wishes to demonstrate his "taste" to the canning company is a culture consumer.)

An *emotional listener* uses music as a stimulant or compensation and cares not about music's intellectual aspects, while a *resentment listener* uses music as a form of protest against existing musical or social conditions. Adorno suggests that a jazz lover is a resentment listener.

Many listeners believe *music is entertainment* and no more. They often are addicted to music listening as a background event.

Finally, Adorno identifies people who are musically *indifferent, unmusical,* or even *antimusical.* Such people have been turned away from music by unpleasant childhood experiences.

Adorno believes that music is primarily an intellectual event, although he does state that one must understand music's social characteristics in order to understand music.

In contrast to the view that there is music which is "good" because of its structure, there is a view that music which is preferred is preferred because of its individual values and utilities rather than any inherent goodness. Whereas Adorno indicates that a criterion of individual taste would deprive "great" music of what makes it great, Chancellor (1975) says that all art is ambiguous and acquires its value from subjective, pluralistic, and relative determinants. Hamm, Nettl, and Byrnside (1975) tie music to society and culture and allow for individual utility and personal identification. In its extreme, such a view is a manifestation of a *referential* (Meyer; Reimer) or a *contextual* (Schwadron) aesthetic position: Music is meaningless except to the extent that it communicates extramusical messages. There is a school of aesthetic *relativism* (Schwadron), which allows for different value systems for different musical styles and recognizes the importance of musical structure while allowing for cultural and functional variability in musical preference.

Individual critics, musicians, and listeners will continue to explain musical preferences on the basis of inherent musical properties, but it is more fruitful psychologically to study preference in terms of people's expressions of preference. "Good" music is good because it is *desirable* in terms of a person's mood, background, training, experience, prejudices, and beliefs. Some people want complexity. Some want simplicity. Some preferences are predictable; others are not. It all depends on the person making the choice.

EXISTING MUSICAL PREFERENCES

There is no formula for predicting individual musical preferences, although there are tendencies for particular groups to prefer particular musical styles. Most investigation has been directed toward preferences for classical music.

Investigations generally have relied on some sort of polling of representative groups and analyses of what is performed. A few studies have related listener characteristics to musical preferences.

Any measure of musical preference is risky. People may not respond honestly to questions regarding their preferences; reasons for attending performances selectively include nonmusical ones such as social visibility. Examining record collections may be useful, but individuals vary in the extent to which they can afford recordings. Possession of a recording tells little about how often it is heard. Analyses of what is performed or aired (over radio) are subject to biases of conductors and patrons of the arts. Scholarly discussions of music reflect musical preferences, but with editorial bias.

Attempts to apply magnitude estimation (see Chapter Two) have been made. Aesthetic judgments may be prothetic in nature; investigators have observed psychophysical phenomena, such as the tendency to hear the second member of a pair of ambiguous stimuli as having "more" of the property in question, in affective judgments (Koh, 1965; 1967). Magnitude estimation may offer a more explicit preference measure in the future.

The studies discussed below are representative of preference investigations.

Surveys

Keston and Pinto (1955) investigated the musical preference of 202 college students in terms of relationships between preference, as indicated by preferential choices of musical excerpts, and eight variables: introversion-extroversion, masculinity-femininity, age, educational level, sex, formal musical training, music recognition ability, and intelligence. Musical training, music recognition, and introversion were related significantly to preference. In scoring their preference measure, Keston and Pinto equated a choice of the classical music excerpt (rather than the "pop" concert, "dinner" music, or popular music excerpt) with a "correct" answer. The study showed that people with greater amounts of musical training and experience who were willing to spend the time required for concentrated listening tend to prefer classical music. It must be stressed that this is *correlational* evidence, an indication that there are tendencies for people scoring highly on one variable to score highly on others. Correlation means relationship, not causality. Training, recognition, and introversion do not cause a preference for classical or any other music.

One cannot study musical preferences for long without encountering Farnsworth's (1966) famous eminence rankings. Based on polls of American Musicological Society members in 1938, 1944, 1951, and 1964, the rankings list composers of classical music in order of their perceived eminence. "Eminence" apparently is interpreted in terms of contributions to music history and worthiness of study. In 1964, the "top five" composers were, in order, Bach, Beethoven, Mozart, Haydn, and Brahms. The rankings, relatively stable across the sampling years, show a notable absence of twentieth century composers. The American Musicological Society is hardly representative of "typical" listeners, and Farnsworth's polls have been criticized, but they do show that musical preferences within one style have some degree of consistency— they are not solely a matter of the whimsey of individual scholars. Eminence and preference are not necessarily the same thing, of course. Farnsworth (1969) reports in his text polls showing less than perfect relationship between perceived eminence and enjoyment of particular composers. On one occasion, preference may be based on eminence; on another it may be based on enjoyment.

Poland (1970) analyzed three music history texts, two music theory texts, Farnsworth's rankings, and the then most recent issue of the Schwann catalog.* He noted the thirty composers cited most frequently in each text, Farnsworth's top thirty, and the thirty composers receiving the most space in Schwann. The seven sources yielded a total of only seventy-one composers, which indi-

---

*The *Schwann Long Playing Record Catalog*, published monthly by W. Schwann, Inc. of Boston, lists available recordings by composer and title. The relative amounts of space required to list the works of various composers provide some indication of those composers' popularities as indicated by demands of the marketplace.

cates considerable agreement regarding whose music merits attention in the opinions of the various authors, the sample completing Farnsworth's surveys, and the recording industry.

Correlations among the individual sources' citations of works by the seventy-one composers showed that eminence and preference may be two different things. Farnsworth's rankings correlated —.31 with the Schwann catalog listings (the minus sign is an artifact of 1 being "high" in the rankings) while the Schwann listings correlated at least .76 with all other sources.

Poland counted the total number of citations for each of the seventy-one composers in the combined five texts. He listed the sixty composers who had at least one full column of Schwann listings. The two lists were not identical, but there were remarkable similarities when each list was analyzed by composer nationality and historical period. About 59 percent of the combined citations were works of German composers. Ten percent were French works; 9 percent were Russian, 7 percent were Italian, and slightly less than 3 percent were American. The remaining 12 percent accounted for the rest of the world, and all those citations were to European composers' works with the exception of Villa-Lobos, a Brazilian.

About 19 percent of the combined citations were baroque; 26 percent were classic, and 34 percent were romantic. Because one music history text gave more attention to pre-baroque music than the other texts, the list based on the texts showed 0.3 percent for the period 500 BC to 1450, 3.8 percent for Renaissance, and 17 percent for "modern" (1915-1955) works. The corresponding percentages for the Schwann-based list were zero, zero, and 20.

Fifty-two percent of the text citations were to just eleven composers, nine of whom were German. Just five composers had one-third of all citations; in order, they were Beethoven, Bach, Mozart, Brahms, and Haydn. Poland's investigation suggests that the core of music study is built around works of "the three B's" plus Mozart and Haydn. Perhaps preferences are perpetuated.

The apparent reverence for the past, which emerges in descriptive research such as that of Farnsworth and Poland as well as in analyses of orchestral programs, is troublesome to fans of contemporary music. People wonder whether there is a "gap" between composer and audience and to what it might be attributable.

J. Mueller (1967) believes that comtemporary composers and audiences indeed are separated by an "aesthetic gap" which is a twentieth century phenomenon, not an event recurring throughout music history. The claim that "good" music never was appreciated initially is not substantiated. Mueller's evidence includes favorable initial criticism of the works of Beethoven and others and the rate of new works' appearances in European concert programs of the nineteenth century. New music never is equally new; novelties vary in their public interest and adoption. The contemporary composer often is more experimental and pays a price through nonconformity which strains the audience's ears. Mueller suggests that modern composers need to make more effort to understand society.

A group of Dutch orchestral concert subscribers generally were satisfied with the programs according to an analysis of survey findings (De Jager, 1967). Beethoven was the most popular composer; contemporary composers collectively were the most disliked. Modern music was more disturbing to older people who had lesser amounts of education and did not play an instrument.

Although inherent musical properties do not guarantee "good," "great," or "truthful" music, many people may prefer the lyric melodies, predictable tonal and harmonic patterns, symmetric rhythms, extensive repetitions, and orchestral colors available in the music of eighteenth and nineteenth century composers. The widespread availability of recordings of many styles and eras means that twentieth century composers must compete with the music of previous generations (Hamm, Nettl, and Byrnside, 1975).

Closed-Mindedness

People who are dogmatic, generally resistant to change, and rather authoritarian sometimes are labelled as *closed-minded*. Variability in acceptance and admiration of new music is more than a matter of degree of closed-mindedness, but closed-minded individuals may be less willing to accommodate new music because of their difficulty in forming conceptual systems. In one study (Mikol, 1960), open– and closed–minded listeners with similar musical backgrounds evaluated works of Schoenberg and Brahms. There were no differences in reaction to Brahms, but the closed-minded subjects reacted more negatively to Schoenberg than did the open-minded subjects. An attempt to replicate the results with music of Bartok did not succeed.

Zagona and Kelly (1966) studied the reactions of forty-four highly dogmatic and forty-four lowly dogmatic individuals to an abstract film featuring lines and colors in motion synchronized with jazz. Subjects' ratings showed that the highly dogmatic persons were less accepting of the film.

Convergence Toward One Popular Style

Preferences for popular music have not been assessed to the degree they deserve. The view that popular music appeals only to some broad undifferentiated mass, victimized by an inferior culture, simply is false; all people, including teenagers, have specific and individual tastes (Denisoff, 1976). With the onset of television, radio stations and their advertisers began to cater to particular audiences; stations now specialize in "Top 40," soul, country-western, rock, folk, "beautiful music," and other styles (Peterson and Davis, 1974). "Top 40" listeners tend to be younger than average while "beautiful music," i.e., "easy listening," listeners tend to be older.

A major musical preference phenomenon is the development of separate American popular music cultures during the past quarter century. From roughly 1930 to the early 1950s, popular music was aimed predominantly at an adult white middle class culture. Music popular with one generation generally was popular with another. Country-western, black, and folk styles were alive and well, but they had only a regional appeal. From about 1955 on, popular music became more fragmented. Country, soul, and folk styles acquired national audiences; rock music became the music of youth. Each musical style has its own values and sociological bases (Hamm, Nettl, and Byrnside).

In visiting music classrooms, the writers have noticed that overt group musical preferences narrow with advancing grade level. First, second, and third graders generally will listen to brief excerpts of a variety of musical styles without undue protest. A trained soprano, ethnic musics, and ambiguous electronic sounds are accepted. In fourth grade and beyond, students will cover their ears, cringe, and look around to ascertain that sufficient numbers of peers are doing the same thing. The preferred music becomes rock.

An increasing preference for rock music with advancing grade level was demonstrated clearly by Greer, Dorow, and Randall (1974), who studied the rock versus nonrock listening of 134 children, nursery school through sixth grade. Each child spent ten minutes with a device containing keys which he or she could press to hear either rock music (eight 75-second excerpts of a local station's "top twenty") or nonrock music. Nonrock meant eight 75-second symphonic music excerpts for nursery school children, second graders, and third graders. Nonrock meant classical piano excerpts for first, fourth, and fifth graders; the sixth graders' nonrock excerpts were Broadway show tunes. Total listening time increased steadily with grade level, with significant increases between nursery school and first grade, second and third grade, and fifth and sixth grade. Listening time for rock increased steadily, with an especially large increase between third and fourth grades; other significant increases occurred between nursery school and first grade, and between fifth and sixth grades. Nonrock listening time increased significantly between nursery school and first grade, but it *decreased* significantly between third and fourth grades. There were no significant differences between rock and nonrock listening time at the nursery school and first grade levels, but beyond first grade, rock was preferred consistently. Although this study was limited to two schools in one metropolitan setting, additional studies (Greer, Dorow, and Hanser, 1973; Greer et al., 1973) suggest decreasing interest in nonrock music with advancing grade level.

The assessment of attitudes toward music, conducted as part of

The National Assessment of Educational Progress,* supports the trend noted by Greer et al. It reveals an increased preference for rock from nine-year-olds to thirteen-year-olds to seventeen-year-olds.

Summary of Existing Preferences

Existing preferences for Western music, then, are such that there is a tendency to prefer music of the eighteenth and nineteenth centuries as far as art music is concerned. Such preferences may result in part from contemporary composers' excessive deviations from compositional norms as well as personal qualities of the listeners. Popular music, often ignored when musical preferences are studied, requires more investigation. In the elementary school years preferences appear to converge toward rock music, which may make education in a variety of musical styles difficult.

SOCIETAL INFLUENCES ON MUSICAL PREFERENCES

Musical preferences are more than interaction of inherent musical characteristics and individual psychological and social variables. There are societal pressures which influence preference. A person making a musical choice considers opinions of other persons who are significant in his or her life, as well as cultural messages in and about the music.

Two experiments by Greer, Dorow, and Hanser (1973) suggested that teacher approval may influence young children's preferences. Thirty-nine second and third graders changed from a pretest preference for rock to no post-test difference between rock and symphonic music in a study of instrument discrimination training. Twenty-four nursery school children changed from either lack of a pretest preference or a preference for rock to a

---

*The National Asessment of Educational Progress is a project of the Educational Commission of the States. It was developed in collaboration with the National Center for Educational Statistics of the Department of Health, Education and Welfare. Additional funding was provided by the Carnegie Corporation and the Ford Foundation's Fund for the Advancement of Education. The project surveyed the educational attainments of nine-year-olds, thirteen-year-olds, seventeen-year-olds, and adults between the ages of twenty-six and thirty-five. The music assessment was conducted in 1971-72.

post-test preference for symphonic selections in a similar study. Dorow's (1977) study of fourth and fifth graders replicated and extended the findings of the Greer et al. 1973 study.

Rigg (1948) attempted to alter preference by introducing propaganda associating certain music with Nazi Germany. Three compositions of Wagner, one of Beethoven, one of Franck, and one of Sibelius were played twice for three groups of listeners. Each group initially heard the compositions without comment. One group then was given favorable information about the German selections. Another group received unfavorable propaganda-based information; the third group received neither favorable nor unfavorable information. After the second hearing, all groups showed increased enjoyment of the compositions, as indicated by a five-point scale, but the largest gain was in the favorable comment group. The unfavorable comment group had the least gain.

Popular music of the mid-1950s was classified according to the relationship of the lyrics to five stages of adolescent lovemaking: prologue, courtship, a honeymoon period, a downward course, and an abandoned lonely stage. The lyrics, appropriate to a limited and predictable love cycle, provided a conventional language for formulating adolescent expectations and self-conceptions (Horton, 1957).

Johnstone and Katz (1957) found that teen-age girls' musical preferences were influenced by their peers. Highly popular girls conformed more closely to neighborhood norms regarding particular songs and disk jockeys than did less popular girls. In a higher socioeconomic neighborhood, the girls who dated frequently preferred songs suggesting "blues" and deprivation, while girls who dated infrequently preferred songs suggesting "happy" or "indulgent" love. In a lower socioeconomic neighborhood, all girls, regardless of dating frequency, preferred songs suggesting happiness and indulgence.

Inglefield (1974) found that eighteen ninth graders showed an overall tendency to alter their expressed musical preferences to conform to those of acknowledged peer leaders. Those subjects who were more otherdirected than innerdirected, more in need of social approval, and more dependent than independent, as identified by personality tests, tended to be the greater conformers. The most conformity was to expressed jazz preferences, next to folk music, thirdly to rock, and least to classical music. Inglefield believed that jazz elicited the most conformity because it generally is alien to adolescent musical environments, while classical music elicited the least conformity because of well-established negative judgments. Conformity studies must be interpreted cautiously because public expression of a preference in accordance with what a respected peer says does not guarantee private acceptance of the peer's judgments. Nevertheless, the pressures to conform in musical judgments are real; they are discussed more fully in Chapter Eleven.

A symposium on new patterns of musical behavior of the young generation in eighteen industrial societies sought to examine the phenomenon of "pop music" and its sociological implications (Bontinck, 1972). Although many of the symposium papers reflected personal observations, more or less informal surveys, and even speculation, it is apparent that popular music is associated with a particular youth subculture in most of the nations represented. The extent to which these subcultures influence the musical preferences of youth in the respective societies is unclear, but the authors suspect that such influences are great.

ALTERING PREFERENCES

Musical preferences may be altered. One's less preferred style may become a more preferred style, and a listener's range of choices may be broadened. Much music requires learning through formal instruction before a listener can expect more than some sort of sound bath. K. Mueller (1970) stressed that listeners cannot hear accurately because they are not taught to hear musical details. The potential for developing and expanding preferences through education was noted by Duerksen (1968), who, in an extensive study of thematic recognition ability, observed that the typical student, college and high school, indicated some positive response toward classical and jazz music as well as rock, popular, and folk styles.

An early descriptive study by Valentine (1913) showed children with greater amounts of musical training approaching adult standards of interval judgment at an earlier age than children with relatively little training. Interval preferences are a miniscule part of musical preference, but Valentine's study often is cited as evidence that children's musical judgments can be accelerated in an adult direction.

Seventh graders who were encouraged to be creative in activities related to contemporary music outscored a control group who followed the existing curriculum guide on a test of musical understanding (Archibeque, 1966), although all seventh graders in the study developed an interest in contemporary music regardless of prior training, grades, or initial attitudes.

Repetition, a process for making the unfamiliar familiar, may be useful in altering and expanding musical preference. Mull (1940) played obscure piano pieces by Bach, Chopin, and Brahms to thirty undergraduate musicians. Each piece, one per composer, was played three times, and listeners reported "direct aesthetic responses" by raising their hands at "high spots." Of the fourteen regions found especially pleasant by fifteen or more listeners, nine were repetitions of thematic material. With repeated hearings, as the music became more familiar, the lengths of the "high spots" increased. Listeners became aroused by anticipation of newly familiar sections and raised their hands in anticipation.

Getz (1966) found that seventh graders' preferences for string ensemble excerpts increased over ten weeks as a result of familiarity through repetition. Faster tempos usually elicited greater preference.

Schuckert and McDonald (1968) asked twenty children, four to six years old, to choose between a classical example and a jazz example. Eight preferred the classical example, twelve preferred jazz. During four quiet play periods each child was required to hear his or her less preferred style. A retesting showed the choices altered to eleven for classical, nine for jazz—not statistically significant, but in the direction predicted by the researchers.

Familiarity through repetition will not guarantee an increase in preference. In Hornyak's (1966) study, 1300 elementary, junior high school, and high school students in a Midwestern city attended concerts which included four woodwind quintets by contemporary American composers. Attempts were made to familiarize student groups with the less traditional music by playing tapes of the music in advance. Familiarity increased the positive responses of elementary students to the contemporary compositions, but it made no difference for the junior high pupils. The high school students showed a *less* positive response as a result of preliminary hearing.

Musical preferences can be altered, but the direction of alteration as well as the means is not always predictable. The philosophical question of *should* preferences be altered is not answered satisfactorily. Music educators and critics should remember that musical preferences result from a complex interaction of personal and social factors, all of which are not under the control of any one institution. An expansion of preferences may be attempted in educational settings with reasonable chances of success, but a reordering of musical preferences in some arbitrary direction is questionable.

SUMMARY

The major points of this chapter include the following:
1. Musical preferences result from a complex mixture of musical and human characteristics.
2. "Good" music may be "good" because of inherent structural aspects; it may be "good" because of what people say about it in context.
3. Preferences may be related to various personality aspects.
4. There are group tendencies in musical preference, particularly for certain predominantly German composers of Western art music.
5. The apparent reverence for the past observed in classical music is a new occurrence in music history; it probably is attributable to perpetuation of tradition through formal education and the widespread availability of music from different eras as well as radical creations of nonconforming contemporary composers.
6. Popular music exists today in several forms, each of which has

its own cultural orientation and sociological base.

7. The preferences of many American school children focus increasingly on rock music with advancing grade levels.

8. Musical preferences may be influenced by respected authorities, extramusical aspects, and peer pressures.

9. Musical preferences may be altered and expanded through education, but the results are not always predictable.

REFERENCES

Adorno, T. W. *Introduction to the Sociology of Music* (E. B. Ashton, Trans.). New York: Seabury Press, 1976.

An Assessment of Attitudes Toward Music. Denver: National Assessment of Educational Progress, 1975.

Archibeque, C. P. Developing a taste for contemporary music. *Journal of Research in Music Education*, 1966, *14*, 142-148.

Berlyne, D. E. *Aesthetics and Psychobiology.* New York: Appleton-Century-Crofts, 1971.

Bontinck, I. (Ed.). *New Patterns of Musical Behavior of the Young Generation in Industrial Societies.* Vienna: International Institute for Music, Dance, and Theatre in the Audio-visual Media, 1972.

Cattell, R. B., & Anderson, J. C. The measurement of personality and behavior disorders by the I.P.A.T. music preference test. *Journal of Applied Psychology*, 1953, *37*, 446-454.

Chancellor, G. R. Aesthetic value in music: Implications for music education from the classic literature of the field (Doctoral dissertation, Northwestern University, 1974). *Dissertation Abstracts International*, 1975, *35*, 6493-A. (University Microfilms No. 75-7886)

DeJager, H. Listening to the audience. *Journal of Research in Music Education*, 1967, *15*, 293-299.

Denisoff, R. S. Massification and popular music: A review. *Journal of Popular Culture*, 1976, *9*, 886-894.

Dorow, L. G. The effect of teacher approval/disapproval ratios on student music selection and concert attentiveness. *Journal of Research in Music Education*, 1977, *25*, 32-40.

Duerksen, G. L. A study of the relationship between the perception of musical processes and the enjoyment of music. *Council for Research in Music Education*, 1968, *12*, 1-8.

Farnsworth, P. R. Musicological attitudes on eminence. *Journal of Research in Music Education*, 1966, *14*, 41-44.

Farnsworth, P. R. *The Social Psychology of Music* (2nd ed.). Ames: Iowa State University Press, 1969.

Getz, R. P. The effects of repetition on listening response. *Journal of Re-*

search in Music Education, 1966, *14,* 178-192.

Greer, R. D., Dorow, L., & Hanser, S. Music discrimination training and the music selection behavior of nursery and primary level children. *Council for Research in Music Education,* 1973, *35,* 30-43.

Greer, R. D., Dorow, L. G., & Randall, A. Music listening preferences of elementary school children. *Journal of Research in Music Education,* 1974, *22,* 284-291.

Greer, R. D., Dorow, L. G., Wachhaus, G., & White, E. R. Adult approval and students' music selection behavior. *Journal of Research in Music Education,* 1973, *21,* 345-354.

Hahn, M. E. A proposed technique for investigating the relationship between musical preferences and personality structure. Unpublished doctoral dissertation, University of Kansas, 1954.

Hamm, C. E., Nettl, B., & Byrnside, R. *Contemporary Music and Music Cultures.* Englewood Cliffs, N.J.: Prentice-Hall, 1975.

Hornyak, R. R. An analysis of student attitudes towards contemporary American music. *Council for Research in Music Education,* 1968, *8,* 1-14.

Horton, D. The dialogue of courtship in popular songs. *American Journal of Sociology,* 1957, *62,* 569-578.

Inglefield, H. G. *Conformity Behavior Reflected in the Musical Preferences of Adolescents.* Paper presented at the meeting of the Music Educators National Conference, Anaheim, California, March, 1974.

Johnstone, J., & Katz, E. Youth and popular music: A study of the sociology of taste. *American Journal of Sociology,* 1957, *62,* 563-568.

Keston, M. J., & Pinto, I. M. Possible factors influencing musical preference. *Journal of Genetic Psychology,* 1955, *86,* 101-113.

Koh, S. D. Scaling musical preferences. *Journal of Experimental Psychology,* 1965, *70,* 79-82.

Koh, S. D. Time-error in comparisons of preferences for musical excerpts. *American Journal of Psychology,* 1967, *80,* 171-185.

McMullen, P. T., & Arnold, M. J. Preference and interest as functions of distributional redundancy in rhythmic sequences. *Journal of Research in Music Education,* 1976, *24,* 22-31.

Meyer, L. *Emotion and Meaning in Music.* Chicago: University of Chicago Press, 1956.

Mikol, B. The enjoyment of new musical systems. In M. Rokeach (Ed.), *The Open and Closed Mind.* New York: Basic Books, 1960.

Mueller, J. H. The aesthetic gap between consumer and composer. *Journal of Research in Music Education,* 1967, *15,* 151-158.

Mueller, K. H. The other side of the record. *Council for Research in Music Education,* 1970, *21,* 22-31.

Mull, H. K. Preferred regions in music compositions and the effect of repetition upon them. *American Journal of Psychology,* 1940, *53,* 583-586.

Peterson, R. A., & Davis, R. B. The contemporary American radio audience.

Popular Music and Society, 1974, *3,* 299-314.

Poland, W. The content of graduate studies in music education: Music history and music theory. In H. L. Cady (Ed.), *Graduate Studies in Music Education.* Columbus: Ohio State University School of Music, 1970.

Reimer, B. *A Philosophy of Music Education.* Englewood Cliffs, N.J.: Prentice-Hall, 1970.

Rigg, M. C. Favorable versus unfavorable propaganda in the enjoyment of music. *Journal of Experimental Psychology,* 1948, *38,* 78-81.

Schuckert, R. F., & McDonald, R. L. An attempt to modify the musical preferences of preschool children. *Journal of Research in Music Education,* 1968, *16,* 39-45.

Schwadron, A. A. *Aesthetics: Dimensions for Music Education.* Washington: Music Educators National Conference, 1967.

Valentine, C. W. The aesthetic appreciation of musical intervals among school children and adults. *British Journal of Psychology,* 1913, *6,* 190-216.

Zagona, S., & Kelly, M. A. The resistance of the closed mind to a novel and complex audiovisual experience. *Journal of Social Psychology,* 1966, *70,* 123-131.

Chapter Eight

FUNCTIONAL MUSIC

As NOTED IN CHAPTER FIVE, music has served (and still serves) a number of basic functions in society. It is a phenomenon of human behavior and is present in all cultures. Besides aesthetic and expressive functions, music also serves many nonmusical functions.

> Indeed most music is performed for the express purpose of achieving aims wherein the aesthetic is not the primary goal. The *functional music* is far older and more abundant than music played or composed for aesthetic purposes. All primitive music is functional music . . . [and] even today a majority of the reasons given for school music ascribe to its functional goals. (Gaston, 1951/52, p. 60)

While music's general functions were discussed in Chapter Five, the present chapter serves to examine some of the specific *uses* of music today.

Some of the uses discussed are traditional; i.e. they are similar to the uses of music throughout much of the history of Western civilization: in religious rites and ceremonies, to promote social conformity and interaction, to accompany dance, and generally to contribute toward the continuity and stability of a culture. Other uses are directed more specifically toward particular ends. They include industrial, commercial, therapeutic, and educational uses.

It has long been recognized that different types of music serve different purposes. While all of the factors which serve to influence any musical behaviors are variables to be considered, it appears that functional music generally stimulates or suppresses activity. Prior to examination of some of the uses of music is a brief examination of the characteristics of the collative characteristics of music which appear to cause it to stimulate or suppress behavior. It should be recognized, however, that individuals' responses to these collative characteristics also are influenced by previous experiences with the characteristics. Within a cultural setting people learn to react in certain ways to certain types of music. While the exact nature of the interaction between learning and the collative characteristics is not clear, observation of reactions to the two basic types of music suggests that differential response patterns are real, regardless of the degree of influence coming from learning or the collative characteristics themselves.

CHARACTERISTICS OF STIMULATIVE AND SEDATIVE MUSIC

All music exists on a continuum between highly stimulating, invigorating music and soothing, sedating music (Gaston, 1968, p. 18). Music therapists and others concerned with using music to influence behavior essentially are concerned with either stimulating or suppressing activity, and the type of music selected for influencing the desired behaviors generally reflects different structural characteristics.

Stimulative Music

Music which stimulates or arouses listeners has a strong energizing component. "For most people it is rhythm that provides the energy of music, be it great or small" (Gaston, 1968, p. 17). Lundin (1967, p. 172) and Farnsworth (1969, p. 83) both suggest that tempo, an important attribute of rhythm, is of primary importance in influencing mood response to music.

Rhythm characterized by detached, percussive sounds stimulates muscular action. March and dance music has definitive and repetitive rhythm which appears to stimulate physical movement. The more percussive, staccato, and accented the music, the greater the apparent physical response to it. Whenever the underlying beat is clearly defined, even a casual listener is likely to respond with some overt-physical response.

While rhythm, and particularly tempo, appears to be the predominant energizing factor, dynamic level also appears to serve as a stimulator. Louder music seems to stimulate greater response activity than softer music. Other musical attributes such as pitch level, melody, harmony, texture, and timbre also may help energize music, but the extent to which these variables contribute toward the driving, energizing force of music is less clearly understood than for rhythm and dynamics.

Sedative Music

Music which soothes, calms, or tranquilizes behavior appears to rely on sounds which are nonpercussive and legato. Its melodic passages are sustained, legato, and generally have a minimum of rhythmic activity. The most important rhythmic attribute is the underlying beat, which is usually monotonously regular but subdued. Lullabies are the primary example of functional sedative music. They are comprised of sustained legato melodies, but with a quiet, steady underlying beat. They also reflect other characteristics of sedative music. The dynamic level usually is quite soft, the tempo is generally much slower than for stimulative music, and the frequency range appears to be quite limited.

Evidence of Differential Response to Stimulative and Sedative Music

Apparently individuals concerned with using music for functional purposes have long recognized the differential response to the two types of music, but they have not gone to great lengths to corroborate the effects through research.* Certainly music used by the military throughout history to incite troops into battle reflects the characteristics of stimulative music, as does music of today's pep bands and marching bands. On the other hand, melodies used to soothe infants reflect characteristics of sedative music. March music reflects different characteristics than romantic music. Responses to adjective checklists, taken as indicators of mood response to music, reveal quite different lists of adjectives for stimulative and sedative music. Applause at concerts generally is louder for stimulative music than for sedative music.

The bulk of the limited research particularly focused on com-

---

*An exception to this might be some of the research conducted by consultants for the Muzak™ Corporation. This research will be discussed later in the chapter.

parisons of responses to the two types of music was conducted in the 1940s and 1950s at The University of Kansas by some of Gaston's students. His (1952; 1968, pp. 18-19) reviews of this research revealed that nearly all studies found significant differences in response to the two types of music. Drawings and paintings by both children and adults while listening to two types of music were readily classified by judges according to the type of music to which they were drawn. Postural response to the two types of music revealed that subjects sat more erect when listening to stimulative music than when listening to sedative music. Clinical observation of the effects of sedative music on patients in a hospital ward resulted in "an observable sedative effect for the ward as a whole." Several studies of physiological response to stimulative and sedative music also revealed significant differences in response rates.

In summary, examples of music used throughout history, in everyday life today, and in a limited number and variety of research studies reveal differential response to stimulative and sedative music. The application of this knowledge and the subtlety with which it is applied for particular uses comprises the balance of the discussion in this chapter. Some of these functions capitalize on music's ability to stimulate while others capitalize on its ability to soothe. These applications are discussed as they pertain to music in ceremonies; "background" music; commercial, industrial, and therapeutic uses of music; music to facilitate non-musical learning; and music as a reward for behavioral change.

MUSIC IN CEREMONIES

Ceremonial music reflects one of the earliest functional uses of music. It is a part of primitive cultures today just as it has been throughout history. Apparently music is viewed as an integral part of ceremony and does much to lend to the formality of such occasions. Virtually all types of ceremony incorporate music in one way or another, be they religious, military, state, athletic, or commercial.

Musselman (1974, p. 129) notes that music has functioned more consistently and more positively in religious ritual than in any other area of life in Western civilization, even to the extent that religious music now comprises one of the longest and richest musical traditions. The specific function of music in religious ceremony tends to vary with its place in the ceremony, as evidenced by the principal sections of the highly formalized Mass of the Roman Catholic Church. Anglican and Lutheran services also have music as an integral part of the service.

Churches of a more evangelical tradition, such as the Methodist, Baptist, and Presbyterian denominations, also include music as part of the services, but they appear to place less emphasis on observance of corporate sacraments than do the Roman Catholic, Anglican, and Lutheran services; instead, they appear to involve the congregation much more directly. Hymn singing appears to be a direct way for drawing the congregation into the service.

Music in religious services appears to serve several functions: at times it serves as a signal to stimulate the congregation to respond in a certain way. At other times quiet organ interludes are used to help establish a mood of reverence or tranquility. Congregational singing serves to draw people together, while choir anthems appear to lead the worshipers to reflect on the beliefs and values of the religion and its implications for them as individuals. Special religious ceremonies are accompanied by special music. Certainly weddings, funerals, and special religious days are made more meaningful by music designed to enhance the significance of the occasion. While some of these uses of music in religious ceremony may be more "persuasive" than "ceremonial" in function, they nevertheless indicate the importance of music in religion.

Music also has been a traditional part of military and state ceremonies and, as in religious ceremony, it has served a variety of functions. Perhaps the traditional function of military music has been to inspire and heighten interest in the military cause and to stimulate troops to battle. That music for the military traditionally has been band music characterized by percussion and fanfare is more than coincidental. Such music appears to have a highly stimulative effect. Even today, the military and state ceremonies of most nations include music of the military band rather than string music.

Music in military and state ceremony not only is used as a signal to draw attention to a particular part of the ceremony, such as playing "Hail to the Chief" to signal the arrival of the President of the United States, but it also is used to create a feeling of patriotism and to commemorate particular occasions that are considered important. Music serves to heighten the immediate importance of the occasion as well as to contribute toward the memorableness of the occasion.

Many occasions other than religious and military also include ceremonial music. Major sporting events nearly always include ceremonial music. The opening and closing ceremonies of the Olympic Games always involve special music, and the medal ceremonies include the playing of the national anthems of the recipients' countries. Major high school, college, and professional sports open with ceremonial music. Music of marching and pep bands, while not always ceremonial music *per se,* serves an important function for sporting events. Nearly any queen (or king) crowning ceremony, whether a high school homecoming event or a Miss World beauty contest, incorporates music into the ceremony. Folk festivals, while perhaps not ceremony in the ritualistic sense, usually rely heavily on music as an integrative force as well as a way for heightening the memorableness of the occasion.

From this cursory review of the use of music in ceremony, it is apparent that music has been an important part of ceremony. While the effects of ceremonial music have not been examined from a "scientific" perspective, the fact that music has been and continues to be a part of most ceremonies attests to its functional value.

"BACKGROUND" MUSIC

Although "background" music has been used in both religious and secular settings for centuries, it has been with the advent of electronically reproduced music that background music has come to be so prevalent in society. The type of function background music serves varies greatly for individuals. Background music is used in a wide variety of settings, some of which will be discussed in subsequent sections of this chapter. In some settings it is used systematically while in others music of various styles appears to be played informally and indiscriminately.

Background music, sometimes called "mood music," "easy listening," or "beautiful music," is any music played while the "listeners" are primarily engaged in some task or activity other than listening to music. Musselman (1974, p. 93) notes that it is "intended to be heard but not actively or purposefully listened to." The function it serves varies not only with individual listeners but also with the nature of the task or activity with which they are involved.

Individuals use background music informally and for various reasons. Often they select a favorite style of music, perhaps an "easy listening" or "popular music" (usually meaning rock) radio station or some tape or disc recordings, and let the music play continuously while they are engaged in reading, studying, driving, working in their home or on a job, or doing any number of various activities. Functions for this type of music appear to be more varied than for systematically applied background music; further, little or no thought appears to be given to the function the music is serving—the individual, if asked, often replies merely that he or she "likes" to have some background music while reading, driving, working, or whatever. However, it appears that such informally used background music may serve a variety of functions. An individual may use the music to break the monotony while he or she is engaged in some task which requires little concentration; another might use the music to alleviate feelings of loneliness or to help establish a particular mood, perhaps of reverie or relaxation. Background music also is used to mask other unwanted sounds. When entertaining, some people play background music to help establish an atmosphere conducive to stimulating conversation. Although the effects of such informal uses of music have not been studied to any extent, they apparently are considered valuable by the individuals involved; otherwise, there would not be such widespread usage of music in this way.

Aside from recent uses of music in therapeutic and educational situations, the most extensive and systematic application of background music for functional purposes has been by the Muzak

Corporation. This corporation, established in the 1930s, has capitalized on music's effects as background music and developed a vast international business which transmits music into offices, businesses, industries, and many other types of public and commercial environments in more than twenty countries. It appears that much of the background music heard in businesses, doctors' offices, and other public places is produced and programmed by the Muzak Corporation, although some background music may be radio, privately developed tapes, or perhaps that of other companies. Because of its prevalence, a brief discussion of the characteristics of Muzak's music follows.

Central to Muzak's programming is their concept of "stimulus progression" music, fifteen-minute segments of recorded music designed to provide a psychological "lift"; i.e. the musical segments reflect a "sense of forward movement and change, designed to mitigate tension, boredom, melancholy and fatigue" (Muzak, 1976). Depending on the nature of the tasks or environment for which the music will provide a background, these segments are played either in alternating periods of fifteen minutes of music and fifteen minutes of silence or "continuously," i.e. with two-minute interludes of silence between each fifteen-minute musical segment.

Each fifteen-minute segment includes a sequence of five or six specially recorded instrumental pieces with progressively increasing stimulus values. The "stimulus value" is a composite of the effects of four variables: tempo, rhythm classification of popular music, instrument groupings, and number of instruments used. Although the empirical basis by which the stimulus values were originally derived is not known, Muzak has published "stimulus progression charts" which show that increased tempo reflects increased stimulus value, certain meters and rhythm styles have greater stimulus value than others, certain instrument groupings are of greater stimulus value than others, and an increase in the size of the ensemble (texture change) results in increased stimulus value. Popular music is selected, arranged, performed, and recorded to meet certain characteristics for each of the four variables, after which it is sequenced into fifteen-minute segments with increasing stimulus value.

Whether it is Muzak or some other music, background music for other groups of people has become a part of the contemporary environment, and the basic function of such music appears to be to "humanize the impersonal atmosphere of the environment" (Musselman, p. 96). Public places such as airline and bus terminals, restaurants, hotel lobbies, doctors' and dentists' offices; and public conveyances such as subways, buses, and airplanes provide music as a familiar and welcome relief to the aloneness, anxiety, or nervousness that individuals sometimes feel in situations with large crowds of strangers or when in anticipation of a somewhat unknown or threatening event.

Background music in industry also is becoming more prevalent. Where workers are involved in simple repetitive tasks, the music can serve to break the monotony. In situations called "vigilance tasks," which require alertness on the part of a worker, music can serve an "arousal" function. The onset of fatigue and decline in efficiency which occurs twice a day in the normal eight-hour workday routine, called the "industrial efficiency curve," can be combatted to a degree with appropriate background music. (These industrial uses of music will be examined more fully below.)

The white-collar worker's environment also includes background music. In some relatively quiet offices, background music is used to raise the overall sound level to mask the effects of occasional sudden noises which are distracting. In some offices, the environment may be too quiet for maximum efficiency and comfort of the workers. The quietness might inhibit freedom of conversation. In these cases music may serve to provide privacy for conversations within a large open space. Musselman (p. 96) notes that the acoustical factors alone may help this situation. Normal human speech covers an intensity range of between 30 and 75 decibels and a frequency range from 100 to 7500 Hz. Background music, above the lower limits of these ranges but well below the upper limits, tends to render speech inaudible beyond a few feet, thus providing a semblance of privacy for conversation. In other situations, however, where spoken communication is essential, background music may interfere if the music emphasizes the frequencies corresponding to that of consonants, which roughly are between 500 and 4800 Hz.

Although background music is intended to serve some special-ized functions such as those noted above, perhaps its ultimate value in nearly all situations is to humanize the environment. Music in Western culture is essentially a nonthreatening, satisfy-ing phenomenon. While scientific documentation of the effects of background music may be lacking, it is apparent that it is believed to be valuable by many individuals, including those who provide the money to make it available. Such beliefs lend validity to Musselman's (p. 96) statement that background music has the "practical economic effect of improving efficiency, morale, and safety, and of increasing productivity among employees or satis-faction among customers."

COMMERCIAL USES OF MUSIC

The range of musical enterprise which could be considered commercial is great. Conceivably concert artists, composers, per-formers, and teachers could be viewed as engaged in musical ac-tivity for commercial reasons. On the other hand, some musical enterprise appears to be more obviously concerned with using music for financial gain. This section examines four particular uses of music which appear to have financial gain as a major concern: (1) background music in places of business, (2) music for com-mercials, (3) music for television and movies, and (4) music as entertainment.

Mentioned briefly in the discussion of background music, the use of music in stores, shopping centers, restaurants, and other places where members of the public come as customers has be-come prevalent in contemporary society. While no research is available to demonstrate any particular effects on sales, it appears that businesses have recognized music's value in humanizing an environment. Just as lighting and decorating, music has come to be viewed as an essential means for making an environment at-tractive to customers. Apparently music facilitates the creation of a pleasant, nonthreatening, but subtly active atmosphere which is conducive to attracting customers and stimulating business.

Music for radio and television commercial advertising has almost become a business in itself, even to the point that there are composers who specialize in writing such music. Commercials usually last between fifteen and sixty seconds. Radio commercials involve both verbal and musical sounds while television commercials include verbal and musical sounds as well as visual-verbal information and visual images. The intent is to persuade the listener (and viewer) of the value of the product and to cause him or her to remember it. The fact that commercials are brief interruptions within or between some continuing programs calls them to a listener's attention. Toddlers playing in a room with television playing often will interrupt their playing to listen to and view the commercials. The verbal message of a commercial often is a song the melody of which is "catchy." Depending on the nature of the product, the melody may reflect varying degrees of stimulative characteristics; other commercials, however, use music as background to help create a particular mood relevant to the type of product being advertised. Apparently music is valuable in facilitating interest in and memory of products, and there appears little likelihood that this functional use of music will diminish in the future.

Musselman (p. 103) maintains that one of the most important uses of music in Western culture is to enhance the emotional qualities of words, actions, or images in film and television dramas. While some might argue that this use of music is more "artistic" than "commercial," it is clear that television and film music in itself has become a huge commercial enterprise. Composing, scoring, and performing such music is a multimillon dollar business.

Television and film media are a theatre of illusion. The intent is to stimulate the viewer to perceive or imagine a sense of reality, something which appears to be substantially aided by music. The more successfully this is accomplished the greater the commercial success of the production.

The function of music in film and television has been summarized by Musselman (pp. 103-106). The most basic uses are to fill silence, mask unwanted sounds, and encourage empathy for the figures on the screen. Music which fulfills these functions generally must be consistent with the mood and tempo of the story.   Another use is to imitate or suggest sounds of natural phenomena: Perhaps the most important function of music in film and television is to lend to the continuity of the story.   The traditional practice is to identify certain distinctive themes or motifs with particular persons, places, or ideas in the story and to use these themes with reappearances of the person, place, or idea or whenever they are to be remembered.   Television serials or weekly shows also are readily identified by their distinctive musical themes.   That such themes are readily recognized by the general public is reflected by the apparent popularity of marching band football halftime shows based on themes from television shows.   Music also provides continuity to film and television dramas by serving as a cushion or transition between scenes with quite different emotional implications.

The dependence on music to heighten the emotional impact of a scene represents another major use of music in film and television.   Music usually is used to build suspense rather than dispell it.   Musselman (p. 106) typifies this use of music in a television western:

> We are looking over the shoulder of a cowboy who is scanning the distant horizon.   Suddenly a lone horseman appears there, silhouetted against the rising moon.   Is he friend or foe?   The cowboy cannot tell for sure, but a sudden loud (*sforzando*) dissonance warns us that danger is imminent.

Without question, background music has become a vital and functional part of the film and television industries, and the commercial success of the industries is due in no small part to effects of music on audience response.

Perhaps the greatest commercial success with music is the field of entertainment, particularly the recording industry.   While persons working in the popular music field are considered "artists," most appear to develop their art for commercial rather than artistic ends.   The concern is to develop a style that "sells," even if artistic values have to be compromised.   As Musselman (pp. 141-142) notes, artists and composers of popular music are engaged in a commercial enterprise resulting in music which can survive *intensive* exposure for a relatively short period of time, whereas art or classical music both require and survive *extensive* exposure.

As may be evident, commercial uses of music serve financial ends as well as other ends. Certainly the entertainment value of popular music and film and television music is great. The point of the present discussion, however, has been to bring to light perhaps the most prevalent functional use of music in contemporary society.

INDUSTRIAL USES OF MUSIC

Although some might argue that industrial uses of music have their roots in work songs of more primitive times, early uses of music in industry were primarily recreational. Industries in the early decades of this century sponsored bands, orchestras, choirs, ukulele clubs, harmonica bands, mandolin clubs, and other types of musical performance organizations. Such organizations apparently were viewed as having a beneficial effect on worker morale, although as Lundin (1967, p. 292) notes, assessment of the actual value of such organizations was difficult.

Beginning in the 1930s, music began to be introduced into the actual work situation, and since then psychologists and industrial managers have been trying to assess its effects. A review of studies conducted during the 1930s and 1940s has been provided by Soibelman (1948, pp. 173-203). More recent reviews of such studies have been provided by Uhrbrock (1961), Lundin (1967, pp. 291-303), and Farnsworth (1969, pp. 217-219).

A variety of criteria for "effectiveness" of music on industrial workers has been employed: worker output, attitudes, morale, absenteeism, safety, health, as well as feelings of tiredness and unpleasantness. Many of the studies reviewed, however, do not meet contemporary criteria for quality research, leading Farnsworth (p. 219) to caution that "claims made for industrial music can be generalized only with some hazard. Perhaps the most promising area is that of worker morale." Soibelman (1948) was even more cautious: She made no generalizations from her review. Uhrbrock (1961) concluded that music's effectiveness in increasing worker production had not actually been proven.

Lundin, also cautious in his generalizations, does venture several observations, one of which is contrary to that of Uhrbrock. Based on several studies conducted in 1940s, he concludes that music does increase production for certain types of factory work, although he notes that the specific reasons for this are unclear. A second effect, he notes, is that music tends to relieve monotony, although there is an inverse relationship between complexity of the work task and the effects in this regard. A third generalization Lundin makes is that worker attitudes are related to any beneficial effects music has in industry.

Two more recent studies (Konz, 1964; Devereux, 1969), have provided little insight into the issue. Konz studied the effects of background music on twenty noncollege women's performance of repetitive tasks. Using each subject as her own control, he found no significant effect on the productivity of the group as a whole. Devereux studied the effects of background music on both output and attitude of personnel working on both routine and complex activities. Subjects were thirty-one telecommunications operators. Music was played at a ratio of twenty-four minutes on to six minutes off. Results indicated no significant differences in either worker output or attitude.

Literature, including research conducted by consultants, published by the Muzak Corporation, not surprisingly, reports a number of beneficial effects of music in industry. A 1974 Muzak publication (no author or editor) cites five selected case histories on the effects of music on workers. The studies were conducted at various times between 1958 and 1973 in the Black & Decker Manufacturing Company, Blue Shield/United Medical Services, Bulova Watch Company, Mississippi Power & Light Company, and an unnamed major appliance manufacturer. While the particular criteria for effectiveness, i.e. the dependent variables, varied from study to study, the common conclusions were that Muzak had a beneficial effect on both productivity and attitude. It should be noted, however, that statistical tests of the significance of the differences in "before-after" comparisons were not included in the reports of these studies, even though mean differences on productivity criteria appeared to be "large." The conclusions appeared to be warranted, although the statistical rigor was inadequate.

Regardless of the lack of clearcut statistical data to support the claims stated in their promotional literature, it is apparent that Muzak has been well received in the business world, which in itself attests that many believe that beneficial effects accrue from the use of Muzak's music. A Muzak brochure lists more than 100 major corporations which use Muzak.

To generalize regarding the effects of music in industry is difficult. When so many variables are involved, it is unwise to make too specific claims regarding its effect on productivity. On the other hand, virtually all studies that asked workers whether they liked having background music while working reported that a large majority did prefer to have the music. Apparently, music does have some positive effects, particularly in relieving boredom on certain types of monotonous tasks. Perhaps its greatest value, however, is in humanizing the work environment and thus alleviating some of the undesirable affects of monotony, tension, and fatigue.

THERAPEUTIC USES OF MUSIC

Although healing, soothing, and persuasive effects of music have been espoused throughout the history of Western civilization, it has been only within the past few decades that music has come to be systematically used in therapeutic situations. Michel (1976, p. 5) notes that it has come into widespread use in the United States only since about 1946. The National Association for Music Therapy (NAMT) was founded in 1950.* The development of music therapy as a profession has been coordinated and promoted through the NAMT. Accreditation as a Registered Music Therapist (RMT) is awarded through the NAMT. This accreditation "provides the basic standard for employment under civil service and merit systems in many states, counties, and cities" (Michel, p. 11).

---

*For a review of music therapy organizations in other countries, see D.E. Michel's *Music Therapy: An Introduction to Therapy and Special Education Through Music.* Springfield, Thomas, 1976, pp. 98-105.

Music therapists today are professionally trained individuals who use music as a medium to help influence desirable behavioral changes in individuals with behavioral disorders. Behavioral disorders, as defined by Michel (p. 15), are basically social disorders because they are reflected in relationships between the individual who needs therapy with others. The causes for behavioral disorders may have their roots in physical and mental disabilities, disease, and stress from everyday life. Principles which underlie therapeutic uses of music are:

1. *The establishment or reestablishment of interpersonal relationships*
2. *The bringing about of self-esteem through self-actualization*
3. *The utilization of the unique potential of rhythm to energize and bring order* (Gaston, 1968, p. v)

Michel (pp. 11-13) notes that music therapists have two particular uses of music with which to work: (1) the basic power of music to stimulate or soothe activity and (2) music's traditional functional values as a socializing agent and as a symbol or vehicle for expressing patriotism, religion, or fraternity.

Although the uses of music in hospitals include a variety of specializations for patients with particular needs, music therapy today is essentially an activity therapy. The RMT is a member of the professional team, usually headed by a psychiatrist, which outlines the therapeutic program of the individual patient. Music therapy, as one among several activity therapies, may be selected as the particular activity, or one of the activities, through which behavior changes will be sought. A particular value of activity therapy is that it requires an interpersonal relationship between therapist and patient.

The particular music activities selected for individual patients are determined by the music therapist who takes into consideration many factors including the recommendations of the therapeutic team, the patient's disabilities and behavioral disorders, the objectives for the therapy, and the patient's musical background and interests. While musical goals often are established, they are secondary to the behavioral and social goals established by the therapeutic team. The music therapist must select musical activities which capitalize on music's stimulative and socializing strengths to get the patient actively involved while at the same time subtly working toward meeting the desired changes in behavior.

That such an approach in a relatively young field has difficulties in documenting the effects of therapy via carefully controlled experiments is understandable. The clinical approach necessary in activity therapy lends itself more to case study research than experimental research.

Further, since music therapy often is used in conjunction with other therapies, it is difficult to attribute any effects solely to the music; also the personality of the particular music therapist is an important variable. A review of the research literature on particular uses of music in therapy is far beyond the scope of the present discussion. However, the NAMT is quite concerned with having a strong research base. During the 1950s and into the early 1960s, a series of *Music Therapy* yearbooks were published. Beginning in 1964, the yearbooks were superseded by the *Journal of Music Therapy* which is published four times yearly. A landmark publication in the field was Gaston's (1968) *Music in Therapy* which reviewed the status of music in therapy as it pertained to some of the major issues in the profession. It examined philosophy, practice, and research as they related to the foundations of music in therapy and music therapy for mentally retarded children, physically disabled children, children and adolescents with behavioral disorders, adults with behavioral disorders, and geriatric patients. More recently, Michel (1976), on whom the present discussion has relied heavily, has provided an excellent review of the current status of music therapy as a profession. A particularly valuable resource for persons interested in music therapy research is Eagle's (1976) *Music Therapy Index*. Published by the NAMT, the index contains 2,099 bibliographical entries of articles published between 1960 and 1975 inclusively. It is international and interdisciplinary in scope, the entries being drawn from 422 periodicals. A second volume which includes articles since 1975 is scheduled for publication during the summer of

1978.   Readers interested in more information regarding music therapy are encouraged to examine the sources cited above.

While it is obvious that music therapy is a relatively new application of music in a functional way, it appears to have a stronger research base than other functional applications of music.   Its value as an activity therapy is recognized and it appears that research, training, and other standards for the profession are high, thus strengthening the position of the profession within the medical and paramedical community.   In conclusion, there is little doubt that the ideals and principles under which music is used in therapy make music therapy one of the most, if not *the* most, valuable application of music in a functional way.

MUSIC TO FACILITATE NONMUSICAL LEARNING

Many claims have been made regarding the effects of music on nonmusical learning.   Many students (of all ages) claim that they study more effectively while listening to music.   Music educators faced with program cutbacks in schools are seeking new ways to justify music's position in the curriculum and some have begun to suggest that music facilitates learning in other curricular areas.   An area for which perhaps the most claims have been made is in the teaching of language arts.

A solid research base for these claims appears to be lacking. While some isolated studies yield "significant differences" in favor of approaches using music, there appear to be many more which yield "no significant difference."   Whether these differences are real or are due to the approach or design of the experiments recently has been examined by Wolf (1978); the present discussion relies heavily on her work.

Before examining her reviews of some of the research in the area, it should be noted that music has been used in a number of different ways in attempts to facilitate nonmusical learning.   One method, which will be discussed in the concluding section of this chapter, is to use music or musical activities as a reward for having accomplished a given task.   This method is a part of the behavior modification approach advocated by Madsen, Greer, and Madsen (1975).   Music is used as a reinforcer for nonmusical behavior change.

Of the other approaches involving music to facilitate non-musical learning, perhaps the most basic is that of examining the effects of musical experience and learning on achievement in other subject areas. Wolf labels this approach as *general learning transfer* in which "the study of music serves as a mental discipline which expedites the learning of other subjects" (p. 3). She also notes that the notion of training faculties of the mind had already been discredited by the time of Thorndike. Other studies have investigated *specific transfer learning* on certain tasks common to music and other subjects. An example of a study is that conducted by Madsen, Madsen, and Michel (1975), in which tonal cues were used to facilitate verbal auditory discrimination.

Another approach using music to facilitate nonmusical learning is through the use of background music. While few specific claims are made regarding the effects of this type of music on academic achievement, there appears to be enough interest in the approach that the Muzak Corporation has published a brochure on "how environment can affect the learning process" (Muzak, brochure, no date).

No attempt will be made to review the literature regarding the effects of music on nonmusical learning, but readers are encouraged to examine Wolf's excellent review and status report on the matter. She also reviews studies which examine the effects of music experience on self-concept, personality factors, and certain physical activities.

Wolf notes that there may be measurable effects of music education on the development of cognitive skills and understanding. Most of the research she reviewed reported positive results, but she maintains that the conclusions drawn generally remain unconvincing, primarily due to "obvious inadequacies in the experimental designs and also to the incomplete and equivocal descriptions of the experiments themselves" (p. 21). She concludes her review with the statement that "definitive evidence of the nonmusical outcomes of music education is yet to be provided" (p. 21). The authors concur.

MUSIC AS A REWARD

As noted in the above discussion, there is a growing body of research in which music is used as a reward for behavior change or accomplishment of a given nonmusical task. The bulk of the work in this area has been conducted by Madsen, Greer, and Madsen (1975) and their students; Vance Cotter (1973) also is recognized as one of the pioneer researchers in the area.

The work in this area reflects the behavior modification approach to learning. Learning is viewed as change in behavior and must be observable (see Chapter Ten). Most of the research reflects careful control and isolation of variables.

Cotter (1973) studied the effects of contingent and noncontingent music on the performance of manual tasks in a simulated workshop situation by sixteen moderately retarded adolescent females. Subjects in the noncontingent group, i.e. the one receiving music continuously regardless of their work performance, did not achieve a higher mean work rate, while the subjects in the contingent group, for whom the receiving of music was dependent on work rate, did increase their mean work rate.

Greer, Randall, and Timberlake (1975) compared the contingency effects of music listening, pennies, and no reward on improvement in vocal pitch accuracy and attendance. No significant differences were found between the groups' vocal gain scores, although significant differences were found between the nonreinforced group and the groups receiving music or pennies for attendance. No significant differences in attendance were found between the groups receiving music and the pennies.

Madsen and Forsythe (1975) examined the contingency effects of individual music listening (earphones), group music listening, math games, and no reward on sixth graders' mathematical achievement. Results revealed statistically significant differences in favor of the two groups receiving music. There was no significant difference in the response of the music groups. A subsequent study, in which the contingency for first graders' mathematical achievement was the viewing of televised music lessons, also revealed greater achievement for the group viewing the music lessons than for a control group receiving no reward (Madsen, Dorow, Moore, and Womble, 1976).

The selected studies cited here all suggest that music can function as a reward for achievement of nonmusical tasks. The extent to which these results can be generalized is subject to conjecture. Madsen and Forsythe (p. 31) acknowledge that studies of this type have several problems, including "Hawthorne" and "halo" effects as well as all of the variables presumed to be operating in school settings.* The studies do, however, indicate that music has no less effect than other contrived classroom contingencies.

SUMMARY

The major points of this chapter are:

1. Music which stimulates or arouses listeners has a strong energizing component.
2. The energizing component in music for most people primarily is rhythm, particularly its attribute of tempo.
3. Music which soothes, calms, or tranquilizes behavior is characterized by sounds which are nonpercussive and legato.
4. Reviews of the limited amount of research on the effects of stimulative and sedative music reveals differential response to the two types of music.
5. Music has been a part of ceremonies, particularly religious and military, throughout history.
6. Background music is used informally by individuals as well as for groups of people in public places.
7. The Muzak Corporation has been the most successful proponent and producer of background music.
8. Muzak's "stimulus progression" concept involve fifteen-minute segments of specially recorded intsrumental music with increasing stimulus values from one composition to another as a result of changes in tempo, rhythm classification, instrument

---

*The "Hawthorne" effect refers to an increase in performance derived apparently because a group perceives itself as receiving special treatment; the "halo" effect refers to a bias in evaluations arising from the tendency of an evaluator to be influenced in ratings of specific trait by the general impression of the person being rated.

grouping, and number of instruments used.

9. Commercial uses of music include background music in places of business, music for radio and television commercials, music for television and movies, and music as entertainment.

10. Music in industry has been studied primarily in terms of its effects on employee productivity and morale.

11. Music therapy is an activity therapy through which a music therapist seeks to establish or re-establish interpersonal relationships between the patient and others and helps foster the patient's self-esteem.

12. In pursuing their objectives for patients needing therapy, music therapists capitalize on two basic powers of music: (1) its power to stimulate or soothe activity and (2) its values as a socializing agent and as a symbol or vehicle for expressing patriotism, religion, or fraternity.

13. The National Association for Music Therapy is the accrediting agency for music therapists.

14. There has been a recent surge in research examining the effects of music on nonmusical learning, but results are inconclusive.

15. It has been demonstrated that music can serve as a reward for completion of nonmusical tasks.

REFERENCES

Cotter, V. W. Effects of music on mentally retarded girls' performance of manual tasks. *Council for Research in Music Education*, 1973, *27*, 42-43.

Devereux, G. A. Commercial background music — its effect on workers' attitudes and output. *Personnel Practice Bulletin*, 1969, *25*, 24-30.

Eagle, C. T., Jr. *Music Therapy Index* (Vol. 1). Lawrence, Kansas: National Association for Music Therapy, 1976.

Farnsworth, P. R. *The Social Psychology of Music* (2nd ed.). Ames: The Iowa State University Press, 1969.

Gaston, E. T. The influence of music on behavior. *University of Kansas Bulletin of Education*, 1951-52, *6*, 60-63.

Gaston, E. T. Foreword. In E. T. Gaston (Ed.), *Music in Therapy*. New York: Macmillan, 1968.

Gaston, E. T. (Ed.). *Music in Therapy*. New York: Macmillan, 1968.

Greer, R. D., Randall, R., & Timberlake, C. The discriminate use of music listening as a contingency for improvement in vocal pitch accuracy and attending behavior. In C. K. Madsen, R. D. Greer, & C. H. Madsen, Jr. (Eds.), *Research in Music Behavior*. New York: Teachers College Press, Columbia University, 1975.

Journal of Music Therapy, 1964-, *1*-.

Konz, S. A. Effect of background music on productivity (Doctoral dissertation, University of Illinois, 1964). *Dissertation Abstracts*, 1965, *25*, 4830. (University Microfilms No. 65-853)

Lundin, R. W. *An Objective Psychology of Music* (2nd ed.). New York: Ronald Press, 1967.

Madsen, C. K., Dorow, L. G., Moore, R. S., & Womble, J. U. Effect of music via television as reinforcement for correct mathematics. *Journal of Research in Music Education*, 1967, *24*, 51-59.

Madsen, C. K., & Forsythe, J. L. The effect of contingent music listening on increases of mathematical responses. In C. K. Madsen, R. D. Greer, & C. H. Madsen, Jr. (Eds.), *Research in Music Behavior*. New York: Teachers College Press, Columbia University, 1975.

Madsen, C. K., Greer, R. D., & Madsen, C. H., Jr. (Eds.). *Research in Music Behavior*. New York: Teachers College Press, Columbia University, 1975.

Madsen, C. K., Madsen, C. H., Jr., & Michel, D. E. The use of music stimuli in teaching language discrimination. In C. K. Madsen, R. D. Greer, & C. H. Madsen, Jr. (Eds.), *Research in Music Behavior*. New York: Teachers College Press, Columbia University, 1975.

Michel, D. E. *Music Therapy, an Introduction to Therapy and Special Education Through Music*. Springfield: Thomas, 1976.

Music Therapy Yearbooks, 1951-63. Lawrence, Kansas: Allen Press, 1952-64.

Musselman, J. A. *The Uses of Music, an Introduction to Music in Contemporary American Life*. Englewood Cliffs, Prentice-Hall, 1964.

Muzak Corporation. *Significant Studies of the Effects of Muzak on Employee Performance*. New York: Muzak Corporation, 1974.

Muzak Corporation. *Stimulus Progression* (demonstration recording). New York: Muzak Corporation, 1976.

Muzak Corporation. How environment can affect the learning process. In brochure, *Muzak and Schools*. New York: Muzak Corporation, no date.

Soibelman, D. *Therapeutic and Industrial Uses of Music*. New York: Columbia University Press, 1948.

Uhrbrock, R. S. Music on the job: Its influence on worker morale and production. *Personnel Psychology*, 1961, *14*, 9-38.

Wolf, K. The nonmusical outcomes of music education: A review of the literature. *Council for Research in Music Education*, 1978, *55*, 1-27.

Chapter Nine

MUSICAL ABILITY

STUDY OF MUSICAL ABILITY occupies a prominent place in psychology of music. Identifying ability and predicting the likelihood of musical success are traditional concerns of music educators as well as psychologists. Studying musical ability is complicated by lack of a definition, diverse criteria for musical success, and measurement uncertainties. This chapter discusses conflicting terms, differing views of musical ability, selected influences, and measurement and prediction.

EXTENDED DEFINITIONS

"Ability" suggests being "able" to do something. A person with musical ability is able to perform, create, or perhaps, analyze music if given the opportunity. Unfortunately, the terms "talent," "musicality," "capacity," and "aptitude" are interchanged with ability, and opinions differ regarding the permissible degree of interchange. The following definitions represent the authors' views.

Talent is an imprecise term, designating some obvious indication of ability, usually in performance. A violinist who can perform the Mendelssohn concerto from memory after seeing the music once obviously is talented. A young child with an unusually accurate and extended vocal range may be talented. Talent implies something more than ability: While almost anyone has some musical ability, fewer people are talented. To say that someone lacks musical talent does not mean that that person is *unable* to have a satisfactory musical experience.

Musicality also is imprecise. It refers to a state of being "musical," of being sensitive to changes in a musical stimulus. For inexperienced performers, it may mean a tendency to taper phrases and vary dynamic levels without direction from a teacher. It may simply mean interest in music.

Capacity refers to a portion of a person's ability which he or she possesses as a result of genetic endowment and maturation. To the extent that musical capacity increases, it increases regardless of environmental influences. Superior auditory discrimination ability may be a matter of capacity.

Musical *aptitude* includes capacity plus the result of environmental influences other than formal musical education. It refers to what a person can do musically without regard for musical achievement. Since much concern for musical ability relates to predicting a person's musical success prior to opportunity for musical training, musical ability's measurement problems often are problems of measuring aptitude.

Musical *ability* is what a person is "able" to do musically as a result of capacity, environmental influences, and formal instruction. A person who already has profited from formal instruction may continue to profit. Ability is the broadest of the terms and allows for the greatest diversity of measuring techniques.

MUSICAL ABILITY: SPECIFICS OR GENERAL?

Musical ability's multifaceted nature suggests questions regarding its constituent factors. What are they? Is there a loosely related cluster of relatively narrow abilities which comprise musical ability? It there a general musical ability factor which pervades most specific musical tasks? Unfortunately, the answer to these questions is, "It depends."

Factor analysis is a technique for extracting common core variables or *factors* from a matrix of correlations among several tests which are believed to measure different aspects of the psychological property of interest. Various tests may measure the same thing in different ways; they will "load" on an identified factor to the extent that they are functions of that factor. Factor analysis condenses many observations to a few explanatory constructs. The results depend on the particular tests, the mathematical strategies employed, and the judgment exercised in naming the factors. Factor analysis is one logical tool for assessing the structure of musical ability, but results are inconsistent.

In one representative study, Wing (1941) administered seven measures of his own construction to over 2,000 children and approximately 300 adults. The tests required the subjects to (1) indicate how many tones a chord contains; (2) indicate which tone is changed in a repetition of a chord, and (3) in a repeated phrase; (4) select the member of a pair performed with more appropriate accentuation, (5) harmonization, (6) dynamic contrasts, and (7) phrasing. The test data yielded three factors: general musical ability, a judgment factor related to analysis and synthesis, and a judgment factor related to harmony and rhythm.

In a study of similar vintage, Karlin (1942) administered a total of thirty-three tests in pitch, loudness, timbre, time, auditory analysis and synthesis, auditory and visual memory, age, and intelligence to 200 high school students. Unlike Wing, Karlin found no general factor.* The thirty-three tests yielded eight identifiable factors, including (1) pitch-quality discrimination, (2) loudness discrimination, (3) "auditory integral for perceptual mass," (4) auditory resistance, (5) speed of closure, (6) auditory span formation, (7) auditory and visual memory span, and (8) incidental closure. Karlin concluded that auditory ability requires more than auditory acuity and that rhythm is not primarily an auditory factor.

Two pioneering music psychologists engaged in a controversy that never has been resolved because of musical ability's elusive nature and varied criteria. Carl Seashore (1938) maintained that musical ability is a matter of inborn capacity in six loosely related areas involving sensory discrimination. His tests, discussed below, essentially are tests of psychophysical skills. James Mursell (1937) believed in an "omnibus" theory of musical ability. He never published a test of musical ability, but he later criticized Seashore's concept of loosely related specifics. Mursell insisted that musical ability is an all-pervasive ability which can be developed and improved through training. With time, it has be-

---

*Farnsworth (1969) indicates that British factor analytic studies characteristically find a general factor while American studies do not. Wing is an Englishman; Karlin is an American.

come evident that musical ability is more than loosely related sensory skills, but the general musical ability factor remains elusive.

A person who is musically able can apply diverse skills to particular musical situations. Whether such skills are specific or general is a matter of perspective. How such skills may be nurtured, regardless of specificity or generality, is perhaps a more important question.

SELECTED INFLUENCES ON MUSICAL ABILITY

How, without formal instruction, does musical ability develop? Is it a matter of what is *in* or what is *around* the person? As with all nature vs. nurture questions, the answer is that *both* count in varying but unknown degrees.

Auditory Acuity

Music is an aural art form, so it appears logical that sufficient hearing is an essential part of musical ability. Hearing impaired individuals will have difficulty experiencing music in a normal manner. Various hearing ailments are viewed with alarm by musicians. However, musical ability bears little relationship to hearing acuity.

Sherbon (1975) administered tests of melody, harmony, visual music recognition, musical memory, pitch, loudness, and timbre to sixty undergraduate students, thirty music majors and thirty nonmusic majors. Each subject had his or her hearing threshold determined and was tested for diplacusis.* The music majors outperformed the nonmusic majors on all but the loudness and timbre tests. However, the two groups did not differ in acuity or diplacusis, and neither acuity nor diplacusis showed a significant relationship to any of the seven sets of test scores. From the standpoint of being "able" to accomplish the tasks Sherbon required, superior hearing ability made no difference.

The view that musicians have weak auditory skills and compensate for them with vigorous artistic effort is unsubstantiated (Farnsworth, 1941).

---

*Diplacusis, of the type Sherbon tested, is a condition in which a particular frequency sounds with a different pitch in each ear.

Genetics

Genetic endowment for musical accomplishment is unlikely except to the extent that genetic endowment may contribute to overall abilities. What Farnsworth (1969) calls "D.A.R.-like studies," showing how Bach and Mozart were in "musical families," are as much evidence for a stimulating musical environment as they are for a strain of musically superior beings. No musical gene or chromosome has been found.

Belief that musical ability is largely innate and presumably genetically influenced does persist. Bentley (1966), basing his view in part on highly diverse levels of musical ability observed in relatively homogeneous groups of children, maintains that musical abilities are mostly a matter of innate capacity.

Recently, a genetic relationship (not cause) to musical ability has been hypothesized by Scheid and Eccles (1975), who believe that the physical size of the planum temporale in the brain's right hemisphere is an indicator of genetically-coded musical ability. Their belief is based on hemispheric asymmetries, clinical studies of patients undergoing lobectomies or severance of the corpus callosum, and dichotic listening tests purporting to show more right than left hemisphere involvement in music processing.* The planum temporale is located just behind the primary auditory cortical area and can be observed without a microscope. Scheid and Eccles suggest postmortem examinations of brains from individuals of high and low musical ability. If the planum temporale can grow with environmental stimulation, such postmortem evidence would not be valid unless the cadavers had equal stimulation while alive.

There are differences in people which are not of an environmental nature, of course; it is silly to pretend that anyone can do anything, given the right opportunities and education. Someone whose adult height is 150 cm (about 4 ft 11 in) is not likely to play center in the National Basketball Association; a child born

---

*One hemisphere, generally the left, is superior for sequential, analytic, time-ordered processing, such as speech, while the opposite hemisphere is superior for holistic, spatial processing, such as musical contours. This often is oversimplified and misinterpreted; hemispheric dominance is discussed in greater detail in Chapter 11.

with Down's syndrome (mongolism) is unlikely to earn a living as a concert artist.* Nevertheless, until evidence for influence of the planum temporale or any other genetically determined physiological structure accumulates, any genetic relationship to musical ability will remain tenuous.

Physical Features

Physical features such as teeth alignment and lip, hand, and finger sizes may influence performing ability regarding particular instruments. The upper lip protrusion known as a Cupid's bow makes it difficult to form the characteristic flute embouchure. Children with tiny fingers have difficulty covering clarinet fingerholes, and a pronounced overbite makes a trumpet embouchure difficult. Specific instrumental ability is only a part of musical ability, however. If physical influences on musical ability are important, they must relate to many aspects of musical behavior.

Home

There are grossly insufficient data regarding the musical development of children: some are discussed in the next chapter. There obviously are influences of the home's musical stimulation on musical achievement and development of certain musical skills; absolute pitch acquisition via imprinting, discussed in Chapter Two, is an example. In an interesting descriptive study, Simons (1964) observed gross responses to musical stimuli, pitch and rhythm imitation, and free-play activities of twelve pairs of same sex twins (five male, seven female; aged 9 to 31 months) and twelve matched singletons (of similar sex and age) in their home environments. Both groups responded the most to rhythmic stimuli, less to melodic stimuli, still less to harmonic stimuli, and least to dissonant music. The older singletons generally showed greater amounts of response than younger singletons, but the older twins did not consistently respond more than the younger twins. The singletons as a group showed significantly more response to music than the twins. Evidently, constant com-

---

*This does not mean that such a child can never have any satisfactory experience with music.

panionship of a nearly identical child may have some detrimental relationship to musical response, but it is unwise to generalize that family size and age proximity of the children influence musical ability.

Creativity

Composition obviously requires creativity, in the sense of constructing a new arrangement of sounds. Performance may be a creative act (although some say it is more recreative), and a person can listen in creative ways. Attempts to explain musical ability in terms of creativity have been unsuccessful because neither term is defined adequately.

In an often-cited study, Getzels and Jackson (1962) identified twenty-six Chicago area private school students as a high creativity group: They scored in the top 20 percent on the researchers' creativity measures, but they were below the top 20 percent in intelligence, according to school records. A high intelligence group, containing twenty-eight students from the same school, scored in the top 20 percent in intelligence but were below the top 20 percent in creativity. Among their findings, Getzels and Jackson reported: (1) both groups were superior to the school population in school achievement and did not differ in motivation to achieve, (2) teachers showed a preference for the high intelligence group, (3) the creative students were less success oriented in an adult sense, (4) the creative students had more humor and were more prone to take risks, and (5) the creative students were more able to fantasize.

Of particular interest here is the view of creativity which the measuring techniques imply. Creativity was identified through tests requiring multiple associative responses to stimulus words, suggestions of novel and nonstereotyped uses for common objects, detection of simple geometric figures hidden within complex patterns, composition of endings for four fables, and composition of mathematical problems from four paragraphs containing numerical statements.

The two student groups were compared for fantasy via stories written about pictures and pictures drawn to portray given situations. Running throughout is the presumption that the creative student is inventive, nonconforming, and prone to unconventional and even bizarre ideas. For example, a creative student, when asked to depict children playing tag in a schoolyard, submitted a blank white paper and said that the children were playing during a blizzard. The student describing a picture of a man in an airplane seat as a scientist, travelling to the moon, who is about to be consumed by a mass of protoplasm, which he mistakenly believes is a pillow, also was creative. Or were they sarcastic? Any student with a sense of humor and ability to spot absurdities in daily life probably could be highly creative if creativity is synonymous with inventiveness.

Guilford (1957) stressed that creative ability is not uniform. It requires a number of factors, as does intelligence. Particularly important for the artist are fluency, flexibility, originality, and evaluative factors. Moore (1966) concluded that creativity requires above average intelligence but is not synonymous with intelligence.

Creativity may be defined in terms of creation, divergent thinking, problem solving, or something mystical. In one opinion, creativity is in the eyes and ears of the beholder. If something is *judged* as "creative" rather than ordinary, unmusical, "wrong," or bizarre, it *is* creative (Radocy, 1971).

Musical ability may be related to creativity in many facets of music, but divergent thinking, inventiveness, and bizarre behavior are hindrances in the context of ordinary musical development and instruction. Creativity may characterize the musically able, but without discipline and direction creativity is insufficient to make a person musically successful.

Intelligence

Intelligence has been examined as an important influence on musical ability. It seems reasonable that an intelligent person is better able to cope with musical problems, if intelligence is defined as a means of coping with intellectual demands of the environment. As with creativity, definition problems have clouded the relationship of intelligence and musical ability. Different measurement tools imply different definitions.

One may cite cases of so-called idiots savant as evidence that intelligence is not requisite for musical ability. An idiot savant is a person of subnormal intelligence who displays remarkable ability in one or more narrow areas. Anastasi and Levee (1960) report a case involving musical talent in a thirty-eight-year-old man. The subject, brain damaged from encephalitis, walked at eighteen months and did not talk until his fifth year. He hummed tunes before he talked, and a speech therapist taught him to talk by using song lyrics. As an adult, the subject was sexually immature, unable to read beyond a fifth-to-sixth grade level, and generally lazy, except for his music. He disliked children and anything else that disrupted his schedule, and showed excessive, apparently nonintentional echolalia.* The man had exceptional keyboard ability. The only time he appeared to concentrate was when he played the piano, often from six to nine hours daily. He was an excellent sight reader and could play by ear. He had a preference for music of the classic period. Although he could not interpret abstract reading, he had a phenomenal verbatim memory for printed passages and events which were one month or more in the past.

The existence of such idiots savant shows that intelligence in the ordinary sense is not required for musical ability. Gordon (1968) reported that musical aptitude scores often related only slightly to intelligence, although, in European studies, performance ratings related more highly to intelligence. He found (not surprisingly) that his own musical aptitude measures were better predictors of musical success, as measured by etude performance, teacher ratings, and a notation test after three years of instruction, than were intelligence tests. But the logic that intelligence *ought* to be related to musical success persists.

Sergeant and Thatcher (1974) demonstrated that apparent weak relationships between tests of musical ability and intelligence likely are a statistical artifact caused by the less-than-perfect reliability and validity of the tests. Correlation techniques, often

*A person with echolalia immediately repeats what another person just said to him or her.

used to relate musical ability and intelligence, are such that a relatively small change in absolute rank on one variable as compared with absolute rank on another variable can produce a spuriously low relation. The authors conclude, on the basis of three experiments employing various measures of intellectual and musical abilities, where data were analyzed via analysis of variance and trend analysis, that all highly musical people appear to be highly intelligent, but not all highly intelligent people are musical. Musical ability requires an interaction between intelligence and appropriate environmental stimulation. Phillips (1976) also suggests a close relationship between musical ability and intelligence, believed to result from a common environmental cause: A home promoting musical ability also is likely to promote intelligence.

Sex and Race

Sex presents an apparent paradox regarding musical ability. Girls dominate in many school musical organizations, which can be verified by examining membership lists and attending concerts and festivals. Many college music majors are females. Yet, except for certain types of vocalists, most professional performers and conductors are males. This is a result of sexual stereotyping and discrimination, not any inherent sexual differences in musical ability.

Gilbert (1942) administered musical aptitude measures to 500 male and 500 female college students in the Northeastern United States. In general the females outscored the males, but not when musically untrained females were compared with untrained males. Only 231 males had any musical training; their average amount was two years. Four hundred females had an average of three-and-one-half years of private lessons. The social stereotype of women being more "artistic" was a self-perpetuating one, in Gilbert's opinion, as a result of musical training being given more readily to females. (It must be recognized that most of his subjects, male and female, attended expensive private schools and were from high socioeconomic levels.)

On the basis of data gathered in the creation, design, and improvement of music aptitude tests for elementary school children, Bentley (1966) concluded that there are no inherent sexual differences in musical ability. At certain ages, many boys begin to associate musical activity, particularly singing, with feminine roles as a result of classroom social stereotypes.

Figgs (1976), reviewing literature on sexual discrimination and stereotypes, concluded that women have been encouraged to excel only to a certain degree, be dependent, and avoid specialization. Stigmas regarding who should play certain instruments and who should occupy certain roles in music education have not dissipated. Human differences in musical ability exist, but sexual differences are a cultural artifact.

Racial and ethnic characteristics influence musical ability only to the extent that particular cultures encourage musical development in designated directions. There are no inherent influences: Blacks do not necessarily "have rhythm," all Italians are not singers, and all Hungarians are not violinists.

Summary

Musical ability is not influenced significantly by hearing, genetics, and physical features, provided minimal perceptual and physical capacities are present. Sex and race are irrelevant psychologically, although not necessarily sociologically. Creativity is too ill-defined to be very helpful in the prediction of musical ability, but it is hard to be musically able, idiots savant to the contrary, without being intelligent. The constituents of musical ability vary with how they are conceptualized, defined, and measured. Although the major determinants of musical ability are not understood, it probably results from interaction of audition, physical coordination, intelligence, and experience. Attempts to measure and predict musical ability have yielded interesting descriptive information.

MEASUREMENT AND PREDICTION

Lack of a clearcut definition of musical ability encourages varied measurement methods. Musical ability is defined operationally, rather than constitutively, by the particular means of measurement. (An operational definition specifies how a trait will be recognized in a specific instructional or research setting, while a constitutive definition is a dictionary-style definition.) Some tests stress basic discrimination skills; others require more "musical" tasks. Some measures require prior musical achievement. Instrument manufacturers have published "tests" on which almost anyone who is minimally literate may score well.

This book is not a measurement text; only three of the available measures are discussed below. Readers who wish to investigate other available tests should consult the three available textbooks (Whybrew, 1971; Lehman, 1968; Colwell, 1970) and scan *Dissertation Abstracts International.* Test development remains a common doctoral research project.

Some Approaches

Musical ability may be assessed, particularly by an experienced observer, by means of educated guessing. Children vary in the extent to which they actively seek to make and listen to sounds. Children with musically successful older brothers and sisters may be successful themselves. Any child who asks for musical experiences should be welcomed and encouraged. But educated guesses may be misleading, particularly if they stress overt indicators. Discovering "latent" musical ability requires a more formal assessment. Three representative tests are discussed in detail to illustrate approaches to formal measurement.

The *Seashore Measures of Musical Talents* (Seashore, Lewis, and Saetveit, 1960) appeared initially in 1919 and were revised extensively in 1939. Only slight changes have occurred since. The term "measures" rather than the singular reflects Seashore's view that musical ability consists of loosely related specific sensory capacities. Each particular measure must be interpreted as a measure of one narrow skill; the six measures together yield a musical profile, which shows a pattern of auditory acuity. There is to total score possible on the Seashore tests.

The Seashore pitch, loudness, time, and timbre tests all require judgments of paired tones. The subject respectively must indicate whether the second tone is higher or lower, stronger or weaker, longer or shorter, and same or different in comparison with the first tone. Pitch stimuli are based on a 500 Hz standard; the smallest difference is 2 Hz (a 9 cent interval), which approaches a jnd for pitch discrimination. Loudness stimuli, all 440 Hz, vary in intensity level by as little as 0.5 db. The timbre stimuli are altered by varying the third and fourth partials of a 180 Hz complex tone; the smallest change from the standard is a simultaneous 0.7 db decrease and a 4.0 db increase in the third and fourth partials respectively. All the differences are subtle enough that the results may be influenced by the fidelity of the sound reproduction system and acoustical aspects of the testing environment. Plomp and Steeneken (1973) demonstrated the variability of sound pressure level in reverberant sound fields and the place dependence of sound sensations for steady-state tone.

The Seashore rhythm and tonal memory tests require pattern recognition and comparison. Short paired bursts of 500 Hz tones in five-note, six-note, or seven-note patterns comprise the rhythm test; the subject must indicate whether the second pattern is the same as or differs from the first. In the tonal memory test, paired three-note, four-note, and five-note organ sequences are presented; no difference between adjacent tones is smaller than a whole step. The subject must identify which tone differs in the two presentations.

Seashore believed that there was a physiological limit to auditory abilities, and that consequently, scores on his tests would not change appreciably over time except as a function of misunderstood directions and experience in test taking. Investigators attempting to improve Seashore-measured skills by training the subjects have obtained various results, but there is no question that many individuals can raise their scores after training. For example, Wyatt (1945) trained sixteen adults, eight musicians and eight nonmusicians, who did not score well on several administrations of the Seashore pitch test. Training procedures, adapted to each individual, featured the use of tunes, repetition, imitation, and feedback. Several post-training testings showed that the musicians gained, on the average, 49 percent of the maximum possible gain. The nonmusicians' average gain was 26 percent, but they nevertheless scored higher after training than the musicians did before training.

For the person who equates musical ability with the Seashore tests' perceptual tasks or believes that such tasks are an important part of musical ability, the *Seashore Measures of Musical Talents* are a useful tool. They are fairly reliable and are valid for what their creators claim to measure. There are other, more "musical" approaches, which, depending on the test user's philosophy, may be "better."

Wing (1961), whose factor analytic study was described above, developed the *Standardised Tests of Musical Intelligence*. Although the Wing is a battery of seven tests, there is a total score possible, which is appropriate because Wing found a general factor of musical ability. All of Wing's stimuli are piano tones; some of the subjects' tasks require a greater degree of memory.

The chord analysis and pitch sections of Wing's battery require the subject respectively to evaluate individual chords for the number of tones contained therein and to indicate whether the second of paired chords contains a tone higher or lower than the first chord.

The memory, rhythmic accent, harmony, intensity, and phrasing sections require comparisons of paired melodies, some of which are rather lengthy. In the memory section, the subject must indicate which one of three to ten tones is altered in the second rendition. The others require the subject to indicate if the second melody is the same or which he or she prefers regarding the property in question.

Wing tried to make his tests musical while psychologically adequate. He believes that musical ability, as measured by his tests, is largely innate, not necessarily related to intelligence, and not influenced by environment (Wing, 1954). This perhaps is going too far in light of other evidence.

Wing's test is amusing to many American listeners because of the characteristics of the recorded voice and some problems with the audio quality. However, the test is an interesting one for a person who believes in the importance of melodic, harmonic, and rhythmic discrimination.

Gordon's (1965a) *Musical Aptitude Profile* is one of the more recent published tests and is perhaps the most comprehensive prediction measure. Each of the seven subsections, each of the three major sections, and the total battery all yield a score. The subject's basic task is to evaluate paired phrases; the stress is on what Gordon calls *imagery* or *sensitivity*. All stimuli are played on string instruments.

The tonal imagery section contains a melody subsection, in which the subject must indicate whether the second phrase is an embellished melodic variation of the first ("same") or a different melody, and a harmony subsection, in which the subject labels the second phrase as having a lower voice the same as, or different from, the lower voice of the first.

One subsection of rhythm imagery requires the subject to indicate whether the second phrase's tempo accelerates, retards, or stays the same. The second rhythm imagery subsection asks for a same-different comparison regarding metrical accents.

Gordon's musical sensitivity section contains three subsections. In all, the subject must indicate which of two performances sounds better. In the phrasing subsection, musical expression is varied. Endings differ, rhythmically and melodically, in the balance subsection. In a so-called style subsection, tempo differences predominate.

Gordon's test is lengthy and expensive, but it is thorough and has an excellent manual. Gordon based the test on eight years of research and believes that it minimizes musical achievement (Gordon, 1965b). Several investigations, mostly by Gordon's students, attest to the *Musical Aptitude Profile's* predictive validity. The person who believes that sensitivity to tonal and rhythmic variation and nuance in a musical context is a vital aspect of musical ability would find Gordon's battery useful.

The Seashore, Wing, and Gordon batteries illustrate approaches to measuring musical ability. More precisely, they are measures of musical *aptitude*, intended to assess ability without requiring specific musical knowledge. In order for a person to use these or any other tests, he or she must be convinced of the tests' *validity*.

Validity

A test's validity refers to how well the test measures what it is supposed to measure. Validity must not be confused with *reli-*

ability, the consistency with which a test measures. A test must be reliable in order to be valid, but a test may be highly reliable without being valid.

Any respectable published test is accompanied by a manual which includes reliability estimates and an explanation of how they were obtained. There are four common ways of estimating test reliability in classical test theory, which applies to nearly all the musical ability measures. Three ways rely on relating two sets of scores; the other is a matter of interitem consistency.

Parallel-forms reliability, in which scores from alternative forms of the same test administered to the same people are correlated, is one method. Test-retest reliability, in which the same test is administered twice to the same people and the scores are correlated, is another. When only one administration of one form is practical, two halves of the test may be correlated and the resulting correlation coefficient adjusted in accordance with a compensating formula; this is called split-halves reliability. Kuder-Richardson reliability, computed in accordance with a formula, makes use of proportions of examinees answering each item correctly. Each reliability technique has its strengths and weaknesses. The most authoritative discussion of classical reliability techniques is in Stanley (1971); simpler discussions may be found in educational measurement texts such as Lindvall (1967) and Mehrens and Lehmann (1973).

Reliability estimates range, in theory, from −1.00 to +1.00, although negative estimates are rare. The closer to +1.00, the more reliable is the test. There is no magic criterion, but a published measure should have reliability in the .80s before it is considered especially useful, in the writers' opinion.

Given sufficient reliability, a test must have some satisfactory rationale for *why* it is a test of whatever it is supposed to test in order to be valid. Since musical ability is not defined clearly, no ability measure is completely valid.

If a measure of musical ability is valid as a predictor of musical success, a logical way to validate such a test is to administer it to a large representative sample, measure the sample's success later, and look for strong positive relationship between test scores and musical success. This is called criterion-related or predictive validity, and the problem often becomes one of the criterion's validity. Musical success often means accomplishment in a formal music instruction setting. Children particularly may be "unsuccessful" musically because of organizational and personality problems rather than musical problems. Teacher ratings are influenced easily by nonmusical variables. Correlating a new with an old test presumes that the old test is sufficiently valid.

Validity may be a matter of how well a designated body of material is represented in the test. This is called content validity and is more readily appropriate for achievement than for ability measures. It requires a fairly complete specification of just what a musically able person should be able to do.

Construct validity, the extent to which a test measures ability in accordance with underlying theoretical constructs of ability, is difficult to establish. Invalidity may be a failure of the test or a failure of the theory.

The prospective test user must examine the validity claims for the test under consideration and determine whether such claims are personally acceptable.

Importance of Nonmusical Variables

Given the facts that musically able people may be able in other areas and that musical success may be judged with nonmusical criteria, it is reasonable to examine the idea that additional nonmusical variables might increase the accuracy with which musical success may be predicted.

Multiple regression analysis is a statistical technique for determining the amount of variance in a criterion variable predicted by two or more predictor variables and the degree to which each predictor bears a significant relationship to the criterion. Rainbow (1965) used teacher ratings of apparent student musical "talent" and "awareness" in a university laboratory school as a criterion variable for a multiple regression study. His fourteen predictor variables were:

(1) pitch discrimination
(2) tonal memory
(3) rhythm

(4) musical memory
(5) academic intelligence
(6) school achievement
(7) sex
(8) age
(9) musical achievement
(10) musical training
(11) home enrichment
(12) interest in music
(13) relatives' participation
(14) socioeconomic background

The first three predictors were measured by appropriate Seashore sections; the fourth predictor was measured by a section of the *Drake Musical Aptitude Tests* (Drake, 1957) in which the subject indicates whether repeated melodies are the same or change in key, rhythm, or individual tones. Variables five and six were assessed via combinations of standardized tests administered routinely in the school. Musical achievement was measured with the *Kwalwasser-Ruch Test of Musical Accomplishment* (Kwalwasser and Ruch, 1927), which primarily is a test of visual notation reading skills.

The upper and lower 20 percent ability groups, in accordance with teacher ratings, were compared for each variable. A significant difference existed between the groups for each variable except sex and age. The multiple regression analysis gave somewhat different results for different grade levels. For ninety-one elementary students (grades four through six), the significant predictors of teacher ratings were pitch discrimination, tonal memory, interest in music, and socioeconomic background. For 112 junior high school (grades seven and eight) students, academic intelligence, sex, musical achievement, and relatives' participation in music were the significant predictors. For eighty-eight high school (grades nine through twelve) students, the significant predictors were pitch discrimination, tonal memory, home enrichment, and interest in music. For the total group of 291, significant predictors were tonal memory, academic intelligence, musical achievement, home enrichment, interest in music, and socioeconomic background. Rainbow concluded that these last three significant predictors for the total group are important extramusical variables for prediction purposes.

Multiple regression analysis is an extension of correlation; the prediction-criterion relationships are not evidence of causality. Although Rainbow's choice of measures may be questioned, particularly for musical achievement and the criterion variable, the importance of his study is its evidence that musical ability in one operational definition is more than a matter of traditional facets.

Whellams (1970) used discriminant function analysis, a technique for assessing the relative strengths of variables which discriminate between two criterion groups. In one study, the number of terms in the Royal Marines School of Music was the strongest discriminator between a group of below and above average Junior Musicians, as identified by their grades. In another study, comparing buglers and Junior Musicians of two levels, strong discrimination weights were found for nonmusical variables, especially algebra scores. Whellams concluded that musical aptitude batteries need aural-musical and nonmusical tests.

Particularly when the musically able person is viewed as a person capable of achieving musical success in some academic setting, the use of nonmusical variables as predictors of musical ability appears especially propitious. Variables of academic skills and home environment are the most promising.

What Should We Measure?

Measurement and prediction of musical ability presently is best handled by a combination of tools. A combination of a reliable and valid battery stressing various realistic musical skills and assessments of intellectual ability, academic achievement, environmental stimulation, and, where necessary, physical attributes offers the best formal approach to predicting musical success. There is no substitute for providing an *opportunity* for success, of course; the chance to do something usually is the best predictor of whether a person is able to do something.

RELATION TO EDUCATIONAL PHILOSOPHY

Blacking (1973) discusses at length the musical culture of the Venda people of South Africa. The Venda stress the functional effectiveness of music. Music is a social experience more than a technical experience, and the Venda, while recognizing that some people are better performers than others, do not consider the possibility of *anyone* being unmusical. The listener as well as the performer has an important musical function. A musical elite, by Western standards, does not exist in Venda culture.

Interest in selection and construction of a musical elite is natural in a competitive society, particularly when resources are limited. If there are only so many school instruments available for beginners, it makes sense to issue them to students who are likely to profit from instruction. If a conservatory can accept a limited number of students, it makes sense to admit those who demonstrate a strong possibility of attaining a musical career.

But the risk of allowing an "unmusical" person to try to play an instrument or develop sophisticated listening skills hardly is in the same class as allowing an apparently low ability potential pilot to fly an airplane. Pursuit of a musical career by a person lacking successful musical achievements is dubious, but a child who has had no musical training should not be denied musical opportunity. We know enough about musical ability to know that it has many facets. We do not know enough about it to use it as a barrier. And music educators should not be desirous of establishing musical barriers.

SUMMARY

The major points in Chapter Nine include the following:
1. Musical ability is a broad term which includes capacity (whatever a person is born with that promotes musical ability), aptitude (capacity plus results of environmental stimulation), and results of previous instruction.
2. Musical ability has a number of components, but they have not been identified precisely.
3. Musical ability does not vary significantly as a function of hearing acuity.

4. Environmental influences probably play a greater part in determining musical ability than do genetic influences, but there are innate differences in people.
5. Physical features, such as teeth, lips, and hands, are related only to particular aspects of musical ability, generally regarding performance on particular instruments.
6. Creativity is ill-defined and its relation to musical ability, except for composition, is uncertain.
7. Intelligence probably relates strongly to musical ability; although all highly intelligent people are not musical, all highly musical people are intelligent.
8. Sex and race have no bearing on musical ability except to the extent that social stereotypes hamper or promote particular persons' abilities.
9. There are numerous measures of musical aptitudes and abilities; three of the best known are the Seashore, Wing, and Gordon tests.
10. Some tests, such as Seashore, test basic sensory discriminations, while others, such as Wing and Gordon, test musical discrimination at a more contextual level.
11. A musical ability test's validity is critical and often uncertain because of varying standards and techniques.
12. To be valid, a test must be reliable.
13. The most logical way of establishing an ability test's validity is to show a relationship between test success and musical success.
14. Nonmusical variables such as academic achievement and home enrichment may enhance the likelihood of predicting musical success.
15. The use of musical ability to establish unnecessary educational barriers is not recommended.

REFERENCES

Anastasi, A., & Levee, R. F. Intellectual defect and musical talent: a case report. *American Journal of Mental Deficiency*, 1960, *64*, 695-703.

Bentley, A. *Musical Ability in Children and its Measurement*. New York: October House, 1966.

Blacking, J. *How Musical is Man?* Seattle: University of Washington Press, 1973.

Colwell, R. *The Evaluation of Music Teaching and Learning.* Englewood Cliffs, N.J.: Prentice-Hall, 1970.

Drake, R. M. *Drake Musical Aptitude Tests.* Chicago: Science Research Associates, 1957.

Farnsworth, P. R. Further data on the Adlerian theory of artistry. *Journal of General Psychology,* 1941, *24,* 447-450.

Farnsworth, P. R. *The Social Psychology of Music* (2nd ed.). Ames: Iowa State University Press, 1969.

Figgs, L. The ms mess. *Kansas Music Review,* 1976, *38* (3), 24-25.

Getzels, J. W., & Jackson, P. W. *Creativity and Intelligence: Explorations with Gifted Students.* New York: Wiley, 1962.

Gilbert, G. M. Sex differences in musical aptitude and training. *Journal of General Psychology,* 1942, *25,* 19-33.

Gordon, E .E. *Musical Aptitude Profile.* Boston: Houghton-Mifflin, 1965. (a)

Gordon, E. E. The musical aptitude profile: a new and unique musical aptitude test battery. *Council for Research in Music Education,* 1965, *6,* 12-16. (b)

Gordon, E. E. A study of the efficiency of general intelligence and musical aptitude tests in predicting achievement in music. *Council for Research in Music Education,* 1968, *13,* 40-45.

Guilford, J. P. Creative abilities in the arts. *Psychological Review,* 1957, *64,* 110-118.

Karlin, J. E. A factorial study of auditory functions. *Psychometrika,* 1942, *7,* 251-279.

Kwalwasser, J., & Ruch, G. M. *Kwalwasser-Ruch Test of Musical Accomplishment.* Iowa City: University of Iowa Bureau of Educational Research, 1927.

Lehman, P. R. *Tests and Measurements in Music.* Englewood Cliffs, N.J.: Prentice-Hall, 1968.

Lindvall, C. M. *Measuring Pupil Achievement and Aptitude.* New York: Harcourt, Brace and World, 1967.

Mehrens, W. A., & Lehmann, I. J. *Measurement and Evaluation in Education and Psychology.* New York: Holt, Rinehart, and Winston, 1973.

Moore, R. The relationship of intelligence to creativity. *Journal of Research in Music Education,* 1966, *14,* 243-253.

Mursell, J. L. *The Psychology of Music.* New York: Norton, 1937.

Phillips, D. An investigation of the relationship between musicality and intelligence. *Psychology of Music,* 1976, *4* (2), 16-31.

Plomp, R., & Steeneken, H. J. M. Place dependence of timbre in reverberant sound fields. *Acustica,* 1973, *28,* 50-59.

Radocy, R. E. Thoughts on creativity. *Kansas Music Review,* 1971, *33* (5), 16-17.

Rainbow, E. L. A pilot study to investigate the constructs of musical aptitude. *Journal of Research in Music Education,* 1965, *13,* 3-14.

Scheid, P., & Eccles, J. C. Music and speech: artistic functions of the human brain. *Psychology of Music,* 1975, *3* (1), 21-35.

Seashore, C. E. *Psychology of Music.* New York: McGraw-Hill, 1938.

Seashore, C. E., Lewis, L., & Saetveit, J. G. *Seashore Measures of Musical Talents.* New York: The Psychological Corporation, 1960.

Sergeant, D., & Thatcher, G. Intelligence, social status, and musical abilities. *Psychology of Music,* 1974, *2* (2), 32-57.

Sherbon, J. W. The association of hearing acuity, diplacusis, and discrimination with music performance. *Journal of Research in Music Education,* 1975, *23,* 249-257.

Simons, G. M. Comparisons of incipient music responses among very young twins and singletons. *Journal of Research in Music Education,* 1964, *12,* 212-226.

Stanley, J. C. Reliability. In R. L. Thorndike (Ed.), *Educational Measurement* (2nd ed.). Washington: American Council on Education, 1971.

Whellams, F. S. The relative efficiency of aural-musical and non-musical tests as predictors of achievement in instrumental music. *Council for Research in Music Education,* 1970, *21,* 15-21.

Whybrew, W. H. *Measurement and Evaluation in Music* (2nd ed.). Dubuque, Iowa: W. C. Brown Company, 1971.

Wing, H. D. A factorial study of musical tests. *British Journal of Psychology,* 1941, *31,* 341-355.

Wing, H. D. Some applications of test results to education in music. *British Journal of Educational Psychology,* 1954, *24,* 161-170.

Wing, H. D. *Standardised Tests of Musical Intelligence.* The Mere, England: National Foundation for Educational Research, 1961.

Wyatt, R. F. Improvability of pitch discrimination. *Psychological Monographs,* 1945, *58* (2). (Whole No. 267)

Chapter Ten

MUSIC LEARNING

"L EARNING MUSIC" is a major enterprise. Incidental learning occurs through radio, television, and films. Songs are conveyed within and across generations through oral traditions. Formal instructional programs are offered in most American school systems; private music teachers of varying statures work throughout the world. "Learning music" includes learning to perform, analyze, evaluate, create, and rearrange music. Such a major activity has a surprisingly sparse research base.

Many studies of music learning are "contests": Method A vs. Method B. Will students in School X learn a set of musical skills "better" by programmed instruction or a traditional method? Did the students who were told the results of a pretest learn "better" than those who were not? Such studies are useful in their particular instructional settings but they rarely are based on learning theory or tell much about how people learn music.

Teaching or instruction may be confused with learning. Elegant presentation of a musical concept or principle is not learning. No matter how attractive and expensive the instruments, books, or other instructional paraphernalia, they are not learning. Learning requires action on the part of the learner.

This chapter offers extended definitions of key terms which are particularly important in a rational discussion of music learning. After briefly describing relevant neurophysiological activity, the chapter overviews selected learning theories. Tentative sketches of musical development in childhood are presented. Three somewhat traditional topics—memorization, tonal memory, and eidetic imagery—also are discussed. A concluding section suggests applications of psychological principles to music learning.

EXTENDED DEFINITIONS

The terms *learning, reinforcement, goal, motivation,* and *concept* are selected for definition because, in the writers' opinion, they have proved troublesome to musicians discussing learning. Other terms appear in context.

Learning

Learning is hereby defined as an observable change in behavior, due to experience, which is not attributable to anything else. This definition is patterned after that offered in Hilgard and Bower's (1975, p. 17) authoritative text.

Without a behavioral change between times A and B, no learning has occurred in that time span. Someone who already can recite major and minor key signatures cannot learn to do it, although he or she obviously learned the signatures in the past. Furthermore, learning, from the standpoint of someone who must ascertain learning in another individual, requires observable evidence. Showing a student how to produce a trumpet tone is insufficient; learning has not occurred until the student produces the tone. Some recognize so-called latent or hidden learning, i.e. the student "knows" but cannot or has not expressed what is "known." From the behaviorist's standpoint, latent learning is nonexistent: If an individual "knows," he or she can demonstrate the knowledge.

The qualification of "not attributable to anything else" is necessary to exclude behavioral changes resulting from maturation or genetic programming. An infant does not learn to breathe; it happens "naturally." An adolescent boy does not learn to grow facial hair; such secondary sexual characteristics result from maturation. Beament (1977) believes that even a component of musical activity, called *musicality,* or the *potential* for musical activity is inherited. (Beament's "musicality" is analogous to "capacity" in Chapter Nine.)

Any musical behavior requires learning. The forms of particular behaviors are influenced by genetic and maturational processes or lack thereof; consider the qualities of men's and women's voices and the seventeenth century castrati. But people do not organize, analyze, or perform specific musical sounds as a result of instinct or secreted hormones. They learn to react to and with music.

Reinforcement

Reinforcement is both a process and an entity. It is viewed here as a means of increasing the likelihood of a behavior. Reinforcement may be positive, as in awarding a high quality performance a first division rating, or negative, as in releasing a student from a boring study hall to go to the practice room.* A teacher may reinforce; reinforcement may occur without planning. Attempts to chastise a student for turning left when the rest of the band turned right may result in positively reinforcing attention. Reinforcers may be primary, in the sense of meeting some immediate biological need, or secondary, in the sense of virtually anything of momentary or future utility to the organism. An action may be reinforcing in itself.

Individuals vary in what is reinforcing and how often reinforcement is necessary. One of the most difficult, perhaps impossible, tasks in music or any other education is to arrange optimal reinforcement situations.

Goal

A goal is something toward which an organism directs its behavior. It may be long-term and elegant, such as desiring to become the conductor of the Philadelphia Orchestra; it may be short-term and mundane, such as desiring to leave rehearsal in time to reach the supermarket. Goals may be related to biological survival or psychological needs. All *purposeful* behavior is directed toward a goal, which is not necessarily obvious, spiritually uplifting, or "important."

Word games regarding *objectives* vs. goals may have some appeal to curriculum writers. An objective generally is a desired

---

*In general, *positive* reinforcement is a *welcomed* (by the organism) occurrence as a consequence of an organism's behavior; *negative* reinforcement is *removal* of an *unwelcomed* occurrence as a consequence of behavior. Negative reinforcement is not punishment, which is an unwelcomed occurrence as a consequence of behavior.

result of instruction and is more specific than a goal.   Objectives require more formal specification.*

Motivation

To want to reach a goal is to be motivated.   Motivation often connotes halftime pep talks from the coach and preconcert admonishments from the conductor, but motivation may occur through a variety of biological, social, and psychological stimuli.   Motivation can be self-initiated.   Hart (1975, pp. 92-93) believes that motivation arises naturally in the brain and that the concept of motivation as externally imposed stimulation is misleading.

Motivation may be related to reinforcement; if a consequence of behavior is reinforcing, the organism may be motivated to repeat that behavior.

Concept

A concept is an internal organizational creation which enables a learner to classify objects and events with sufficiently similar attributes into one category.   Concepts may be highly specific, such as an instrumentalist's concept of a German bassoon sound, or vaguely broad, such as a young child's concept of music.   Concepts are unique to an individual; no one person's concept of Beethoven, periodicity pitch, hearing, or turkey dinners is exactly like any other's.   Attempts to promote conceptual learning are attempts to facilitate formation of categories in accordance with relevant classification cues.

NEUROPHYSIOLOGICAL ACTIVITY

The brain and central nervous system are vital to human learning.   The basic neurochemical processes of message transfer and memory storage are involved inherently in learning.   Only a few aspects of neurophysiology are treated here.   Readers desiring more intensive and extensive information should consult the neurophysiology chapter in Hilgard and Bower (1975), Pribram

---

*Readers desiring more information regarding *objectives* of musical learning should consult the following: J. D. Boyle (Comp.).   *Instructional objectives in music.*   Vienna, Va.: Music Educators National Conference, 1974.

(1971), and Deutsch and Deutsch (1973). An interesting and informative (albeit antibehavioristic) discussion of the brain's evolution and organization is Hart's (1975) *How the Brain Works.*

The basic neural message is in the form of variations in electrical voltage. Any given neural cell or *neuron* may carry a message to its *axon,* which may stimulate the *dendrites* of other neurons across gaps known as synapses. Incoming signals may be *excitatory* (a kind of "go" order) or *inhibitory* (a "stop" order). If excitory signals exceed inhibitory signals by a certain amount, the neuron will fire. A diagram of a neuron appears in Figure 10-1.

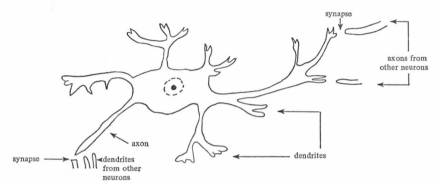

Figure 10-1. A diagram of a neuron. The dendrites are receivers, the axon is a transmitter.

The process by which neural signals are transmitted from one neuron to the next is a matter of chemistry. The transmitting neuron emits through its axon a substance, often acetylcholine, which croses the synapse to the dendrites* of the receiving neurons. If stimulation is sufficient, the receiving neuron fires, and an enzyme, often cholinesterase, neutralizes the acetylcholine, thereby clearing the synapse for further action. Networks of neurons function together, as a result of genetic programming and experience, to communicate between receptors and the brain. All stimulation, including sounds from Handel's *Messiah,* a beginning oboe class, and chirping crickets, results in squirts of a transmitter substance.

Musical inputs, as all sensory inputs, stimulate neural structures. During such stimulation, desoxyribonucleic acid (DNA), the genetic memory molecule, produces ribonucleic acid (RNA), which appears in the glia (non-neural cells embedded in neural tissue) after stimulation. This *consolidation* process may be the basis for long-term memory (Pribram, 1971, pp. 37-38). Current sensory information may be compared with the stored representative record of prior experience, thereby guiding the organism's musical behavior (Pribram, p. 49).

Vital to neural transmission and memory consolidation is sensory inhibition, as described comprehensively by Von Bekesy (1967), who noted that (pp. 133-134) "a good observer is one who has the ability to inhibit the unnecessary phenomena." Sensory inhibition, more pronounced for stronger stimuli, eliminates unwanted information. Chapter Two noted the ear's reduced sensitivity to low frequency sounds. This prevents hearing one's own heartbeat and blood circulation sounds loudly. The eye's insensitivity to infrared light prevents people from seeing light resulting from self-radiation. A sensation of vibration does not extend along the skin as far as the actual physical disturbance. Inhibition of basilar membrane activity is necessary in order to obtain the relatively precise pitch sensations characteristic of human hearing. Sensory inhibition results in a funneling and sharpening of neural information without which human learning, as it exists currently, would be impossible.

The brain is the major control center of human learning. This marvelous collection of ten to thirty billion neurons, organized into its two cerebral hemispheres, midbrain, and cerebellum, monitors body states, controls movements, and conducts continuous search-and-match missions. Regardless of one's theoretical position regarding learning, the brain must be responsible for organization through experience of neural structures present at birth. Learning theory has shown surprisingly little interest in the brain and its evolutionary development (Hart, 1975).

---

*Axon to cell body (soma) and even dendrite to dendrite transmission are possible in some instances.

BASIC LEARNING THEORY

The major classifications of learning theories are the stimulus-response and cognitive theories. Distinctions may become imprecise and blurred in practice, but, essentially, stimulus-response theories view learning more in terms of behavioral sequences, habit acquisition, and trial-and-error, while cognitive theorists are more concerned with central brain processes, cognitive structures, and "insightful" problem-solving (Hilgard and Bower, pp. 23-25). No one theory accounts for all the facts; no surviving theory is completely without utility. Learning theory does not offer instant explanations and solutions to music learning problems (Lathrop, 1970), but a theoretical framework is useful, even if it is difficult to generalize from theory to "tricks that click."

Stimulus-response theories discussed below include those of Thorndike, Pavlov, Guthrie, Hull, and Skinner. Classical Gestalt psychology and Piaget represent the cognitive school. Humanism and social learning, difficult to classify, also are treated briefly. The authoritative bases for the discussion include, in addition to the theorists' works, Hilgard and Bower, Bugelski (1971), and LeFrancois (1975).

Thorndike

Edwin L. Thorndike (1874-1949) believed in an actual, albeit ill-defined, connection between a stimulus and a response. Such a connection or *bond* could be established and strengthened by following a desired stimulus-response connection by a satisfying state of affairs. Thorndike's *Law of Effect* originally said that connections were weakened if followed by an annoying state of affairs, but the law was modified to stress the positive aspects. Reinforcement in the form of reward is critical in Thorndike's system.

Established connections may be strengthened through practice; this is the *Law of Exercise*. Thorndike saw no use in practice without reward, however. The student who has excessive amounts of unsupervised practice time between lessons likely is practicing without reward.

Much of Thorndike's theoretical construction was based on laboratory work using the puzzle box, a device for confining an animal, usually a cat, which can escape if it somehow pulls on a latch inside the box. Cats usually do not like confinement which is not self-imposed, and release from such a situation is a satisfying state of affairs which rewards the action(s) leading to release. Learning thus is a matter of mechanical trial-and-error attempts, although some responses are more likely than others.

Also part of Thorndike's system are the *Law of Readiness,* essentially stating that once an organism is ready to do something doing it is rewarding, the *spread of effect,* in which responses close in time to a rewarded response also are learned to some degree, the concept of *belongingness,* saying that rewards should be perceived by the learner as part of the learned event, and the principle of *prepotency of elements,* stating that more vivid or salient stimuli are likely to lead to learning.

Thorndike's "bonds" are nonexistent physically, and his theory has a hard time accounting for varying degrees of learning difficulty. From the standpoint of promoting music learning, his positions regarding reinforcement and the need to specify just what is to be learned are important. Further information is available from Thorndike himself in *The Fundamentals of Learning* (1932).

Pavlov

Ivan Petrovich Pavlov (1849-1936) was a Nobel Prize-winning (1904) physiologist who turned his attention to studying reflexes. He is the father of the classical conditioning paradigm (ding-slurp), refined to a high degree in his famous dog experiments. Pavlov, limited by the technology available to him, was unable to refine his views regarding cortical irradiation, how incoming stimuli are represented in the cortex. But his conditioning techniques are and will remain contemporary.

The basic classical conditioning paradigm operates as in Figure 10-2. An existing linkage between an unconditioned stimulus and an unconditioned response is exploited by *preceding* the unconditioned stimulus, often by about three seconds, with a potential conditioned stimulus. The conditioned stimulus, signaling the onset of the unconditioned stimulus, eventually can elicit the response without benefit of the unconditioned stimulus. The response then is conditioned. Pavlov exploited the hungry dog's unconditioned response of salivation to the unconditioned stimulus of meat powder and was able to condition salivation to stimuli such as bells, time passage, tones, and combinations thereof by preceding meat powder with the desired potential conditioned stimuli. The precision of the conditioned response could be increased until a very slight difference in time or tonal frequency could prevent a response.

(1)   US———►UR

(2) (CS)   US———►UR

(3)   CS———►CR

Figure 10-2. Pavlovian or classical conditioning. (1) An unconditioned stimulus elicits an unconditioned response; (2) the conditioned stimulus precedes the unconditioned stimulus; (3) eventually the conditioned stimulus elicits the same response which now is a conditioned response.

Generalization of the conditioned response to similar stimuli is both a strength and a weakness. A Pavlovian cannot allow learners to "get by" or "pass" because they "have the idea" with rough approximation. Stimulus differentiation and discrimination must be forced by withholding the unconditioned stimulus except for the particular desired condition.

Conditioned responses will extinguish with continued omission of the unconditioned stimulus. They may, however, reappear suddenly or spontaneously recover.

One must not consider conditioning as limited to "lower" animals. Conditioned responses are common events in human life. Student fear of particular teachers, reaction to particular functional household objects at certain times of day, and special behaviors of trained troops or marching bands are possible examples of conditioning.

It is very difficult to apply Pavlov's system, because the requisite unconditioned stimulus–unconditioned response links are seldom apparent and extinction of undesirable stimulus generalization by withholding the unconditioned stimulus is not always practical. Nevertheless, the tremendous power of the conditioning paradigm and the opportunities for its occurrence, desirable and undesirable, should be of concern to anyone responsible for developing musical behaviors.

Details of many of Pavlov's experiments are presented vividly in his *Conditioned Reflexes* (1927).

Guthrie

E. R. Guthrie (1886-1959) stressed contiguity, as did Pavlov, but he found the classical conditioning paradigm too restrictive. Rather than substituting one stimulus for another, Guthrie conceptualized the stimulus as being conditioned to the response. The response that removes or significantly rearranges the stimulus ("shuts it off") becomes linked to that stimulus.

For Guthrie, responses were *movements,* covert as well as overt. The essence of his theory is that stimuli or a stimulus responded to with a movement will be followed by that movement in the future. The full associative strength of a stimulus and a responding movement is gained when the initial association is made. This one trial learning paradigm at first glance seems inapplicable to complicated tasks, such as playing an instrument, but Guthrie solved that problem by noting that complicated tasks require separately learned responses to myriads of stimuli.

Guthrie's one trial learning means that reinforcement is important because it protects behavior from new associations; strengthening of response in the Thorndike sense is nonexistent. Practice brings improvement because movements can occur in response to a greater variety of stimuli, not because of strengthening responses. Completely identical stimulus configurations never occur.

Learning, for Guthrie, was habit formation. Such habits, which are stimulus-response linkages, never can be broken. The cigarette smoker who stops smoking *replaces* his or her smoking with something else. The student who finally stops playing F sharp incorrectly as F in a particular piece replaces the wrong note with the right note. Guthrie's methods of replacing habits include presenting the stimulus ordinarily eliciting the "bad" habit at a faint level and gradually increasing its strength. This threshold method is used when a person conquers a fear of spiders by having caged hairy tarantulas and other spiders gradually brought closer and closer until the former spiderphobe can handle them. Another way to replace a habitual response is to fatigue the subject by having him or her respond repeatedly until the undesirable response is replaced by no response. Another method is to present the stimulus which elicits the "bad" habit in contexts where the person is unable to respond.

Guthrie was a fluent writer and speaker, not overly concerned with rigid scholarly inquiry or extensive quantification. His theories are criticized, but they are sufficiently flexible, in Hilgard and Bower's (p. 120) opinion, that they are hard to attack through experimentation. The utility of a Guthriean interpretation of learning probably lies in the concepts of habit replacement and the all-or-none occurrence of parts of a complex learning task at definite points in time.

Guthrie's *Psychology of Learning* (1952) may be consulted for further information regarding his system.

Hull

Clark Hull (1884-1952) attempted to construct a quantitative model of behavior. For Hull, learning proceeded in an incremental manner, small steps at a time, as an organism works toward a goal. The organism is motivated toward that goal by a drive. As the goal is approached, drive is reduced, and that reduction is reinforced. Each response made as the goal is approached becomes a stimulus for another response. A chain of successive responses is used in reducing a drive and approaching a goal. Anticipation of reward is crucial in Hull's system; the closer the goal, the more active the learner's responses.

An organism learns many habits; they have various strengths and are arranged in *habit family hierarchies,* which are ordered patterns of response. The habit family closest to the particular need will perform the necessary function, and the individual habits with the greatest strengths will be utilized first.

Hull allowed for latent learning. Learning may occur as habits are established before the learning is observable.

Motivation is the basis for reinforcement, which in turn serves as both a drive and a reward. Performers may be motivated to perform well at some future date and be "driven" toward that goal. Successful rehearsals are reinforcing. All the while existing habits are used and new habits are formed, each to take its place in an appropriate habit family hierarchy.

Hull attempted to be very precise and systematic. He created many symbols and quantifications, which, with time, have been easy to fault, but he was a major inspiration to other theorists. The idea of gradual approach to a goal and, again, the importance of reinforcement are useful to someone planning a long-term musical learning experience.

The reader wishing to learn more about Hull should consult appropriate chapters in Bugelski and Hilgard and Bower prior to reading Hull's (1943) *Principles of Behavior*.

Skinner

B. F. Skinner (1904-   ) is a strict behaviorist: That which is not observable is superfluous to understanding, predicting, and controlling human behavior. To understand the Skinnerian view of learning, one must understand operant conditioning and reinforcement schedules.

Operant conditioning is the basis for chaining behavior in the Skinnerian model. It differs from classical conditioning in that the organism *emits* a response rather than having it elicited by the stimulus. The emitted response is called an operant; the operant is strengthened and made more likely if reinforced.

If an encaged pigeon pecks at a particular spot and receives food as a consequence, the pigeon is more likely to peck at that spot again and can learn to do it whenever food is required. If a cat escapes from a cage by a certain combination of movements, that combination is more likely to occur when the cat is recaged; the cat can learn to escape. If a baby "discovers" that dropping a toy from the crib brings Mother's solicitous attention, the baby is more likely to drop the toy again; the baby learns to fetch Mother. In these and similar instances of operant conditioning, a behavior occurs "naturally" and is reinforced. Skinner chains behavior through a series of selective reinforcements with remarkable results.

Reinforcement may occur continuously or intermittently. In continuous reinforcement, each and every emitted response is reinforced, or, if extinction of the operantly conditioned stimulus-response connection is desired no response is reinforced. Intermittent reinforcement occurs in two main classes, interval and ratio, each of which features reinforcement only for specified instances.

In a fixed interval reinforcement schedule, the first response occurring after a fixed amount of time is reinforced. Responses observed in laboratory animals often show time discrimination after awhile; responses cease immediately after reinforcement and accelerate to a high rate just before the next reinforcement is due. Responses are more uniform under variable interval reinforcement schedules, where the time spans vary at random. Hilgard and Bower (p. 215) indicate that responses developed under variable interval schedules are unusually resistant to extinction.

In ratio schedules, reinforcement is provided for the nth (n usually equals ten or more) response after the prior reinforcement. The ratio is *fixed,* so that every nth response is reinforced, or it is variable, so that n is continually changing.

The proper reinforcement schedule added to opportunities arranged in the proper sequence virtually guarantees the stimulus discrimination and response differentiation necessary for learning to perform clearly structured tasks. Skinner's work is a basis for linear programmed instruction, in which learning proceeds, relatively error-free, in small sequential steps according to a structured presentation of the material.

Skinner has been rather unsuccessful in accounting for verbal behavior, particularly regarding speech development. His description of emotions as a set of operations alarms "humanists." There is much to learn from his reinforcement schedules, however. Constant praise, as most experienced music teachers recognize, becomes ineffective; a variable praise schedule will, in the long run, motivate more students to higher goals. Secondary reinforcers, such as verbal praise, do work with human learners, and a careful structuring of reinforcement is a powerful learning aid.

Skinner has many publications; his 1938 and 1953 texts are particularly useful for acquiring detailed knowledge of his system. His *Beyond Freedom and Dignity* (1971), in which he makes the point that people are not "free" because they always are controlled by the environment operating through the laws of behavior, has been criticized negatively.   Skinner believes that systematic planned positive controls would be more beneficial to human beings than the quasi-random controls which presently exist. Some place faith in "human will" and regard Skinner's views as tyranny.   Others merely wonder who will do the planning.

Gestalt Views

The German word Gestalt may mean shape or form as an attribute or as an entity in itself.   The Gestalt psychologists, of whom Kohler, Wertheimer, and Koffka were the leaders, were interested primarily in perception.   Perception extends to learning; in the Gestalt view, learning is a matter of perceptual organization.   The clarity of past organization improves present organization.

For the Gestalt advocate, problem solving is structuring and restructuring relations.   Insightful behavior, generally not considered by stimulus-response learning theory advocates, is recognized in Gestalt theory; insight requires the proper relations.

Learning requires coherence rather than association.   The essence of Gestalt learning theory is the *Law of Pragnanz* (compactness), which states that psychological organization is toward "good" or 'harmonious" figures.   Just what a "good" or "harmonious" figure *is* is somewhat clarified by the four sublaws of the Law of Pragnanz.

The *Law of Proximity* states that grouping elements to make a figure is in accordance with the elements' nearness or proximity to each other.   The pattern 11 11 11 11 is more likely to be grouped as four twos rather than two fours or one two and two threes.

If not overridden by proximity, objects or events with similar attributes, such as shape, color, or timbre, will be grouped together in accordance with the *Law of Similarity*. A musical idiom containing groups of four sixteenth notes, as in

often is heard as a duet when played by one instrument such as a clarinet: The last three notes of each group are in a different register than the first and are within a semitone; they are "similar." (From a frequency standpoint they also are "proximate.")

The *Law of Common Direction* refers to grouping on the basis of extrapolated completion. The incomplete lower case cursive letter *d* easily can look like *cl,* but it can be read as a *d* from the context of the word. Incomplete notes and clefs abound on music manuscript, but experienced players generally have no difficulty interpreting them.

The *Law of Simplicity* refers to a perceptual preference for smoothness, regularity, and symmetry as compared with roughness, irregularity, and asymmetry; it relates to making perceptual order out of chaos.

People who do not care for the essentially mechanistic nature of stimulus-response theories may use the term Gestalt only in the sense of antibehaviorism and speak lovingly of insight, meaningful learning, and the whole being greater than the parts. This is unfortunate because a Gestalt view of learning is positive. Music learning can be promoted by facilitating perceptual organization; for example, music manuscript which violates the principle of rhythmic spacing is asking for trouble, especially with inexperienced performers, because of the Law of Proximity. The Law of Simplicity suggests that a teacher should begin "music appreciation" with novice listeners by using music with predictable and readily perceivable forms. Perceptual organization can be fostered without appeal to mystic cognitive processes.

Kohler's (1929) text is a good source for exploring Gestalt viewpoints.

Piaget

Jean Piaget (1896-   ), trained as a biologist, is a developmental psychologist who founded a theory of *genetic epistemology*, a result of formal logic and psychology. Piaget observed children in their natural settings, often with a clinical rather than an experimental viewpoint, and hypothesized four developmental stages through which all children must pass. Movement from one stage to the next results from maturation and learning.

From birth to approximately two years of age,* the child is in the *sensorimotor* stage. Objects initially have no existence when they are not in the newborn child's immediate environment; by about age one an object acquires a permanence in the child's thinking. Piaget divides the sensorimotor stage into six substages; essentially, the child moves from a type of motor intelligence to a more symbolic intelligence as reflexive behavior is replaced by voluntary movements.

The *preoperational* stage, roughly ages two to seven years, is characterized by illogical and incomplete concepts and the lack of reversibility, i.e. ability to understand that a given operation can be undone by an inverse operation. This stage is dominated more by perception than reason. Children will say that a higher or wider container contains more beads than a lower or narrower container despite seeing equal amounts of beads placed individually in each container. The preoperational stage also is characterized by a peculiar transductive reasoning. As LeFrancois (p. 214) indicates, transductive reasoning enables a child to go from particular instances to particular instances, as in assuming that two animals which give milk must belong to the same species.

The stage of *concrete operations*, roughly ages seven to eleven years, is when a child learns to conserve. Conservation is recognition that changes can occur in an object's form or spatial arrangement without changing the object's other attributes. If two identical shot glasses are filled to the same height (water is sufficient) and the liquid from one glass then is placed in a test tube while the liquid from the other is placed in a wide shallow pan,

---

*Children vary greatly in when they reach each stage and how long it takes to pass through them. The ages are only a rough approximation, and a child of a given age never should be tagged automatically as being in a certain stage.

the amounts of water are still equal, but a nonconserving child will insist that one or the other container contains more liquid. When the liquids are returned to their corresponding original containers, the same child readily will agree that the amounts are the same, but he or she just as readily will insist that one container "has more" if the shot glasses are again emptied into the test tube and pan.

Conservation has interested some music researchers, partly because children in the concrete operations stage often are beginning formal musical training and conservation is necessary for form perception and musical analysis. Pflederer (1967), after intensive research, identified five types of musical conservation: (1) *identity,* when thematic material maintains its essential characteristics across various permutations, (2) *metrical groupings,* in which meter recognition and discrimination are maintained despite changes in note value distributions within measures, (3) *augmentation and diminution,* recognition that respective lengthening and shortening of a melodic passage's note values does not change the basic tonal relations, (4) *transposition,* where a change of frequency level does not alter perception of tonal configurations, and (5) *inversion,* in which an inverted simultaneous or successive interval is recognized.

On the basis of data from forty children, Rider (1977) reported acquisition of rhythmic conservation, as indicated by a child's ability to tell that an accompanying drumbeat remained constant (MM = 60) while a song was played at three different tempi (MM = 60, 120, 240), at a mean age of 6.1 years. Area conservation, as indicated by ability to recognize that four cubes occupy an identical area on a sheet of paper regardless of whether they are adjacent to each other or scattered across the paper, was acquired at a mean age of 7.6 years. Volume conservation, as indicated by a task similar to the above shot glass example, was acquired at a mean age of 8.1 years. Ability to tell that a drum and bell playing alternately on the odd beats (and even beats in $\frac{4}{4}$ meter were at the same tempo as when they both were played only on the odd beats) indicated tempo conservation; its mean age of acquisition was 8.3 years. Rider's data must be interpreted cautiously because he used children with developmental difficulties, as well as because of variable acquisition ages, but the *order* of acquired conservations is important: Tempo conservation may indicate the approaching end of the concrete operations stage.

Conservation's arrival time will vary greatly with individuals. All aspects of all the developmental stages must occur; attempts to accelerate conservation or any other aspect are highly questionable.

Concrete operations are characterized by thought processes dependent on a concrete framework.   Once a child moves to more formal, propositional thinking and can combine various grouping operations, he or she is in the *formal operations* stage.   This usually occurs from eleven to fifteen years of age.   The adolescent can now consider diverse possibilities, make "what if" judgments, and organize principles into networks.   In short, he or she can now reason as an adult.

Equilibration is the self-regulated process which is the basis for psychological development and learning in Piaget's system.   It includes the functions of *assimilation*, in which a new environmental experience is accepted into the existing cognitive structure, and *accommodation*, in which the cognitive structure is altered to take cognizance of a new reality.   Learning problems may result from assimilation occurring rather than accommodation because of ignored details in a "new" stimulus.

Piaget's work strongly suggests the importance of presenting material to a child in a way in which he or she is ready to handle it.   Excessively hypothetical questions (what if . . .) without concrete referents are unsuited to a child in the stage of concrete operations.   One must be well aware that the age approximations are only approximations.

The relevant Hilgard and Bower chapter provides a comprehensive overview of Piaget's theories.   Piaget's *The Psychology of Intelligence* (1950) and *The Psychology of the Child* (1969), co-authored by Piaget and Barbel Inhelder, are detailed discussions of his work and views.

Social Learning

So-called *social learning* "involves the acquisition of those behavior patterns which society expects" (LeFrancois, p. 290). One
learns through imitation and observation just what is expected
and what is not expected in various societal contexts. Continued
social reinforcement promotes imitative behavior.

Models (persons or symbols such as found in magazines and
television) are the stimuli for imitation. Such models can alleviate some needs for trial-and-error learning. Unfortunately for
teachers, models are not always those who teachers might choose,
either in a social or musical sense.

Few educators doubt the wisdom of supplying appropriate
models and opportunities for imitation. Simple dependence on
presenting a model ("Do it *this* way") without ascertaining that
the model is understood and accurately imitated is of course
naive; people really do not learn by osmosis. Even the most
passive learning must be demonstrated before it can be recognized
as learning.

The appropriate LeFrancois chapter is an excellent introduction to social learning. More detail regarding its theoretical basis
is available in Bandura and Walters (1963) and Bandura (1969).

A Humanistic Approach

If one presumes that scientific study of learning in terms of an
organism reacting to the environment dehumanizes people, an
alternative approach may be humanism, as discussed by LeFrancois
(Chapter Seven) and exemplified by Carl Rogers (1951; 1969). In
a humanistic approach, the individual is the central focus of his
or her own activity. The individual reacts as a whole to the world, as
it is experienced, with goal-directed behavior. The basic goal is so-
called *self-actualization,* a "becoming" of whatever one can become, a reduction of distance betwen a perceived and an ideal
self. The "self" aspects of self-actualization—self-regulation, self-
government, free choice—make such a view incompatible with be-
haviorism.

An individual evaluates the information which is received

about himself or herself. Such information is organized and incorporated into self-perception, denied because of its perceived incompatibility with self-perception, or simply ignored because there is no perceived relevance or incompatibility.

Learning, in this view, requires promotion of a positive self-concept. Rogers advocates student-centered teaching, in which the teacher is a facilitator. One must always admire and respect a person because of that person's humanity. Humanism requires humane treatment.

Humanism may place excessive and naive faith in some sort of "basic good" in man, and student-centered teaching may be inefficient in many contexts. People do like to "feel good about themselves," however; musical experiences can enhance an individual's life, regardless of the details of how music is learned. The teacher who uses the music class, lesson, or rehearsal to ridicule students is not practicing sound educational psychology from a humanistic or behavioristic standpoint.

MUSICAL DEVELOPMENT

Extensive normative data regarding the musical development of children are lacking, but there has been some interesting descriptive work.

Kresteff (1963) noted characteristic musical behaviors of children in their first four years. Children's early first-year interest in sound is no clue to future musical development. Free vocalization, with only approximations of up and down, and discrimination between low and high and loud and soft occur during the second year. The third year features more rhythmic movement (in general, rhythmic perception develops faster than tonal discrimination). Awareness of tonal relations, particularly the minor third, at the expense of tonal freedom occurs during the fourth year.

Then, according to Kresteff, comes a growth of tonality in seven stages, varying considerably in their time of appearance. The first stage, the only one constant worldwide, features the pattern *so-mi,** a descending minor third.

---

*For the reader unfamiliar with solfeggio syllables, they are tone syllables attached to particular scale degrees. The syllable *do* goes with the tonal center. As an example, the C major scale tones have the following syllables, in *descending* order: *do* (C), *ti* (B), *la* (A), *so* (G), *fa* (F), *mi* (E), *re* (D), *do* (C).

In the second stage, the characteristic tonal pattern expands to *la-so-mi,* often with a stress on *la.* *Do* is added in the third stage, *la-so-mi-do,* although it does not function as a tonic.

A pentatonic scale, *la-so-mi-re-do,* appears in the fourth stage. There are no fixed tones, and there is no dissonance. The fifth stage adds the octave *do,* so the characteristic tonal relations are now based on *do-la-so-mi-re-do.*

A half-step is introduced in the sixth stage as the syllable *fa* extends the pentatonic scales to a hexacord, *do-la-so-fa-mi-re-do.* With the addition of the leading tone *ti* in stage seven, the diatonic scale is complete.

Petzold (1963) administered tests of tonal configurations, rhythm, and phrasing to children in the first six grades. The children were required to respond with some type of musical performance as evidence of the appropriate musical perception. Findings included a large improvement in musical perception at the sixth grade level, nonsignificant sex differences, and significant effects of musical training and out-of-school experience. Perception of short patterns precedes perception of long patterns, and rhythm has little influence on melodic perception. Considerable variation in perceptual abilities exists within grade levels. Petzold recommended less rote learning of music and more "intelligent thought."

According to Bentley (1966), music's first appeal elicits a spontaneous response, varying from indiscriminate movements to a feeling for the beat. Rhythmic perception precedes concern for tonality. Spontaneous responses lead to what Bentley calls the "apprehension" of music. Tunes become more accurate, and children recognize and have a memory for melodies. One can enjoy music at this level, and some people never advance beyond this stage.

An analytic stage follows for those who do advance; the individual can isolate figures from a tune and learn to recognize intervals. Then come three developmental stages of melodic response: (1) rhythmic coalescence, in which individuals will sing as a group with nearly identical rhythm but not pitch, (2) an appropriate grasp of tonal configurations, and (3) a group coincidence of pitch. All this normally occurs, in Bentley's view, by the time a child is eight years old.

No one has identified an optimal music learning sequence which is influenced by curriculum as well as "natural" musical development. One study with a limited school population (Hufstader, 1977) suggested a learning sequence of timbre, rhythm, melody, and harmony. Timbre discrimination skills were evident at the first grade level. Rhythmic discrimination did not begin to reach criterion until seventh grade.

Using musically untrained children (aged 6-12), younger adults (18-37), and older adults (ages 50-70), Funk (1977) studied recognition of thematic variation, discrimination of variations from themes, and detection of modulation (in tonality). Recognition improved moderately into adulthood, but the older adults performed the most poorly of the three groups. Young children relied heavily on rhythmic cues for recognition. Discrimination was clearly superior in both adult groups; about 80 percent of the time children thought a variation was a theme. Modulation improved with age; tonality apparently is the last of the three skills to develop. Funk concluded that musical structure is largely "invisible" prior to age eight; perception is limited to awareness of rhythm and overall melodic shape. More stimulus attributes are detected and organized as development progresses.

MEMORIZATION OF MUSIC

Memorization of music, in the sense of learning to perform a piece of music in a specific sequence without benefit of notation, attracted considerable attention of early workers in psychology of music. One representative study (Rubin-Rabson, 1937) showed that analytic prestudy of the score was beneficial in memorizing short easy piano pieces. Twenty-four college-age students used one of four memorization methods. Two involved analysis of the music prior to attempts at memorization: In one case, the analysis was prepared by the teacher; in the other, it was student-prepared. A third method featured hearing the music in advance; the remaining method had no prior analysis. Both analytic methods were superior; the student-prepared analysis was especially effective in terms of time required for relearning the material after it initially had been memorized to criterion.

In one recent study involving memorization of piano music (Lo, 1977), college students for whom piano was a secondary performing medium improved their memorization abilities by visualizing four-part hymn scores with eyes closed. Sixteen experimental subjects received two weeks of specific visualization training while fourteen control subjects received only general suggestions regarding memorization.

Memory consolidation, storage of a "record" of experience in the glia, was discussed above. There are at least two kinds of memory, short-term and long-term. A sensory representation resulting from neural reverberation highlights short-term memory, which is lost as a result of time or interference. Long-term memory requires consolidation and storage. It may be effected negatively by similar meanings but not by similar perceptions. There may be an intermediate-term memory, overlapping long-term and short-term, which plays a role in music memorization (Tallarico, 1974).

Optimal musical memorization strategies vary with the learner as well as the music and the performing medium. No particular method has any automatic superiority. Musical performance is a psychomotor as well as an intellectual skill, and memorization may be attained as a matter of physical or musical sequences or combinations thereof.

TONAL MEMORY

Tonal memory (sometimes called musical memory) is the skill used in recalling a tonal sequence across time. It may require a relatively short time span, as in comparing a first and second version for melodic identity on a musical aptitude test, or a relatively long time span, as in "drop the needle" games dreaded by many music history students. Tonal memory involves both spatial and temporal aspects. The necessary degree of tonal memory accuracy varies with musical context.

Bergan (1966) investigated a simple form of tonal memory. The subject's task was to match a 932 Hz standard tone by adjusting a variable tone after an interval of silence between standard and variable. Independent variables included stimulus intensity level, length of silence, feedback provided to the subject, and sensory stimulation of the subject. Respective findings included superior performance when adjustment followed the standard tone almost immediately. Training at levels of 50 and 25 db was superior to 75 db; auditory feedback was superior to visual, and sensory stimulation made no difference. Bergan recommended immediate overt responses in learning to match pitches.

Pitch matching, as exemplified in the Bergan study, requires tonal memory for a certain pitch sensation. When active vocal or instrumental production of a sound is required, one is uncertain whether inability to reproduce the stimulus correctly is a tonal memory problem or a musical production problem.

Development of accurate tonal memory for pitch sequences probably is fostered by recognition of successive intervals. Jeffries (1967) found that random, as opposed to sequenced, presentation of intervals resulted in superior interval recognition and retention. Delayed knowledge of results appeared slightly more effective than immedate knowledge of results in the Jeffries study.

Tonal memory, in the sense of recognizing alterations of melodic fragments, may be improved through vocal or keyboard percussion instruction in seven-year-old children (Buckton, 1977).

Peculiar phenomena can occur when auditory patterns vary in loudness. In one study (Ptacek and Pinheiro, 1971), white noise patterns were presented to thirty normal-hearing subjects under binaural, monaural, and dichotic listening conditions. Each pattern contained three 130 msec elements; 200 msec separated each element. Seven seconds separated each pattern, which was one of six configurations of "loud" (50 db SPL)* and "soft" (45, 40, 35, or 30 db SPL) elements. The configurations, presented in random order, included soft-loud-soft, loud-soft-loud, loud-loud-soft, soft-soft-loud, loud-soft-soft, and soft-loud-loud. It was found that subjects needed a 10 db difference within a pattern in order to recognize it half the time. Unexpectedly, 30 to 40 percent of the errors were complete pattern reversals or mirror images, e.g. re-

---

*The 50 db SPL were in relation to the individual subject's hearing threshold.

porting loud-soft-loud for soft-loud-soft. Reversals were more common for symmetrical patterns; listening conditions did not matter. The subjects' success was unrelated to musical training; the strange pattern reversal, in the researcher's opinion, may result from sensory inhibition causing underestimation of sudden increases and overestimations of sudden decreases in loudness levels. The particular laboratory conditions of this study are unlikely in a musical context, but it reminds musicians that strange perceptual anomalies can confound tonal memory.

Tonal memory in musical contexts usually is considered as a matter of pitches and melodic contours, but other sound dimensions can influence the saliencies of the individual tones. Webster, Woodhead, and Carpenter (1973) trained four groups of six young men to identify sounds purportedly representing ships. Each sound, which varied in four dimensions, required categorization as a member of the "red" or "blue" force, a warship or a merchant ship, nuclear or diesel powered, and running at full or half speed—each particular naval characteristic was keyed to a particular sound dimension.

The four dimensions, each with two values, were source waveform, fundamental frequency, number of formants,* and formant frequency. The sounds either contained all harmonics or only odd harmonics, built on fundamentals of 90 or 142 Hz. The formant frequencies were low (600 Hz, or 600 and 1550 Hz) or high (940 Hz, or 940 and 2440 Hz). All variations were steady-state aspects; attack, decay, and sonance were constant.

The "ships" which were easiest to identify were those represented by the higher fundamental, all harmonics, and two high formants. "Ships" represented by the higher fundamental, all harmonics, and one low formant were hardest to identify. In general, fewer confusions were made between any two "ships" as the number of differing sound dimensions increased and as the dimension (single or in combination) changed from formant number to formant frequency to fundamental frequency to waveform. The researchers believed that the listeners made a general

---

*A formant is a complex tone component which is particularly strong. The term also applies to resonance regions which are particularly excitable.

classification along a single dimension which varied systematically with waveform complexity and periodicity.

Ease of tonal memory varies with sequential characteristics as well as sound dimensions. Tonal melodies are easier to recall than atonal melodies; practice (not surprisingly) brings improvement (Long, 1975). Recognition of tonal patterns in altered forms improves with age (Larsen, 1973; Foley, 1975); a perceptual shift in which the salience of individual pitches declines, and contour, interval size, and tonality become more relevant, occurs in many children betweeen the ages of three and six (Sergeant and Roche, 1973). To the extent that it is necessary for melodic recognition, tonal memory does not require exact pitch recognitions. Dowling and Fujitani (1971) found that the recognizability of distorted familiar melodies varied with the type of distortion. Distortion caused few recognition problems when the melodic contour was the same as the original and the relative (but not exact) successive interval sizes were preserved. Recognition was more difficult when only the contour was preserved, and became quite difficult when only the suggested harmonic pattern was maintained. That the pattern rather than particular pitches would suggest a melody is in accordance with the Gestalt organizational laws.

Tonal memory is not understood adequately. It may be developed with practice in recalling sequences under a variety of conditions. Recognition is no substitute for production of a musical sequence because production contains its own problems. Its facilitation is a matter of helping a person tend to relevant contour and intervalic cues as well as pitch discrimination.

EIDETIC IMAGERY

Eidetic imagery is discussed here because it may be beneficial in some music learning tasks; it could have been discussed in the prior chapter because it may enhance musical ability. The term properly refers to the sharp persistence of a visual image after the visual stimulus is removed (Haber, 1969), but it is sometimes used to mean recall of any stimulus to almost hallucinatory intensity.

Haber and his colleagues conducted extensive experiments with children. Eidetic imagery was recognized when the child could move the eyes over where a removed stimulus had been and report details. (Fleeting and indistinct afterimages, similar to what is seen after staring at a glowing light bulb and then looking away, are not eidetic imagery.) One ten-year-old boy, after a thirty-second exposure to an easel-mounted picture showing Alice (in *Wonderland*) looking upward at the Cheshire cat perched on a tree limb, reported details regarding flowers under the tree, Alice's hair and clothing, the position of the cat's paws, and stripes in the cat's tail.

Eidetic images nearly always are lost when the child attempts to move them off the surface where the visual stimulus appeared originally. There usually is no control over the eventual disappearance; images vary greatly in their completeness and duration. It often is difficult to distinguish between true eidetic imagery and memory.

Auditory eidetic images are suggested by such comments as "It's still ringing in my ears," but whether such situations are literally true is highly speculative. Eidetic imagery is an interesting perceptual phenomenon which may assist learning visual aspects of music, but somehow it must be disentangled from vivid memory.

PRACTICAL APPLICATIONS

Consideration of learning theory, experience, and particular problems in music learning suggests specific recommendations in regard to encouraging learning. The following recommendations, while neither complete nor a recipe for successful teaching, are offered as practical suggestions.

Reinforcement

Whether they strengthen a stimulus-response connection, prolong a response, maintain goal-seeking behavior, prevent other responses, or promote a positive self-concept, positive reinforcements generally do *work*. Bennett and Adams (1967) showed that positive reinforcement was more effective than no reinforcement or negative reinforcement in elementary music classes.

Even where criterion behavior is not immediately facilitated, reinforcement may promote attending behavior, as Greer, Randall, and Timberlake (1971) demonstrated with sixth grade students.

Positive comments, music listening, money, candy, stripes on band uniforms, and many other objects and processes may serve as reinforcers. If something desirable (to the learner) happens, the likelihood that it will happen again is increased by reinforcement. An individual's behavior may be self-reinforcing, of course; just what behavior is reinforced is not always obvious.

Constant reinforcement for a learned behavior generally is less effective than random or intermittent reinforcement. Too much time between reinforcements promotes extinction. The teacher should remember this as he or she schedules performances, auditions, dispensation of grades and tokens, and practice schedules.

Practice

Depending on one's theoretical position, one may regard practice as exercising or stengthening stimulus-response connections, applying a learned response to a new stimulus, anticipatory goal-seeking responses, or searching for insight. Regardless, practice is essential in developing musical skills in both performance and nonperformance areas.

The traditional weekly private lesson grossly ignores what is known about learning, particularly with younger students. During the time between lessons, mistakes may be practiced continually with no opportunity for correction until the next lesson. It often is difficult to maintain an incentive to practice without frequent reward. The "music as its own reward" is an unrealistic ideal when one is just beginning to develop musical skills. Frequent short instructional periods should have a higher priority than weekly concentrated instructional periods. Practice sessions are facilitated by comprehensive statements of objectives and models: It is easier to practice if one knows for what he or she is practicing.

The strange belief that the so-called *beta hypothesis* can enhance musical learning should not be taken seriously. Dunlap (1932) believed that negative practice could help a person "unlearn" persistent errors made in psychomotor tasks such as type-writing and piano playing. Negative practice involves the deliberate practice of an error, accompanied by self-admonishment, e.g. "This is wrong. I shouldn't do it this way." Attempts to apply negative practice to music learning, such as Reitmeyer's (1973) attempt with clarinet fingerings have not been successful.

One does not have to be a follower of Guthrie to advocate the importance of practice in varied situations. No two "stimulus conditions"—concert halls, performance dates, stadiums, audiences, adjudicators—are exactly alike.

Concept Formation

Children's confusion of labels may interfere with proper musical conceptualization (Andrews and Deihl, 1968); hence, descriptive use of adequate terminology is important in aiding concept formation. High, low, loud, soft, fast, slow, and other musical terms must be demonstrated.

It is said that many students are unable to tell what they like about music or compare and contrast two compositions because their relevant concepts are incomplete and lack the necessary vocabulary. "It has a beat," a favorite evaluative comment of many junior high school students, is at best an obvious statement and at worst a gross musical oversimplification. Learners need to become explicit; it is not "enough" to "have the idea."

Concrete referents are important for younger learners. Overly abstract and symbolic language is beyond the processing capabilities of many (but not all) elementary school pupils.

Concepts are private, and there is an inherent difficulty in fully expressing an aurally experienced phenomenon orally. Clarity of presentation, explicit examples, models, and emphasis of important musical attributes will facilitate concept formation.

SUMMARY

The major points in Chapter Ten include the following:
1. Learning requires an observable behavioral change, nonattributable to anything else.
2. Teaching and instruction are not learning.

3. Reinforcement, as a consequence of behavior, is essential in most forms of learning, although theoretical explorations differ regarding why.
4. Purposeful behavior is directed toward a goal.
5. Motivation directs the learner toward a goal.
6. Concepts are individual categorization schemes which help to organize experience.
7. Neurons exchange excitatory and inhibitory messages electrochemically across synapses; learning requires neural networks to function together.
8. Neural stimulation may promote memory consolidation via a permanent chemical change in adjacent non-neural cells.
9. Sensory inhibition serves to channel and funnel essential information while suppressing nonessential information.
10. Learning theories may be classified broadly as stimulus-response and cognitive theories.
11. For Thorndike, learning was a matter of establishing and strengthening stimulus-response bonds.
12. For Pavlov, learning was a matter of conditioning stimulus-response linkages and generalizing them.
13. For Guthrie, learning was a matter of connecting stimuli with movements on a one-trial basis.
14. For Hull, learning was establishing habit families as the organism works in small increments toward a goal.
15. For Skinner, learning is a matter of operant conditioning of desired responses through selective reinforcement.
16. In Gestalt theory, learning depends on perceptual organization through proximity, similarity, common direction, and simplicity.
17. For Piaget, learning results from assimilation and accommodation as the child progresses through developmental stages.
18. Social learning is largely imitative behavior elicited by models.
19. Humanism stresses self-actualization through promotion of a positive self-concept.
20. Several descriptions of musical development exist, but comprehensive normative data are lacking.
21. Rhythmic sensitivity precedes tonal sensitivity.

22. Tonal sensitivity is culturally based and proceeds from simple to complex patterns.
23. There is no one superior method for memorizing music.
24. Tonal memory requires practice and emphasis on relevant dimensions.
25. Active tonal production requires more than tonal memory.
26. Eidetic imagery often is confused with vivid memory and probably is more of a visual than an auditory phenomenon.
27. Learning can be promoted by judicious use of reinforcement, varied vocabularies and examples, and frequent instruction.

REFERENCES

Andrews, F. M., & Deihl, N. C. Development of a technique for identifying elementary school children's musical concepts. *Council for Research in Music Education*, 1968, *13*, 1-7.

Bandura, A. *Principles of Behavior Modification*. New York: Holt, Rinehart and Winston, 1969.

Bandura, A., & Walters, R. *Social Learning and Personality Development*. New York: Holt, Rinehart and Winston, 1963.

Beament, J. The biology of music. *Psychology of Music*, 1977, *5* (1), 3-18.

Bennett, L., & Adams, J. A comparative study of the effects of positive and negative reinforcements on the efficiency of musical learning. *Council for Research in Music Education*, 1967, *10*, 39-46.

Bentley, A. *Musical Ability in Children and its Measurement*. New York: October House, 1966.

Bergan, J. R. Factors affecting pitch discrimination. *Council for Research in Music Education*, 1966, *8*, 15-21.

Boyle, J. D. (comp.). *Instructional Objectives in Music*. Vienna, Va.: Music Educators National Conference, 1974.

Buckton, R. A comparison of the effects of vocal and instrumental instruction on the development of melodic and vocal abilities in young children. *Psychology of Music*, 1977, *5* (1), 36-47.

Bugelski, B. R. *The Psychology of Learning Applied to Teaching* (2nd ed.). Indianapolis: Bobbs-Merrill, 1971.

Deutsch, J. A., & Deutsch, D. *Physiological Psychology* (2nd ed.). Homewood, Illinois: Dorsey, 1973.

Dowling, W. J., & Fujitani, D. S. Contour, interval, and pitch recognition in memory for short melodies. *Journal of the Acoustical Society of America*, 1971, *49*, 524-531.

Dunlap, K. *Habits: Their Making and Unmaking*. New York: Liveright, 1932.

Foley, E. A. Effects of training in conservation of tonal and rhythmic patterns on second-grade children. *Journal of Research in Music Education,* 1975, *23,* 240-248.

Funk, J. D. Some aspects of the development of music perception. (Doctoral dissertation, Clark University, 1977). *Dissertation Abstracts International,* 1977, *38,* 1919B. (University Microfilms No. 77-20, 301)

Greer, R. D., Randall, A., & Timberlake, C. The discriminate use of music listening as a contingency for improvement in vocal pitch acuity and attending behavior. *Council for Research in Music Education,* 1971, *26,* 10-18.

Guthrie, E. R. *The Psychology of Learning* (Rev. ed.). New York: Harper and Row, 1952.

Haber, R. N. Eidetic images. *Scientific American,* 1969, *220* (4), 36-44.

Hart, L. A. *How the Brain Works.* New York: Basic Books, 1975.

Hilgard, E. R., & Bower, G. H. Theories of Learning (4th ed.). Englewood Cliffs, N.J.: Prentice-Hall, 1975.

Hufstader, R. A. An investigation of a learning sequence of musical listening skills. *Journal of Research in Music Education,* 1977, *25,* 184-196.

Hull, C. L. *Principles of Behavior.* New York: Appleton-Century-Crofts, 1943.

Jeffries, T. B. The effects of order of presentation and knowledge of results on the aural recognition of melodic intervals. *Journal of Research in Music Education,* 1967, *15,* 179-190.

Kohler, W. *Gestalt Psychology.* New York: Liveright, 1929.

Kresteff, A. D. The growth of musical awareness in children. *Council for Research in Music Education,* 1963, *1,* 4-10.

Larsen, R. L. Levels of conceptual development in melodic permutation concepts based on Piaget's theory. *Journal of Research in Music Education,* 1973, *21,* 256-263.

Lathrop, R. L. Music and music education: a psychologist's view. *Music Educators Journal,* 1970, *56* (6), 47-48.

LeFrancois, G. R. *Psychology for Teaching* (2nd ed.). Belmont, California: Wadsworth, 1975.

Lo, L. N. L. The effect of visual memory training on the ability to memorize music within class piano instruction. (Doctoral dissertation, Indiana University, 1976). *Dissertation Abstracts International,* 1977, *38,* 538A-539A. (University Microfilms No. 77-16, 861)

Long, P. A. Pitch recognition in short melodies. (Doctoral dissertation, Florida State University, 1975). *Dissertation Abstracts International,* 1976, *36,* 3840A-3841A. (University Microfilms No. 76-2664).

Pavlov, I. P. *Conditioned Reflexes.* London: Clarendon Press, 1927.

Petzold, R. G. The development of auditory perception of musical sounds by children in the first six grades. *Journal of Research in Music Education,* 1963, *11,* 21-43.

Pflederer, M. Conservation laws applied to the development of musical intelligence. *Journal of Research in Music Education,* 1967, *15,* 215-223.

Piaget, J. *The Psychology of Intelligence.* New York: Harcourt Brace Jovanovich, 1950.

Piaget, J., & Inhelder, B. *The Psychology of the Child.* New York: Basic Books, 1969.

Pribram, K. H. *Languages of the Brain.* Englewood Cliffs, N.J.: Prentice-Hall, 1971.

Ptacek, P. H., & Pinheiro, M. L. Pattern reversal in auditory perception. *Journal of the Acoustical Society of America,* 1971, *49,* 493-498.

Reitmeyer, J. W. The application of negative practice to the correction of habitual fingering errors in clarinet performance. (Doctoral dissertation, The Pennsylvania State University, 1972.) *Dissertation Abstracts International,* 1973, *33,* 3403A-3404A. (University Microfilms No. 72-33, 201)

Rider, M. S. The relationship between auditory and visual perception on tasks employing Piaget's concept of conservation. *Journal of Music Therapy,* 1977, *14,* 126-138.

Rogers, C. R. *Client-centered therapy: Its Current Practice, Implications and Theory.* Boston: Houghton Mifflin, 1951.

Rogers, C. R. *Freedom to Learn.* Columbus, Ohio: Charles E. Merrill, 1969.

Rubin-Rabson, G. The influence of analytic prestudy in memorizing piano music. *Archives of Psychology,* 1937, *31* (220), 1-53.

Sergeant, D., & Roche, S. Perceptual shifts in the auditory information processing of young children. *Psychology of Music,* 1973, *1* (2), 39-48.

Skinner, B. F. *The Behavior of Organisms: an Experimental Analysis.* New York: Appleton-Century-Crofts, 1938.

Skinner, B. F. *Science and Human Behavior.* New York: MacMillan, 1953.

Skinner, B. F. *Beyond Freedom and Dignity.* New York: Alfred A. Knopf, 1971.

Tallarico, P. T. A study of the three phase concept of memory: Its musical implications. *Council for Research in Music Education,* 1974, *39,* 1-15.

Thorndike, E. L. *The Fundamentals of Learning.* New York: Teachers College, 1932.

Von Bekesy, G. *Sensory Inhibition.* Princeton, N.J.: Princeton University Press, 1967.

Webster, J. C., Woodhead, M. M., & Carpenter, A. Perceptual confusions between four-dimensional sounds. *Journal of the Acoustical Society of America,* 1973, *53,* 448-456.

Chapter Eleven

FUTURE RESEARCH DIRECTIONS

IT IS DIFFICULT to accurately predict future research interests and trends in psychology of music. The previous chapters have presented considerable material which is not thoroughly understood. Identification of a complex tone's pitch, harmony vs. one discrete pitch sensation, rhythmic sensitivity, tonal memory, human musical learning, and aesthetic sensitivity are areas which will continue to require research. New technological refinements, such as in holography, and discoveries in physics, chemistry, and biology may suggest radical revisions of psychological theories and views. Ultimate knowledge is nonexistent.

Four areas have been selected for treatment in this chapter because (1) they have not been treated elsewhere in this text, (2) the research base is somewhat speculative, and (3) in the opinion of the authors, interest will increase in the near future.

PHYSIOLOGICAL ASPECTS

Enjoyment and discomfort of music must be related in some way to the functioning of the brain's limbic system. Another important brain phenomenon is cerebral dominance; it often is assumed mistakenly that music always is a function of the right cerebral hemisphere. As more knowledge of the brain accrues, these will become fruitful research areas.

Limbic System

The limbic system includes the hypothalamus, the amygdala, the hippocampus, and the septal area. It monitors sensory inputs, produces or reduces emotionality, suppresses irrelevant "old" memories, and dispenses sensations of pain and pleasure. The hypothalamus especially is a "reward" center, as demonstrated by electrical stimulation of animal brains. The limbic system does not work independently of the brain's other parts, and detailed understanding must await more general knowledge of the brain (Issacson, 1974, p. 2; p. 62; pp. 115-117; p. 132; p. 219; p. 238).

Roederer (1975, p. 164) suggests that the limbic system may be responsible for enjoyment of music and other art forms. The limbic system can react to neural information processing unrelated to the immediate environment; "thinking" about music conceivably can arouse reward and punishment.

Music resulting from neural redundancy, i.e. people have so many excess neurons that music gives them something to do, is debatable; opinions differ regarding just how redundant the brain is. Hart (1975, p. 54) believes that the brain tends to be redundant while Eccles (1977, p. 147) believes that the concept of neural excess is misleading; the brain is not connected at random or redundantly.

Since emotional, aesthetic, and affective behavior must have a physiological base, just as all behavior, it is reasonable to explore the limbic system as a possible seat of musical enjoyment. We are a long way from saying "People enjoy music because it tickles their hypothalamuses," but it is an intriguing idea.

Cerebral Dominance

The brain's cerebral cortex is divided into two hemispheres. The left hemisphere's usual specialization in spoken language has been acknowledged for over a century, but the right hemisphere's usual specialization in pattern recognition is a recent acknowledgement (Galin, 1976). The fact that the two hemispheres process information in different ways recently has encouraged speculation that education, including music education, may be reformed somehow if proper attention is given to the "neglected" right hemisphere (Samples, 1977; Regelski, 1977). This is at best an oversimplification and at worst a dangerous fad.

Certain evidence does suggest a right hemisphere dominance for music. Kimura (1973) summarized a number of her investigations utilizing dichotic listening, in which simultaneous but

different inputs are presented to the two ears. The physiological
fact that contralateral, i.e. left-to-right and right-to-left ear to
brain information flow is stronger than ipsilateral, i.e. left-to-left
and right-to-right information flow, means that information presented to the *left* ear goes mainly to the *right* hemisphere and vice
versa. Kimura's subjects usually selected the melody presented to
the left ear from a five-melody array more consistently than the
melody presented simultaneously to the right ear.

McCarthy (1969) presented simultaneous triads of spoken
numbers and simultaneous paired tones to college students major-
ing in elementary education. Subjects selected from sets of four
number triads or four groups of tones which two of the set had
been presented for each number or tone trial. Tones were recognized better in the left ear. Numbers were recognized better in
the right ear.

Apparent left-ear right-hemisphere superiority for music processing becomes quite tenuous when consideration is given to the
listeners' backgrounds and the nature of the musical task. Four
particular studies demonstrate that these are highly important
qualifications.

Bever and Chiarello (1974) distinguished operationally between twenty-two musically experienced and fourteen musically inexperienced subjects. All experienced subjects had four or more
years of private lessons and were currently performing, while the
inexperienced subjects had less than three years of lessons, with no
lessons for at least the immediately preceding five years. The investigators presented seventy-two tonal sequences, each containing
twelve to eighteen tones of identical length. A two-tone excerpt
followed each sequence, and subjects indicated whether or not
each excerpt was contained in the immediately prior sequence.
Subjects also indicated whether each entire sequence (other than
the first) had been heard previously. The excerpt recognition
task proved too demanding for the inexperienced listener. Recognition of entire sequences was slightly better in the left ear for the
inexperienced subjects, *but* recognition was clearly superior in the
right ear for the experienced subjects. The particular melodic
recognition task was a Gestalt-like holistic process for the inex-

perienced listener, but it was an analytical task for those with greater amounts of musical training. Hemispheric dominance was a matter of process, not content.

In another relevant study (Papcun et al., 1974), Morse code signals were presented dichotically to experienced Morse code operators and to subjects who did not know Morse code. Each ear received different dot-and-dash patterns of identical length. All subjects were told to which ear they should listen and to write that pattern in an appropriate way. There was a consistent right ear superiority for the experienced operators. The naive subjects also showed a right ear, left hemisphere superiority for those patterns containing seven or fewer elements (a dot and a dash each were considered an element). However, the naive subjects processed the longer patterns with greater accuracy from the left ear. Inexperienced in Morse code, the naive subjects could not maintain the necessary sequential analysis, so they switched to holistic, right hemisphere pattern recognition. Again, hemispheric specialization depended on task nature rather than material nature.

In a superficially apparent contradiction to a left hemisphere dominance for musically trained subjects, Kellar (1977) found that musicians matched simultaneous intervals (perfect fourths, augmented fourths, and perfect fifths) to standards better with the left ear, while nonmusicians performed better with the right ear. The musicians, however, simply were categorizing the intervals, while the nonmusicians were forced to analyze. (See Chapter Two regarding differences in interval perception between musicians and nonmusicians.) In this case, the musicians performed holistically while the nonmusicians performed analytically, so there is no contradiction.

Murray and Rushford (1977) presented 122 paired simultaneous tones to twenty-seven right-handed* graduate music students. One tone, initially in unison at 622.3 Hz, was varied to differences

---

*Dichotic listening studies often are restricted to right-handed subjects to ensure a left hemisphere dominance for speech and analytic tasks. Even left-handed individuals usually have a similarly dominant left hemisphere (Eccles, 1977, p. 205) but the handedness-dominance relationship is uncertain. Depending on the cognitive task's nature, handedness may be associated with increased or decreased hemisphere specialization or with no effect (Beaumont, 1974).

from the constant tone ranging up to 30 cents. The subjects' task was to identify the direction of the change and the ear in which it occurred. A consistent right ear superiority for totally correct responses existed, regardless of frequency difference and direction. There were more wrong ear reports for left ear presentations. Statistically, both ears perceived an identical amount of changes, but *identification* (verbalization) of the changes was more successful for right ear presentations. The task was analytical and the subjects were experienced musicians.

Studies of dichotically presented consonant-vowel combinations have shown differing degrees of left hemisphere dominance, varying with the stimulus portion (Shankweiler and Studdert-Kennedy, 1966; Studdert-Kennedy and Shankweiler, 1970). Somewhat similar differential degrees of hemispheric dominance were found by Rushford-Murray (1977), who presented attack transient (onset), steady-state, and legato transient portions of clarinet, violin, oboe, trumpet, piano, and flute tones to twenty-four right-handed graduate music students. White noise was presented to one ear; the instrumental sound was presented simultaneously to the other. The subjects correctly identified the instrument producing the attack transient more often from their right ears. Steady-state segments were identified equally well from both ears. The legato transients were identified correctly more often from the left ear. Music's spatial and temporal aspects may be related to differential processing modes.

People have brains in which the left hemisphere ordinarily is reserved for analytic processing while the right hemisphere is reserved for spatial processing (Hart, p. 141). Cerebral dominance is largely nonexistent up to four years of age* (Gazzaniga, 1967); beyond that, its development varies greatly (Barr, 1972, p. 16). Neither hemisphere exists in a vacuum regardless of which is dominant; there is communication across a connecting band of nerve tissue, the corpus callosum. Demonstration of hemispheric super-

---

*Recent evidence (Hammer, 1977) suggests that newborn infants may process speech sounds more effectively with the left ear and white noise more effectively with the right ear, as indicated by turning the eyes in appropriate directions during binaural presentations.

iority does not mean that the other hemisphere is uninvolved (Dimond and Beaumont, 1974). Hemispheric dominance as it applies to complex musical phenomena varies with musical training, the way the musical stimulus is presented, and the musical elements within the stimulus (Aiello, 1977). There may be no hemispheric dominance for processing of rhythmic stimuli (Vrtunski, 1977). Before educators can take advantage of known dominance phenomena, much more knowledge of music learning and human brain processes is necessary. Extravagant claims for reforming education via "educating the right brain" are absurd.

PERCEPTION'S ROLE IN MUSICAL PRODUCTION

"If you can sing it, you can play it. If you can't sing it, you can't play it." With such words, some instrumentalists are urged to master sightsinging skills. Ability to produce a desired sound with consistent accuracy probably indicates accurate perception and/or conception of the sound. But the reverse does not hold. Inability to sing or produce a sound does not necessarily indicate inability to perceive it.

Although beyond the scope of this book, more needs to be learned regarding the acoustical aspects of vocal and instrumental tone production to enable musicians to focus on the perceptual, conceptual, and mechanical aspects of performance. Accurate musical production requires a concept of what is to be produced, which should be modifiable by accurate perception. Given accurate perception and adequate conception, there still are the separate acoustical problems of tone production. Even if you can sing it, you cannot necessarily play it. And you might play it without singing it.

SYNESTHESIA

In the authors' experience, synesthesia is a topic that never fails to arouse the interest of psychology of music classes, even during early morning class periods on dreary winter days. The synesthetic experience often sounds bizarre and incredulous to the non-synesthete, but it is perfectly normal for the "chosen few."

Synesthesia is simultaneous response to one stimulus in more

than one sensory mode. A frequency within the audible spectrum
may elicit a color sensation in addition to the auditory sensations.
Auditory perception of a word may be accompanied by a simultaneous taste. Pronounced days of the week or numbers may
elicit color sensations.

The synesthetic experience may not be uncommon. According to Wilentz (1968, p. 316), one authority estimates as many as
14 percent of men and 31 percent of women experience some sort
of simultaneous sensations, usually as combinations of colors and
sounds. Marks (1975) collected synesthetic vowel-color associations from over 400 people.

In one case of synesthesia known personally to the authors, a
female art educator experiences particular colors with particular
frequencies. For example, A is lavender, B is orange, C is red,
D is blue, E is green, F is brown, and G is black. The colors,
seen as bars or bands in the field of vision, are identical for octave
repetitions but are most prominent in the range from

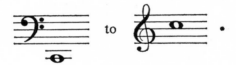

The lady also possesses absolute pitch, of which she became aware
during elementary school at the same time that she became aware
of her synesthesia. Absolute pitch identification occurs directly
from the sound; her auditory sensation precedes her color sensation. Colors do not fuse for harmonic passages; each tone is represented by its color in some way, often in a series of pointillistic
dots. The lady is bothered immensely by light shows in which
the chosen colors do not match her synesthetic color-tone linkages.
She views her synesthesia as an amusing curiosity that is a disad-
vantage in listening to music when she concentrates on the colors
and thereby analyzes the music into overly simple elements.

In an extensive investigation of color-tone linkage in college
students, Karwoski and Odbert (1938) found that approximately
60 percent of 274 subjects reported some sort of color association
for phrases, measures, or chords excerpted from popular music.

Based on their questionnaire reports, thirty-four subjects were selected for intensive individual study. Three classifications or degrees of synesthesia were apparent: thirteen subjects saw colors as vague patterns; twelve saw colors in "meaningful" images from past experiences, and nine saw colored abstractions in great detail. Five of those nine showed remarkable similarity between listening sessions eight months apart, as indicated by their drawings. Only one subject could have the synesthetic experiences with the eyes open. A possible continuum of different degrees of color-tone linkage perhaps should be investigated anew, as should Karwoski and Odbert's findings that some subjects could experience colors only from longer musical segments. In this and another study (Karwoski, Odbert, and Osgood, 1942), the researchers recognized the difficulty of distinguishing between a verbal and a sensory association and apparently were willing to label a verbal relationship as synesthesia.

Consistent verbal color-tone associations, while also found in synesthesia, really are not the same thing, in the authors' opinion. The synesthetic experience is an actual *multisensory sensation,* not simply a *verbal association.* Omwake's (1940) study of 555 school children exemplifies an association study: The subjects matched red, blue, black, or yellow to eight tones and four pieces.

The dominant color associations were:

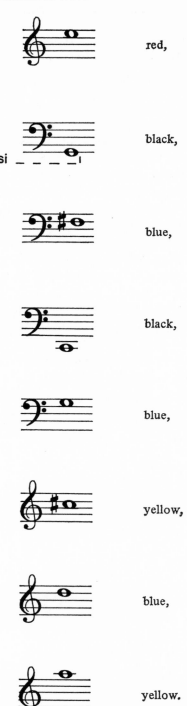

red,

black,

blue,

black,

blue,

yellow,

blue,

yellow.

The lullaby was "blue;" the march was "red." A "melancholy melody" was "black," and ballet music was "yellow." The tendency was for higher tones and "brighter" music to suggest lighter colors.

In another association study (Simpson, Quinn, and Ausubel, 1956), 995 elementary school pupils indicated which of six colors (violet, blue, green, yellow, orange, red) they "thought of" after hearing tones of 125, 250, 1000, 4000, 8000, and 12000 Hz at 40 and 50 db SPL. Yellow and green tended to be associated with higher tones. The 1000 Hz tone suggested red and orange. Blue and violet generally were associated with low tones. No one color elicited a majority (greater than 50%) classification for any tone; the blue-violet combination elicited 51 and 52 percent for 125 and 250 Hz respectively. Decibel and sex differences were trivial.

Two piano players with absolute pitch discovered that they had simultaneous perceptions of tonality and color (Carroll and Greenberg, 1961). One (Carroll) had a color sensation for each key in the chromatic octave. Greenberg did for all keys except E, B, F-sharp, and C-sharp.

Ostwald (1964) indicated that synesthesia may be symptomatic of mental illness when the secondary aspect of the synesthetic experience overshadows or obliterates the "normal" aspect. He cites the case of a thirty-one-year-old woman for whom *all* sounds were accompanied by color. The woman had a sister who had the same experience. Ostwald's patient heard vowels with specific colors, which appeared in specific shapes and consistencies. Single colors accompanied individual tones; color mixtures accompanied chords. "Harsh" words elicited pain. The woman had undergone breast surgery for removal of a small tumor when she was twenty-two, and she had several sexual (in a social sense) abnormalities.

One investigator (McCluskey, 1975) experienced considerable difficulty in exemplifying for himself and others the color-sound associations of his synesthetic wife, who, as many synesthetes, assumes that all people experience the world as she does. Photographs and drawings could not convey adequately the way his wife "sees" in color the pronunciation of her maiden name or nonverbal sounds because depth and perspective were lacking. Short film sequences come closer to portraying the moving colors, in their various shapes and blends.

Sound-color synesthesia, also called *chromesthesia,* is character-ized by a consistent relation between color brightness and the sound's pitch. Low pitches are accompanied by dark colors; high pitches are accompanied by bright colors. The particular colors associated with spoken vowel sounds are fairly consistent: Red and yellow for "ah;" white for "ay" as in "late," "eh" as in "let," "ih" as in "bit," and "ei" as in "beet;" red and black for "o" as in "home;" and blue, brown, and black for "oo" as in "boot." However, tone-color associations are idiosyncratic. Individuals are consistent within themselves, but different individuals disagree regarding whether C, for example, is green, red, or something else (Marks).

Farnsworth (1969, p. 77) indicates that color-tone linkages are elicited by an acoustical stimulus, not by a visual stimulus. Women are more likely to be chromesthetic, and there is a tendency for chromesthesia to run in families.

Synesthesia may represent a basic unity of human sensation, just as Stevens's cross-modality matching (see Chapter Two). Marks suggests that children may learn *not* to be synesthetic as they grow. Verbal-color associations in nonsynesthetes sometimes show a similar consistency. Development of multimedia art forms, understanding of music perception, and experimental aesthetics all would be benefited by a better understanding of synesthesia.

CONFORMITY

Who says something about music may be more important than *what* is said. What is heard in the music may be less important than what the listener is "supposed" to hear. The study of con-formity and acceptance of authority is well established in social psychology, but more work needs to be directed toward con-formity in musical situations.

Conformity in expressed musical taste is exemplified by the Inglefield (1974) study, discussed in Chapter Seven, where junior high school students conformed to peer leaders' expressed musical preferences. More conformity was noted in those students who were otherdirected rather than innerdirected and high rather than low in need for social approval.

Radocy (1975), applying the Asch (1956) model to tonal stimuli, demonstrated conformity for simple sensory judgments of pitch and loudness. (In the Asch study, naive subjects stated which one of three line segments matched a standard after hearing other alleged subjects, in reality the experimenter's confederates, state their matches. Two-thirds of the time, the confederates unanimously stated deliberately wrong answers, thereby placing the subject in a conflict between sensory input and peer pressure.) One hundred thirty-six university music students, assigned randomly to pitch experimental, pitch control, loudness experimental, and loudness control groups, indicated publicly which one of three tones had the same pitch or loudness as a standard for eighteen items. Four confederates, always responding prior to the subject, answered each item correctly during the control condition, but they stated incorrect answers for two-thirds of the items during the experimental conditions. Experimental pitch subjects showed a .30 overall conformity rate for pitch, i.e. in 30 percent of the conflict situations the subject agreed with the confederates' deliberately erroneous responses. The overall loudness conformity rate was .49. Control groups made no erroneous pitch responses and few erroneous loudness responses. Experimental subjects who were retested with the same stimuli in a conventional paper-and-pencil format confirmed that their original erroneous responses were not due to genuine inability to make correct judgments. Trained musicians may defy their own perceptions rather than disagree with their peers.

Authority is a necessary social contigency, and much legitimate learning results from acceptance of authoritarian pronouncements. Authority attached to particular teachers, composers, or critics can influence musical judgments, even to the point of believing that one hears things that are not present in the musical stimulus.

Jascha Heifetz, a violin virtuoso of the pre- and post-World War II era, somehow acquired a reputation, possibly from his facial expression, as a "cold" performer. Farnsworth (1952) played two recordings of an identical composition to two groups of fifty psychology students. One version was performed by Heifetz, the other by Mischa Elman. Half of the students heard the Heifetz version first; half heard the Elman first. They did not know who was playing. When asked to say which recorded performance sounded "colder," the students showed about a fifty-fifty split: Heifetz's version received fifty-one votes. However, in a separate task requiring students to rank Heifetz for coldness as compared with Elman, Yehudi Menuhin, and Fritz Kreisler, Heifetz consistently was ranked as "colder." A judgment based on a performer's name was different than a judgment based on recorded performance. In listening sessions with other groups, Elman was heard as "colder," or the recording played first was heard as "colder." If Heifetz's playing really was "colder," it was not on an auditory basis.

A common finding in performance evaluation was demonstrated by Duerksen (1972), who asked undergraduate students to evaluate two tape recordings of an identical piano performance. Half of the experimental subjects were told that the first performance was by a professional and the second by a student; the other half were told the opposite. Control subjects heard the performance labelled simply as "one" and "two." The experimental subjects consistently rated the alleged professional performance, regardless of performance order, as better, technically and musically. A professional is *supposed* to play better than a student, so Duerksen's subjects heard the professional as better. Control subjects consistently rated the second performance as better.

In an extensive study of performance and musical preference judgments, Radocy (1976) administered "tests," in the form of intentionally ambiguous checklists of vague musical terms, to twenty groups of undergraduate music majors. Performance "tests" required comparison of two piano, two trumpet, and two orchestra performances of identical works. Preference "tests" required comparing obscure pairs of baroque, classical, romantic, and twentieth century examples. Half of the subjects received performance "tests;" the other half received preference "tests."

Each listening group was assigned randomly to one of five bias conditions, differing in degrees and direction of bias. No bias subjects were told only that they were to evaluate two performances or two compositions. Moderate bias subjects were told (prior to hearing) bogus information about the alleged performers or composers; the bias was toward the first or second example in the form of an alleged "professional" or "eminent" composer. For example, the trumpet performances were labelled as the work of a "former symphony player" or a "young graduate assistant." The baroque compositions were billed as the respective works of Handel and Friedrich von Krumpft, or vice versa. Strong bias subjects also were given bogus artist and composer information, as well as reasons why "prior listening groups" had preferred the work of the eminent artist or composer.

The performance experiment showed a significant bias effect, which varied with the different performance media. Sometimes the moderate biases were more effective than the strong biases. The strong bias toward the first member of a paired performance condition always differed significantly from the no bias condition, but the no bias condition did not differ significantly from the strong bias toward the second member condition because no bias subjects tended to hear the second performance as better.*

Results of the preference experiment were not as clear cut; significant bias effects were noted only for the baroque and romantic examples. Agreement with an authority may be less crucial for positive judgment of musical preference than for performance.

Caution is necessary in interpreting this study, but it is apparent that a person in an authoritarian position can use accumulated and imaginary prestige to influence musical judgments. Subjects who allow themselves to hear two identical performances as different or who say something sounds the same when it does not should not be condemned or ridiculed. They only are behaving in a very human manner.

People may not always wish to study themselves. The very idea of deceiving subjects is suspect (Kelman, 1967), and accept-

---

*This, as Duerksen's similar finding for his control subjects, is an example of the psychophysical time error, in which subjects judge the *second* of two relatively similar (or ambiguous) stimuli as having "more" of the property in question.

ance of authority to the point of inflicting apparent harm on fellow humans, as in Milgram's (1974) famous "shock the student if he fails to learn" studies, is frightening. However, humanity is a many-faceted and not always noble condition. Tendencies to conform and accept what is said because of who says it will not disappear because of denial any more than Jupiter lost its satellites because Galileo was censured.

SUMMARY

This chapter's main points include the following:

1. Pleasurable and irritating musical sensations may result from the limbic system.
2. Cerebral hemispheres specialize in different cognitive processes; analytic processes almost always are in the left hemisphere while spatial processes almost always are in the right hemisphere.
3. The dominant hemisphere for music processing depends on the musical task, not on the material.
4. Further research into the nature of musical tasks as well as the brain is necessary before hemispheric specialization can be utilized properly in education.
5. Problems of musical performance are more than perceptual problems.
6. Some people experience multisensory responses to one stimulus; this is synesthesia.
7. Although several synesthetic combinations are possible, the most documented seems to be a color-sound response to an auditory stimulus.
8. True synesthesia is experiencing the multisensations, not merely verbal associations.
9. Synesthesia may prove to be a more normal state of affairs than previously believed.
10. People will alter their musical judgments of preference, performance, and simple sensory discriminations to conform to expressed or implied choices of peers and authority figures.

REFERENCES

Aiello, R. The effect of musical training on cerebral dominance. (Doctoral dissertation, Columbia University, 1976.) *Dissertation Abstracts International,* 1977, *37,* 5388B. (University Microfilms No. 77-6707)

Asch, S. E. Studies of independence and conformity: I. a minority of one against a unanimous majority. *Psychological Monographs,* 1956, *70* (9).

Barr, D. F. *Auditory Perceptual Disorders.* Springfield, Illinois: Charles C Thomas, 1972.

Beaumont, J. G. Handedness and hemisphere function. In S. J. Dimond and J. G. Beaumont (Eds.), *Hemisphere Function in the Human Brain.* New York: Halsted Press, 1974.

Bever, T. G., & Chiarello, R. J. Cerebral dominance in musicians and non-musicians. *Science,* 1974, *185,* 537-539.

Carroll, J. B., & Greenberg, J. H. Two cases of synesthesia for color and musical tonality associated with absolute pitch ability. *Perceptual and Motor Skills,* 1961, *13,* 48.

Dimond, S. J., & Beaumont, J. G. Experimental studies of hemisphere function. In S. J. Dimond and J. G. Beaumont (Eds.), *Hemisphere Function in the Human Brain.* New York: Halsted Press, 1974.

Duerksen, G. L. Some effects of expectation on evaluation of recorded musical performances. *Journal of Research in Music Education,* 1972, *20,* 268-272.

Eccles, J. C. *The Understanding of the Brain* (2nd ed.). New York: McGraw-Hill, 1977.

Farnsworth, P. R. Notes on "coldness" in violin playing. *Journal of Psychology,* 1952, *33,* 41-45.

Farnsworth, P. R. *The Social Psychology of Music* (2nd ed.). Ames: Iowa State University Press, 1969.

Galin, D. The two modes of consciousness and the two halves of the brain. In P. R. Lee, R. E. Ornstein, D. Galin, A. Deikman, and C. T. Tart (Eds.), *Symposium on Consciousness.* New York: Viking Press, 1976.

Gazzaniga, M. S. The split brain in man. *Scientific American,* 1967, *217* (2), 24-29.

Hammer, M. Lateral differences in the newborn infant's response to speech and noise stimuli. (Doctoral dissertation, City University of New York, 1977.) *Dissertation Abstracts International,* 1977, *38,* 1439B. (University Microfilms No. 77-19, 548)

Hart, L. A. *How the Brain Works.* New York: Basic Books, 1975.

Inglefield, H. G. *Conformity Behavior Reflected in the Musical Preferences of Adolescents.* Paper presented at the meeting of the Music Educators National Conference, Anaheim, California, March, 1974.

Issacson, R. L. *The Limbic System.* New York: Plenum Press, 1974.

Karwoski, T. F., & Odbert, H. S. Color-music. *Psychological Monographs,*

1938, *50* (2). (Whole No. 222)

Karwoski, T. F., Odbert, H. S., & Osgood, C. E.   Studies in synesthetic thinking: II. The role of form in visual response to music. *Journal of General Psychology*, 1942, *26*, 199-222.

Kellar, L. A.   Hemispheric asymmetries in the perception of musical intervals as a function of musical experience and family handedness background. (Doctoral dissertation, Columbia University, 1976.) *Dissertation Abstracts International*, 1977, *37*, 4200B. (University Microfilms No. 77-6650)

Kelman, H. C.   Human use of human subjects. *Psychological Bulletin*, 1967, *67*, 1-11.

Kimura, D.   The asymmetry of the human brain. *Scientific American*, 1973, *228* (3), 70-78.

Marks, L. E.   Synesthesia: The lucky people with mixed-up senses. *Psychology Today*, 1975, *9* (1), 48-52.

McCarthy, J. F.   Accuracy of recognition for verbal and tonal stimuli presented to the left and right ears. *Council for Research in Music Education*, 1969, *16*, 18-21.

McCluskey, K. W.   Diary of a synesthete: Christina's color-drenched world. *Psychology Today*, 1975, *9* (1), 50-51.

Milgram, S.   *Obedience to Authority*.   New York: Harper and Row, 1974.

Murray, D. J., & Rushford, K.   *Hemispheric Asymmetry in the Discrimination and Identification of Small Frequency Changes: a Dichotic Listening Experiment*. Paper presented at the meeting of the Music Educators National Conference (North Central and Southwestern Regions), Kansas City, March, 1977.

Omwake, L.   Visual responses to auditory stimuli.   *Journal of Applied Psychology*, 1940, *24*, 468-481.

Ostwald, R. F.   Color hearing.   *Archives of General Psychiatry*, 1964, *11*, 40-47.

Papcun, G., Krashen, S., Terbeek, D., Remington, R., & Harshman, R.   Is the left hemisphere specialized for speech, language, and/or something else? *Journal of the Acoustical Society of America*, 1974, *55*, 319-327.

Radocy, R. E.   A naive minority of one and deliberate majority mismatches of tonal stimuli. *Journal of Research in Music Education*, 1975, *23*, 120-133.

Radocy, R. E.   Effects of authority figure biases on changing judgments of musical events. *Journal of Research in Music Education*, 1976, *24*, 119-128.

Regelski, T. A.   Who knows where music lurks in the mind of man?   *Music Educators Journal*, 1977, *63* (9), 31-38.

Roederer, J. G.   *Introduction to the Physics and Psychophysics of Music* (2nd ed.).   New York: Springer-Verlag, 1975.

Rushford-Murray, K.   Left-right ear differences in the processing of instrument tone segments. *Council for Research in Music Education*, 1977, *52*, 1-6.

Samples, B.   Mind cycles and learning.   *Phi Delta Kappan*, 1977, *58* (9), 688-692.

Shankweiler, D., & Studdert-Kennedy, M.   Lateral differences in perception of dichotically presented synthetic CV syllables and steady-state vowels. *Journal of the Acoustical Society of America,* 1966, *39,* 1256.

Simpson, R. H., Quinn, M., & Ausubel, D. P. Synesthesia in children: association of colors with pure tone frequencies. *Journal of Genetic Psychology,* 1956, *89,* 95-103.

Studdert-Kennedy, M., & Shankweiler, D. Hemispheric specialization for speech perception. *Journal of the Acoustical Society of America,* 1970, *48,* 579-594.

Vrtunski, C. P. Inter- and intra-hemispheric EEG relationships during speech and music rhythm processing. (Doctoral dissertation, Case Western Reserve University, 1976.) *Dissertation Abstracts International,* 1977, *37,* 6383B-6384B. (University Microfilm No. 77-11, 913)

Wilentz, J. S. *The Senses of Man.* New York: Thomas Y. Crowell, 1968.

AUTHOR INDEX

[Citations to jointly authored works are listed by the first author only. For example, the Getzels and Jackson study is listed here only as Getzels.]

SUBJECT INDEX

91